The Changing Landscape of Workplace and Workforce

Edited by Hadi El-Farr

Published in London, United Kingdom

The Changing Landscape of Workplace and Workforce
http://dx.doi.org/10.5772/intechopen.111368
Edited by Hadi El-Farr

Contributors
António Cardoso, Benito Gonzalez Jr., Durgesh Tripathi, Edith Galy, Hadi El-Farr, Hezekiah O. Falola, Jacob Ongaki, Jacques Bughin, Joseph Mukuni, Kevin Sevag Kertechian, Klara Nano Hormez, Manuel Sousa Pereira, Michele Cincera, Nadjete Natchaba, Oluwatunmise O. Ojebola, Sohel M. Imroz, Surbhi Tandon, Sílvia Faria, Ume Rubaca, Álvaro Cairrão

First published in London, United Kingdom, 2024 by IntechOpen
IntechOpen is the global imprint of INTECHOPEN LIMITED, registered in England and Wales, registration number: 11086078, 167-169 Great Portland Street, London, W1W 5PF, United Kingdom

British Library Cataloguing-in-Publication Data
A catalogue record for this book is available from the British Library

Additional hard and PDF copies can be obtained from orders@intechopen.com

The Changing Landscape of Workplace and Workforce
Edited by Hadi El-Farr
p. cm.
Print ISBN 978-0-85466-374-3
Online ISBN 978-0-85466-373-6
eBook (PDF) ISBN 978-0-85466-375-0

For EU product safety concerns:
IN TECH d.o.o., Prolaz Marije Krucifikse Kozulić 3, 51000 Rijeka, Croatia,
info@intechopen.com or visit our website at intechopen.com.

Meet the editor

Hadi El-Farr is an Assistant Teaching Professor of Human Resource Management at the School of Management and Labor Relations, Rutgers University, USA. He also is the director of the online master's in human resource management. Dr. El-Farr received his Ph.D. in Human Resource Management from the University of Leeds, UK, his MBA from the Lebanese American University, and his BBA from the American University of Beirut, Lebanon. He completed several certifications, such as the Professional in Human Resources and the Certificate for Lifelong Learning in Inclusive and Equitable Teaching. Dr. El-Farr teaches courses in Strategic HRM, Staffing, Global HRM, and Organizational Behavior, both in person and online. He delivered several professional training programs, presented at various conferences, and was a keynote speaker at various professional events. Before joining academia, he worked for several years in multiple industries and countries. His research interests are in strategic HRM, knowledge management, artificial intelligence in HRM, and online education. He published several peer-reviewed journal articles and book chapters, mainly in HRM and knowledge management. He has also served as an editor-in-chief, editor, and reviewer for several journals and publishers.

Contents

Preface

As a human resource (HR) professional turned academic, I have always championed the vital link between academia and real-world practice. My journey has been driven by a profound interest in how HR and managerial practices can effectively harness the wealth of knowledge embedded within employees and organizational processes and culture. However, in recent times, the rapid proliferation of contemporary technologies, particularly artificial intelligence, and cyber-physical systems, has shifted my focus. I have immersed myself in understanding the far-reaching implications of these technological advancements on the landscape of work, with a particular focus on the pivotal role of HR. I aim to maximize the benefits and mitigate the setbacks of these changes on employees, ensuring that organizations can navigate the evolving terrain of the modern workplace with agility and foresight.

This heightened interest was further intensified as I, like many of us, navigated through the challenges and unforeseen opportunities brought about by the pandemic. The sudden shift to remote work, balancing personal and professional responsibilities, the quest for work-life balance, and the imperative to safeguard mental health while maintaining productivity and professional growth was indeed a remarkable journey. These experiences have elevated my curiosity about the transformative effects of remote work and contemporary technologies on the fabric of our work environments. It is within this context that this book finds its place—a culmination of my ongoing academic and professional pursuits, aimed at making a modest contribution to addressing the contemporary challenges faced by employees, employers, and policymakers alike.

While the benefits of technological advancements are undeniable, it is crucial to acknowledge the myriad challenges they pose. Do we abandon progress due to its inherent drawbacks? I believe that we cannot reverse the tide of advancement, but we can certainly strive to mitigate its negative impacts and enhance the welfare of our society. With this perspective in mind, this book endeavors to navigate the complexities of the evolving work landscape, offering insights and strategies to confront challenges head-on while striving for a future where technology and humanity coexist harmoniously for the betterment of all. As the academic editor of this book, I am thrilled to embark on an exploratory journey into the multifaceted shifts shaping the landscape of work, the workforce, and the workplace. The dawn of the 21st century has witnessed a rapid acceleration in these transformations, catalyzed by breakthroughs in artificial intelligence, the onset of the COVID-19 pandemic, the evolving values and preferences of contemporary workforce generations, diversity and equity awakening, and an increasing trend in immigration. As we delve into the following pages, we embark on a quest to not only understand the profound implications of these transformations but also to decipher actionable insights that can benefit industry stakeholders, policymakers, and academic researchers alike.

In the opening chapter, the foundation is laid as we explore the driving forces propelling the profound changes in our professional realms. With eloquence, we explore how the advancements of the Fourth Industrial Revolution have ushered in an era marked by unparalleled innovation and disruption. Furthermore, we shine a light on the seismic impact of the COVID-19 pandemic, which not only accelerated existing trends but also underscored the vital need for adaptability and resilience in the face of adversity. Moreover, we investigate the heightened awareness of diversity and equity, sparked by the pandemic's disproportionate impact on various minority groups, including women, working parents, and people of color. Additionally, we highlight the growing concern of brain drain—a phenomenon fueled by increased immigration—exacerbating the alarming skill shortage in developing and emerging economies. Through these insights, we lay the groundwork for a comprehensive exploration of the dynamic shifts shaping our professional spheres.

As we navigate through subsequent chapters, authored by a diverse cohort of scholars from various corners of the globe, we embark on a voyage of discovery. From dissecting the socioeconomic ramifications of artificial intelligence to navigating the intricacies of remote work and alternative arrangements precipitated by the pandemic, each chapter offers a nuanced perspective on the evolving contours of the modern workplace. Furthermore, our exploration extends beyond the realms of technology and pandemic-induced transformations. We confront the pressing imperatives of diversity, equity, and inclusion, probing into the systemic inequalities exacerbated by the pandemic and the imperative for organizational practices that foster inclusivity. Furthermore, we delve into the pressing issue of skill shortages exacerbated by immigration trends and propose policies aimed at curbing this detrimental and escalating phenomenon. Through a meticulous synthesis of theoretical frameworks, empirical evidence, and practical insights, this book aspires to be more than a mere compilation of scholarly discourse. It seeks to serve as a beacon illuminating the path forward in an era characterized by uncertainty and flux.

As we navigate the uncharted waters of the 21st century, may this book stand as a modest contribution to our collective endeavor as academics, professionals, and policymakers to comprehend, adapt, and thrive amidst the ever-evolving landscape of work and workforce.

I would like to extend my heartfelt gratitude to all the authors who dedicated their time and expertise to contribute to this work. Your insights and contributions have enriched the discourse and propelled our understanding of the changing landscape of the workplace and workforce. I also want to express appreciation to the administrators and support staff who diligently facilitated the completion of this project in a timely and professional manner. Your efforts behind the scenes were instrumental in bringing this endeavor to fruition. Last, but certainly not least, I want to thank all the readers who have engaged with our work. Your interest and engagement allow us to share our knowledge and insights, with the hope of collectively advancing the field and making meaningful contributions to practice and academia alike.

Hadi El-Farr
Human Resource Management Department,
School of Management and Labor Relations,
Rutgers University,
Piscataway, United States of America

Section 1

The Fourth Industrial Revolution and the New World of Work

Chapter 1

Introductory Chapter: The Changing Landscape of Workplace and Workforce – An Overview

Hadi El-Farr

1. Introduction

The dynamics of work, the workplace, and the workforce are in a state of perpetual transformation, a process that has been markedly accelerated by the swift advancement and adoption of new technologies. Hence, ongoing research within the academic community is essential to comprehend the effects of these shifts and to offer insights for future research and practical recommendations for industry stakeholders, professional bodies, and policymakers. This book significantly contributes to propelling this discourse forward.

Numerous factors are driving these transformations, with arguably the most influential being the technological advancements of the twenty-first century, such as artificial intelligence. Some scholars have labeled this period as a transition from the third industrial revolution to the fourth, and some even suggest that we are entering the era of the fifth industrial revolution. Another significant factor is the impact of COVID-19 on the nature of work, prompting rapid adoption of new working methods and technological solutions to adapt to the pandemic's challenges. Although the evolution and adoption of these methods and solutions were already underway, the advent of COVID-19 served as a significant accelerant, hastening the rate of transformation.

In addition to the aforementioned factors, younger generations are showcasing different workplace values, such as prioritizing work-life balance and seeking meaningful work. Even older generations are embracing some of these values, reshaping perceptions of work as an integral aspect of life and personal careers. Consequently, many employees favor alternative work arrangements, particularly following the widespread experience during the pandemic's mandates. Some argue that such arrangements, coupled with a heavy reliance on information and communication technologies for task completion rather than in-person interactions, have become the new norm. This has led to a division among employers and business leaders regarding whether to embrace remote work on a large scale or to recall employees to office settings.

Furthermore, societal awareness regarding diversity and inclusion has significantly heightened during the pandemic. In response, numerous organizations have pledged to enhance their diversity and inclusion efforts, with some steadfastly upholding their commitments, while others have not. Also, immigration trends have intensified in the twenty-first century, with individuals from lower-income countries migrating to higher-income nations for improved living standards. This phenomenon has resulted in a brain drain in developing countries, as a substantial portion of their skilled workforce departs, leading to significant shortages in crucial professions, such as medical doctors, nurses, and engineers.

2. The Fourth Industrial Revolution and the new world of work

Every industrial revolution is defined by significant advancements in general-purpose technologies, resulting in leaps in automation, productivity, and abundance. While much of this change brings undeniable benefits, each revolution also brings negative consequences, such as income inequality, increased unemployment, pollution, and the need for workers to adapt their skills.

Many scholars argue that we are currently experiencing the Fourth Industrial Revolution, characterized by key general-purpose technologies like artificial intelligence and cyber-physical systems and many other enabling technologies [1]. Some go even further, proposing that we are entering the Fifth Industrial Revolution, which builds upon the fourth by emphasizing human-machine interaction, further integration of the physical and virtual worlds, and sustainability, leading to advancements in augmentation and personalized mass production [2, 3]. However, the concept of Industry 5.0 is still developing, with some envisioning its general-purpose technologies to include cognitive systems and collaborative robots (cobots) [4, 5].

Professor Klaus Schwab, the founder and executive chairman of the World Economic Forum, is credited with popularizing the term "Fourth Industrial Revolution" or "Industry 4.0." Schwab posited that this ongoing revolution would profoundly alter humankind, asserting that the physical, digital, and biological realms are converging [6]. This transformation is characterized by an unprecedented pace of breakthroughs, technological advancements with wide-ranging and profound impacts, and shifts in production, management, and governance systems [7]. Consequently, significant changes in the landscape of work and the workplace are inevitable.

Industry 4.0 presents numerous opportunities, including enhanced productivity, customization, efficiency, quality of life and work, affordability, and the creation of innovative products and services [7]. However, alongside these prospects come significant challenges. These challenges encompass disruptions in the labor market, leading to both temporary and structural unemployment, increased pressure on workers to continually update their skills, and widening income disparities between low- and high-skilled workers. Moreover, Industry 4.0 fundamentally alters how work is organized, how jobs are designed, how knowledge is managed, and how leadership roles evolve. In light of these developments, this book seeks to address several key questions about Industry 4.0:

1. What are the socio-economic effects of Artificial Intelligence?

2. How can we mitigate the negative impact of Artificial Intelligence?

3. What strategies should be employed to effectively manage knowledge in the Fourth Industrial Revolution?

4. How can leadership strike a balance between the technological and human dimensions within organizations in the current era?

5. What are the essential leadership qualities needed to effectively navigate and lead organizations in the twenty-first century?

6. What key skills and competencies are vital for the workforce to thrive in the era of Industry 4.0?

7. What are the most efficacious strategies and techniques for lifelong learning, particularly for upskilling and reskilling employees, to secure their employability in the future?

3. COVID-19 impact on the workplace and work arrangements

The COVID-19 pandemic has brought about profound changes in the workplace. While alternative work arrangements like remote and flexible working were already gaining traction in organizations, the pandemic undeniably accelerated these trends. The pandemic also triggered a quick shift toward digitalization and increased reliance on information and communication technologies, enabling employees to complete tasks, collaborate, and engage with their work remotely without needing physical presence in the office. This adaptation showcased resilience and inadvertently led to a widespread experiment with alternative work arrangements, revealing both their benefits and challenges. Arguably, several organizational, job, and employee-related factors play a role in either supporting or hindering the positive outcomes of remote and flexible work [8–11].

Furthermore, the pandemic's impact on society and businesses would likely have been far more severe without the technological advancements of Industry 4.0. The crisis accelerated the adoption of these advancements in existing solutions and spurred the rapid development of new ones. Beyond its technological ramifications, the pandemic has highlighted the critical importance of mental health and well-being within the workplace, leading to an increased focus on fostering a healthier work-life balance.

Opinions on the effectiveness of alternative work arrangements vary among organizations and employees. While some organizations continue to advocate for remote work due to perceived benefits such as increased efficiency, productivity, autonomy, and flexibility, others are calling for a return to office-based work [12]. Concerns about reduced employee engagement, productivity, and creativity in remote settings have led some organizations to prioritize a return to the office environment. Employee perspectives on remote work also vary. Some view it negatively, citing issues such as work-life imbalance, dissatisfaction, disengagement, limited career progression, role ambiguity, and increased workloads leading to burnout and turnover. On the other hand, many employees prefer remote work for its flexibility, autonomy, convenience, productivity, and improved work-life balance [13].

As a result, some scholars predict that remote work and other alternative arrangements will become the new norm post-pandemic, given their demonstrated benefits [14]. However, others argue that such arrangements may not be as effective as office-based work for both organizations and employees. Based on the preceding arguments, the book chapters aim to address the following questions:

1. What are the advantages and drawbacks of flexible work arrangements during and after the pandemic?

2. What factors enhance the efficiency and effectiveness of alternative work setups?

3. How can organizations prepare for and effectively support alternative work arrangements?

4. In what ways do technologies and human resource practices enable remote work?

5. What effects does work digitalization have on mental workload and health?

4. Diversity and immigration trends

While everyone experienced economic, professional, and social challenges during the pandemic, the severity and prevalence of these challenges were disproportionately higher for certain groups, particularly women, people of color, and working parents [15]. Issues such as workplace safety, mental health, social isolation, maintaining employability, career progression, and work-life balance presented significantly greater challenges for these groups.

Notably, diversity, equity, and inclusion (DEI) emerged as one of the top societal and political concerns during the pandemic. Although inequalities between diverse and other groups have always existed, the impact of the pandemic underscored these disparities to an even greater extent. The heightened societal awareness surrounding DEI issues exerted pressure on organizations to increase their investment in DEI initiatives and programs, even amidst economic downturns.

The literature explores numerous organizational DEI practices, each varying in effectiveness. These practices encompass diversity training, recruiting, and training minorities for managerial roles, promoting transparency in hiring, performance evaluation, and promotion processes, implementing fair retention strategies, and adopting equitable layoff policies [16]. With the ongoing shift toward digitalization and alternative work arrangements, there is growing concern about how workplace practices will address DEI considerations. As such, the book will delve into managerial and human resource practices within organizations aimed at fostering a diverse and inclusive workplace.

Another critical issue that requires attention is the escalating concern over immigration, particularly the phenomenon of brain drain from developing and emerging economies to more developed nations. This trend is especially pronounced in vital sectors such as healthcare, where the departure of skilled professionals is becoming increasingly prevalent. Skilled workers, being more mobile than their unskilled counterparts, choose destination countries based on factors such as job opportunities, income, colonial ties, immigration policies, stability, and career advancement, among others [17]. Hence, the book will explore the primary reasons for brain drain and suggest policies to mitigate it in developing countries.

5. Conclusion

This book represents a collaborative effort by a multinational group of scholars aiming to contribute to the evolving discourse on the nature of work and the workplace in the twenty-first century. Its chapters offer a blend of literature reviews, theoretical insights, and empirical findings drawn from diverse national contexts.

Employing a range of research methods including case studies, interviews, surveys, and literature reviews, the book provides a comprehensive exploration of the changing landscape of the workplace and workforce.

The initial section of the book delves into the characteristics and impacts of Industry 4.0, with a particular focus on the ramifications of artificial intelligence and other technological advancements. It offers actionable recommendations for policymakers, organizations, and researchers to navigate the associated challenges and leverage the opportunities presented.

The subsequent section shifts its attention to the transformative effects of the COVID-19 pandemic on the workforce, with a spotlight on remote work and alternative work arrangements both during and after the pandemic. This section examines the nuanced benefits and challenges inherent in such arrangements and offers strategies for organizations to optimize their implementation for enhanced effectiveness and efficiency.

The final section of the book is dedicated to exploring the interconnected issues of diversity and immigration, which have emerged as significant global concerns. It underscores the importance of managerial and human resource practices in fostering diversity, equity, and inclusion within organizations. Additionally, this section addresses the escalating trend of brain drain from developing countries and proposes policy interventions aimed at retaining skilled workers and mitigating the associated challenges.

Author details

Hadi El-Farr
Human Resource Management Department, School of Management and Labor Relations, Rutgers University, Piscataway, United States of America

*Address all correspondence to: hadi.elfarr@rutgers.edu

References

[1] Martinelli A, Mina A, Moggi M. The enabling technologies of industry 4.0: Examining the seeds of the fourth industrial revolution. Industrial and Corporate Change. 2021;**30**(1):161-188

[2] Ali S, Al-Sultan H, Rubaie M. Fifth industrial revolution: (New perspectives). International Journal of Business, Management and Economics. 2022;**3**(3):196-212

[3] Kim RY. The fifth wave: The sustainability age and new industrial revolution. IEEE Engineering Management Review. 2024;**99**:1-12

[4] Ali SH, Al-Sultan HA, Al Rubaie MT. Fifth industrial revolution: (New perspectives). International Journal of Business, Management, and Economics. 2022;**3**(3):196-212

[5] Santhi AR, Muthuswamy P. Industry 5.0 or industry 4.0S? Introduction to industry 4.0 and a peek into the prospective industry 5.0 technologies. International Journal on Interactive Design and Manufacturing. 2023;**17**:947-979

[6] Schwab K. The Fourth Industrial Revolution. Geneva: World Economic Forum; 2016

[7] Schwab K. The Fourth Industrial Revolution: What it means, how to respond. 2016. [Online]. Available from: https://www.weforum.org/agenda/2016/01/the-fourth-industrial-revolution-what-it-means-and-how-to-respond/ [Accessed: April 4, 2024]

[8] Mihalache M, Mihalache OR. How workplace support for the COVID-19 pandemic and personality traits affect changes in employees' affective commitment to the organization and job-related well-being. Human Resource Management. 2022;**61**(3):295-314

[9] Sasaki N, Kuroda R, Tsuno K, Kawakami N. Workplace responses to COVID-19 associated with mental health and work performance of employees in Japan. Journal of Occupational Health. 2020;**62**(1):e12134

[10] Galanti T, Galanti GG, Mazzei E, Zappalà S, Toscano F. Work from home during the COVID-19 outbreak: The impact on employees' remote work productivity, engagement, and stress. Journal of Occupational and Environmental Medicine. 2021;**63**(7):426-432

[11] Alipour J-V, Falck O, Schüller S. Germany's capacity to work from home. European Economic Review. 2023;**151**:104354

[12] Erdsiek D. Working from home during COVID-19 and beyond: Survey evidence from employers. In: ZEW - Leibniz Centre for European Economic Research Discussion Paper Series. Mannheim: Leibniz-Zentrum für Europäische Wirtschaftsforschung; 2021

[13] Yang E, Kim Y, Hong S. Does working from home work? Experience of working from home and the value of hybrid workplace post-COVID-19. Journal of Corporate Real Estate. 2023;**25**(1):50-76

[14] Barrero JM, Bloom N, Davis SJ. Why working from home will stick. In: NBER Working Papers Series. Cambridge: National Bureau of Economic Research; 2021

[15] Ellingrud K, Krishnan M, Krivkovich A, Kukla K, Mendy A,

Robinson N, et al. Diverse Employees Are Struggling the Most during COVID-19—Here's How Companies Can Respond. New York: McKinsey & Company; 2020

[16] Dobbin F, Schrage D, Kalev A. Rage against the iron cage: The varied effects of bureaucratic personnel reforms on diversity. American Sociological Review. 2015;**80**(5):1014-1044

[17] Najib M, Salloum A, Juni MH. Brain-drain phenomenon among healthcare workers. International Journal of Public Health and Clinical Sciences. 2019;**6**(3):90-103

Chapter 2

Knowledge Management and Knowledge Leadership in the Fourth Industrial Revolution: Resolving the Automation-Augmentation Paradox

Hadi El-Farr and Kevin Sevag Kertechian

Abstract

As acknowledged by scholars and practitioners, the rise of artificial intelligence and cyber-physical systems has led to a shift from the third to the fourth industrial revolution. Knowledge management as a discipline evolved in the late twentieth century, reflecting the increasing importance of knowledge as a resource in the knowledge-economy era. This chapter explores how organizations manage their knowledge in the fourth industrial revolution, which arguably should differ from how they did in the 1990s. The paper will begin by identifying the major characteristics of the four industrial revolutions. It will then delve into organizations' strategies for managing knowledge during the third industrial revolution. Subsequently, alternative knowledge management strategies will be highlighted to address the changes brought about by the fourth industrial revolution. We claim that organizations might decide to prioritize augmentation or automation, or we propose an organic relationship between both, calling for another approach to managing knowledge: DeParadoxication. By reviewing relevant literature, this chapter proposes a theoretical framework for knowledge management in the twenty-first century.

Keywords: artificial intelligence, industry 4.0, augmentation, automation, knowledge management, leadership, strategy, IT adoption, job design, employee skills

1. Introduction

The rise of the knowledge economy in the 1990s stressed the importance of knowledge as the most critical resource to achieve a competitive advantage [1]. Reflecting the central role of knowledge in production, the term knowledge management was introduced, highlighting the need for organizations to manage knowledge creation and exploitation actively [2]. Knowledge has always been a source of competitive advantage, even before the knowledge economy era. That said, the increased importance rose due to the growth in the service sector and knowledge-intensive industries [1]. Thus, developing advanced information technology solutions and the quality of embedded knowledge in workers, in addition to their willingness to share knowledge and ability to create knowledge, arguably, became more important than financial and physical resources in competition. Stated differently, in the knowledge economy era, products and services are characterized by rapid obsolescence; therefore, the speed of knowledge creation and innovation and the dissemination of knowledge and its widespread use within organizations, among other knowledge-intensive activities, are of greater importance to organizational competitiveness than any other resource [3].

Many scholars argue that we are in the fourth industrial revolution (Industry 4.0), a term made famous by Klaus Schwab, the founder and chairman of the World Economic Forum [4]. The shift from the third to the fourth industrial revolution was caused by the development of several general-purpose technologies (GPTs), which infuse the physical world with the digital and biological [5]. Among those GPTs are artificial intelligence (AI), cyber-physical systems (CPS), intelligent robots, and advancements in nanotechnology and biotechnology, which enabled a major leap in innovation, automation, productivity, quality, efficiency, and customization [5, 6]. With the emergence of the fourth industrial revolution, knowledge management is far from being obsolete. The importance of knowledge in achieving a competitive advantage has been increasing exponentially. Agreeing with some scholars in the field of knowledge management, we argue that the approach to knowledge management should adjust to accommodate the technological advancements of the current era [7].

This chapter will begin with highlighting the major features of the first three industrial revolutions, leading to an in-depth presentation of the fourth industrial revolution. Then, it will present an overview of the knowledge management strategies debated in the third industrial revolution. The chapter will focus then on debating three knowledge management strategies to cater to the fourth industrial revolution. Afterward, the concept of knowledge leadership will be addressed, highlighting the best-fit leadership styles and roles in the digital era. Finally, the chapter will briefly present some technological and human challenges, with a focus on the essential role of leadership in managing those challenges and their interrelations.

2. The first three industrial revolutions

An industrial revolution is marked by technological breakthroughs that lead to substantial shifts in the socio-economic landscape. Such innovations, termed general-purpose technologies (GPTs), can be widely integrated into various industries (pervasiveness), enhance productivity and efficiency (dynamism), and foster innovation and the development of diverse technical applications (complementarities) [8]. In the context of this chapter, we define an industrial revolution as the rise of multiple technological advancements that deeply transform the economy, particularly in terms of production methods, the creation or obsoleteness of new industries, and the impact on the workplace and workforce.

In essence, although the introduction of GPTs during each industrial revolution marks a significant surge in automation, productivity, and efficacy, it is essential to highlight that the pace at which organizations adopt these technologies can vary based on financial constraints and their ability to integrate innovations, among other factors. So, while some enterprises are at the forefront, leveraging cutting-edge technologies, others may still rely on tools from past industrial phases.

Before the first industrial revolution and the factory system, manufacturing took place within the domestic system, also referred to as the putting-out system or cottage industry. Craftsmen produced goods at home or in workshops. Merchant capitalists used to deliver raw materials to craftsmen, who process them into final goods. Then, the merchant capitalist collects the goods, compensates the craftsmen, and sells the products in the market. The domestic system, thus, is characterized by high decentralization, low efficiency, and low production capacity. That said, the knowledge of the entire production process is embedded in the artisan, and the production quality depends on their skill level, with a high ability for customization. Moreover, craftsmen had more control over their schedules and working methods, which meant merchant capitalists had a diminished role in directing the production process.

The Industrial Revolution, a transformative era, unfolded in three distinct phases, fundamentally reshaping society and the economy. The First Revolution introduced mechanization with steam power, the Second ushered in mass production with electricity, and the Third revolutionized industries with digital technology. Each phase marked a significant leap in technological advancement, collectively setting the stage for the modern industrialized world.

2.1 The first industrial revolution

The onset of the First Industrial Revolution, often termed Industry 1.0, can be traced back to the mid-eighteenth century, marked by significant innovations like the steam engine. Initially invented by Thomas Newcomen in 1712, the steam engine underwent transformative enhancements under James Watt in 1769 [9]. The era's primary General-Purpose Technologies (GPTs) included steam and water power, facilitating the shift toward mechanized production. By the mid-nineteenth century, the embrace of steam engines and the factory system intensified, propelling industrialization to new heights by introducing the factory system.

These technological advancements ushered in heightened automation, lessening reliance on manual craftsmanship and amplifying production speed and efficiency. The outcome was a monumental increase in product diversity, volume, and affordability. Steam engines became instrumental across multiple sectors, including textiles, transportation (like steam trains and ships), construction, farming, mining, and glassmaking [9]. This boom spurred a greater need for resources such as coal and iron. Consequently, cities grew as more people flocked to them for factory jobs, replacing the artisan-based workforce of yesteryears. This shift also birthed new socio-economic divisions, notably the working class and the capitalist elites.

However, the gifts of the Steam Age came with their set of challenges. While production and transportation underwent revolutionary enhancements, there were adverse repercussions like heightened pollution, subpar working environments, meager wages, and the exploitation of child labor. These developments further deepened social disparities and introduced a range of societal concerns.

2.2 The second industrial revolution

The late nineteenth century heralded the onset of the Second Industrial Revolution frequently referred to as Industry 2.0, primarily propelled by the innovation of electricity. This pivotal change witnessed the shift from steam to electric power, bringing about a transformative wave in factory automation. The genesis of this transformation can be traced back to 1870 with the invention of electric generators and trains. This period also saw the introduction of assembly lines and a structured division of labor, leading to the large-scale production of goods. The work process became more standardized, tasks more simplified, and labor more task-specialized. In this framework, workers were often perceived as mere cogs in the production wheel, required to possess only rudimentary skills for their specific tasks. One evident advantage of this was the substantial augmentation in productivity and operational efficiency.

Beyond just electrification, this era was marked by groundbreaking advancements in domains like steel manufacturing, chemicals, combustion engines, and communication [9]. This period birthed or significantly enhanced industries like automotive, aviation, construction, agriculture, and the oil and petrochemical sectors.

Building upon the foundations of the First Industrial Revolution, Industry 2.0 further accelerated economic expansion and urbanization. This led to a surge in oil demand, and cities expanded, necessitating enhanced infrastructure. Products became more accessible to consumers due to their increased affordability. However, this period also brought challenges: deteriorating work conditions, rising unemployment, heightened work-related stress, and growing social disparities became more pronounced. Additionally, as with its predecessor, the era was marked by escalating environmental pollution and a worrying trend of resource exhaustion.

2.3 The third industrial revolution

The Third Industrial Revolution, often termed Industry 3.0 or the Digital Revolution, emerged in the mid-twentieth century, marked predominantly by the advent of microprocessors. This era witnessed a pivotal transition from primarily hardware-focused technologies to digitalization, heralding what many consider the dawn of the Information Age [9]. A benchmark moment in this revolution was around 1970 when advancements in computers and automation systems reached a point of widespread industrial application. This period's pivotal General-Purpose Technologies (GPTs) encompassed computers, the internet, advanced electronics, and robotics. This technological surge enabled the automation of complex tasks, fostering an era of specialized production combined with heightened efficiency.

These innovations allowed factories to operate with minimal human intervention. Concurrently, there was significant progress in both nuclear energy and sustainable energy sources. The demands of Industry 3.0 emphasized a more educated and highly skilled workforce, amplifying the importance of advanced education and training programs. Additionally, the revolution ushered in dramatic improvements in communication, knowledge dissemination, storage, and analytical capabilities due to the evolution of information and communication technology.

Digital transformation reshaped numerous sectors, from e-commerce, digital and social media platforms, IT, and telecom, to biotech, 3D printing, green energy, financial services, healthcare, and manufacturing. These sectors have been reshaped through automation, advanced analytics, and advanced manufacturing technology. The ripple effects of Industry 3.0's innovations persist, with many experts positing that we are still navigating this transformative period. A notable societal shift during this time has been a heightened consciousness about work-life harmony, environmental sustainability, and addressing socio-economic disparities.

3. The fourth industrial revolution

In this twenty-first century, it's undeniable that trends toward automation and digitalization are intensifying. However, there's ongoing debate regarding whether we are navigating the Fourth Industrial Revolution or merely witnessing an extension of the Third Industrial Revolution's core technological advancements [8]. Despite differing views, a common consensus is that both productivity and customization are on an upward trajectory, bringing along substantial shifts in employment patterns and technological innovation.

Among those who advocate that we are amidst the Fourth Revolution, many emphasize a suite of interrelated technologies underpinning Industry 4.0, rather than a single predominant one. Prominent among these GPTs are artificial intelligence (AI), big data, the Internet of Things (IoT), cloud computing, machine learning (inclusive of deep learning), advanced robotics, cyber-physical systems (CPS), additive manufacturing, and blockchain [8, 10, 11]. Notably, AI and CPS stand out as particularly emphasized GPTs, as they are also inclusive of most of the previously mentioned GPTs.

The innovations have undeniably left a profound mark across various sectors, ushering in enhanced intelligence in industries such as manufacturing, healthcare, transportation, energy, information and communication technology, as well as commerce. Most job roles will likely see shifts, with further automation of routine tasks and, notably, creative, and non-routine tasks that were once deemed uniquely human. Consequently, there's a growing discourse about the requisite skills for the modern workforce and how frequently these skills might become outdated. This directly influences individual employability and raises concerns about heightened unemployment rates as technology adoption and advancement accelerate. Moreover, Industry 4.0 raises significant concerns about the loss of craftsmanship and an increase in wage disparity [12]. An accompanying **Figure 1** illustrates the core characteristics of the four industrial revolutions, underscoring the consistent rise in automation through each phase.

Given the significant influence of both GPTs and the widespread agreement among scholars regarding their pivotal role in the fourth industrial revolution, the subsequent sections will delve deeper into the realms of AI and CPS. Furthermore, we'll underscore the economic paradigm of this revolution, characterized by a transition toward mass personalization.

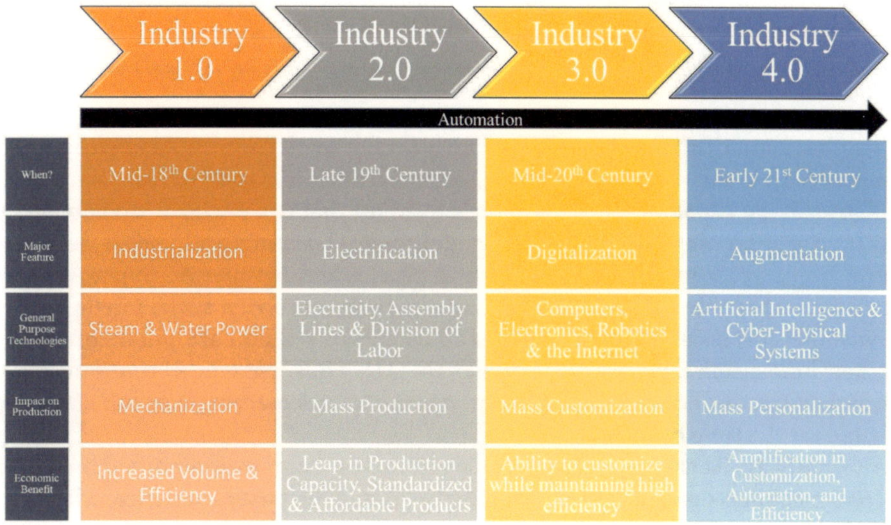

Figure 1.
Major characteristics of the four industrial revolutions.

3.1 Artificial intelligence

AI's definition remains debated, with no universal agreement [13]. Typically, AI is perceived as a system that learns from past experiences, comprehends its environment, modifies based on new data, and makes decisions aligned with its designated objectives. Advanced AI systems exhibit autonomy, implying decision-making without human intervention. Depending on the AI's sophistication, it might replace human activities, ranging from basic repetitive tasks to intricate cognitive ones. The ultimate objective is to enhance prediction quality while saving time and costs [13]. Therefore, a comprehensive AI definition suggests a system capable of partially or wholly substituting human roles, amplifying capabilities beyond traditional automation.

Numerous taxonomies have been proposed by both researchers and professionals. For instance, in 2017 PwC introduced a classification with four AI categories, based on human interaction levels with machine decisions and whether the AI merely automates existing tasks or explores new ones independently [14]. Therefore, the report provided four types of AI: assisted intelligence, automated intelligence, augmented intelligence, and autonomous intelligence, which are demonstrated in the following **Figure 2**.

	With Human Involvement	No Human Involvement
Specific Systems	**Assisted Intelligence** Systems that assist employees in making decisions faster and better, yet they are not capable of learning.	**Automated Intelligence** Systems that automate cognitive existing tasks, yet it is not capable of learning.
Adaptive Systems	**Augmented Intelligence** Systems that augment employee decision-making, and are capable of learning.	**Autonomous Intelligence** Systems that autonomously adapt and act with no human involvement.

Figure 2.
Artificial intelligence forms based on human involvement and level of adaptability (adapted from: [14]).

Another classification is to differentiate between weak (narrow) and strong AI (general) [11]. Weak AI is systems designed and trained for specific tasks with no problem-solving capabilities. Strong AI are systems that can perform intellectual tasks such as reasoning, problem-solving, judgment, learning, and understanding natural language. Some theorized for a third type, which is super AI. Super AI is a system that is capable of duplicating humans in their creativity, social intelligence, and wisdom. It is noteworthy that strong and super AI systems are still theoretical and their innovation might not appear shortly [11]. Thus, current AI solutions may reduce the human element in production, but the total replacement of humans is not probable for the time being (**Figure 3**).

Alternatively, AI can be classified under reactive machines and limited memory. Reactive machines do not have the capacity to learn from past experience, while limited memory AI does have the ability to learn from data input and amend decisions accordingly. A typical example of reactive AI is machine learning models, and a typical example of limited memory is deep learning algorithms. Some added the theory

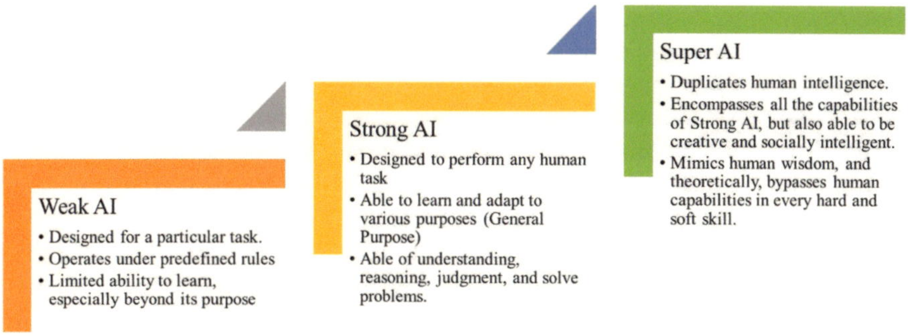

Figure 3.
Major characteristics of weak, strong, and super AI systems.

of mind and self-awareness systems, which might evolve in the future. The theory of mind suggests the development of AI systems that can have emotions, beliefs, desires, and mental capabilities, similar to what we identified before as super AI. Self-aware AI goes one step further by developing systems that have their own consciousness and emotions. Alternatively, AI could be categorized based on its function, such as machine learning, deep learning, neural networks, natural language processing, cognitive computing, robotic automation…etc. (**Figure 4**).

Decision-making in a system necessitates an algorithm, processing power, and relevant data for algorithm training. As algorithms grow more sophisticated and computers advance [15], the quality and quantity of the data become pivotal. A richer dataset ensures superior algorithm outcomes. However, AI concepts, like expert systems, machine learning, and neural networks, aren't novel. Introduced around the mid-twentieth century, their evolution was previously constrained by the absence of substantial data and limited computational capacities [10]. With the advent of big data, permitting extensive data accumulation, coupled with amplified processing

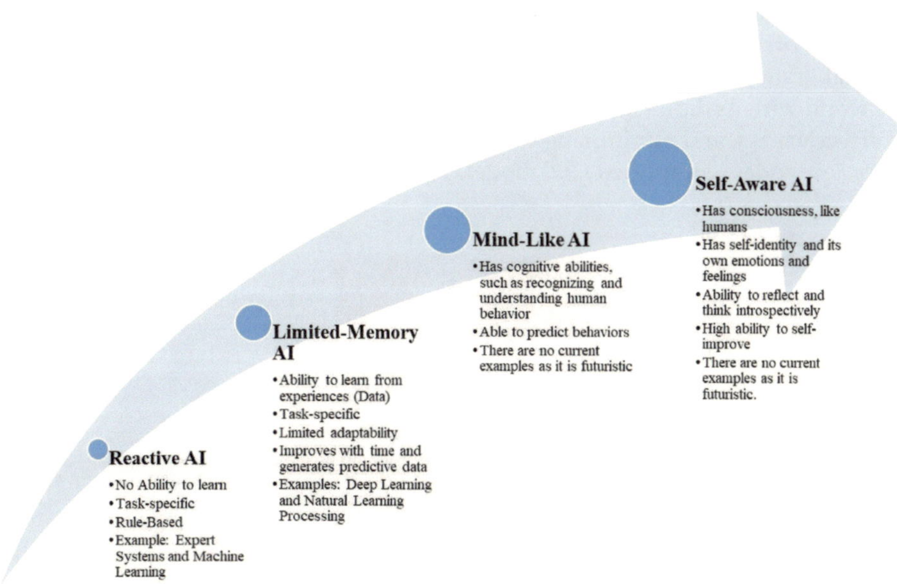

Figure 4.
Major attributes of reactive, limited-memory, mind-like, and self-aware AI systems.

abilities, AI's potential has surged dramatically [13]. Given the expected advancements in data solutions and processing capabilities, future prospects seem brighter.

The era of digitalization witnesses exponential growth in data volume, speed, and diversity. Whether structured or unstructured, harnessing this data for knowledge extraction is invaluable. This extracted knowledge, besides being shareable, is a potent innovation catalyst. However, given big data's sheer volume and complexity, conventional processing tools often fall short. Thus, advanced predictive analytics are essential to derive meaningful insights. The cloud further facilitates efficient big data storage and enhances accessibility, offering computational prowess and diverse IT tools. The pay-as-you-use nature of cloud services eliminates hefty initial IT infrastructure investments, especially benefiting small and medium enterprises with limited investment capacities for intricate IT solutions. Therefore, current AI development and adoption was the result of several technological advancements that are interdependent to achieve the existing systems, and the future ones if they evolve.

3.2 Cyber-physical systems

CPS fuses the realm of physical processes with virtual computations [11]. This is done through several components: sensors, actuators, computation systems (AI systems), and communication networks, which enable them to interact with each other. Sensors are physical endpoints that monitor the surroundings and send data through the network to the computation system. The system will analyze the data and generate decisions to be implemented by the actuators, which are also physical endpoints. Prime examples of CPS include autonomous vehicles, sophisticated self-operating robots, and smart factories.

While CPS encompasses the concept of IoT, it emphasizes a deep synchronicity between hardware and digital computations. IoT refers to a network of devices, each boasting its unique digital identifier on the internet. Linked by specific protocols, these devices gather, disseminate, analyze, execute, and exchange information. This intricate web of interconnected devices amasses a treasure trove of insights, paving the way for further innovation. Beyond mere data logging and sharing, these devices can collaborate to oversee and fine-tune one another. In essence, IoT bridges the tangible world with its digital counterpart, increasing optimization, efficiency, quality, and effectiveness, and minimizing the need for human operators [11]. The following **Figure 5** provides a simplified CPS model.

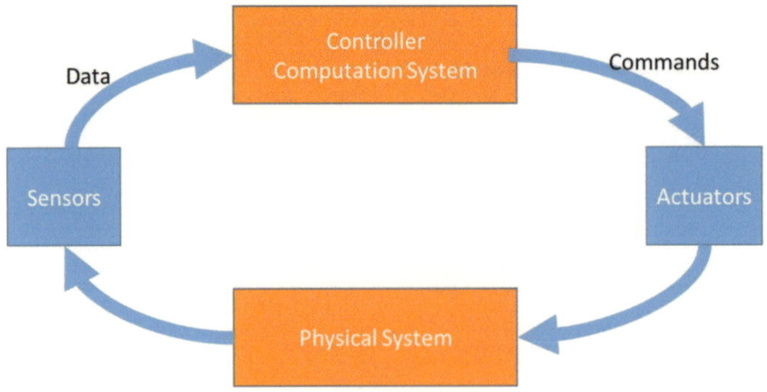

Figure 5.
Simplified model of a cyber-physical system.

3.3 The economic model of the fourth industrial revolution

The GPTs mentioned earlier pave the way for enhanced mass customization in production. They even hold the promise of advancing to mass personalization, where products can be jointly developed with individual customers without driving up production costs. Today's consumers crave personalized experiences. The capability to understand and cater to individual preferences while sustaining large-scale production became feasible primarily due to intelligent systems [12]. These systems have refined customization, evident in platform-based business models, online supply chains driven by real-time demand, and tools that involve customers in the design process [16]. Moreover, organizations that focus on customers rather than products, rely on consumer data and communication, and behavioral analysis to further cater to individual customers [17].

While many companies are yet to fully embrace mass personalization, many are pushing the boundaries of mass customization, aiming to serve increasingly specific niches and ultimately individual needs. Failing to do so might lead them to lose out to competitors, bear higher inventory expenses, and miss out on innovative breakthroughs, potentially eroding their market edge [18].

4. What is knowledge management?

Although scholars differ in defining knowledge management, the consensus is that organizations should seek to extract the maximum value from their existing knowledge and strive to add to their knowledge depository through knowledge creation and acquisition [19]. Doing so will achieve continuous innovation in products and services, which leads to achieving a sustainable competitive advantage. Some scholars presented knowledge management as a system or strategy with supporting processes to flourish knowledge-intensive activities within a firm [20–23]. Others looked at knowledge management as the active management or facilitation of a set of knowledge-intensive activities. A taxonomy of these activities could be grouped under three major ones: knowledge sharing (includes dissemination, usability, and accessibility), knowledge creation, and knowledge codification (includes transformation, storage, protection, and representation) [24]. For some, knowledge management should deal with knowledge as a resource, thus the focus should be on accumulating intellectual assets. Many scholars looked at knowledge management as active management of various knowledge types and their interaction and transformation, such as explicit knowledge vs. tacit knowledge and organizational knowledge vs. personal knowledge [22, 25–27].

Regardless of the definition, knowledge management focuses on two dimensions: information technology and human, and how to manage each and their interaction to maximize innovation, production, revenues, and profitability [28]. Management could flourish knowledge-intensive activities, whether embedded in humans and networks, information systems, or a combination of both, through formal and informal mechanisms. Formal mechanisms include strategy formation, processes, systems, rules, and procedures, and Informal mechanisms include the organizational culture, which includes norms and behaviors within and across teams and networks [28, 29].

4.1 How knowledge was managed during the first and second industrial revolutions?

Before Industry 1.0, the putting-out system was highly dependent on the embodied and embrained knowledge that is embedded in the craftsman. Rarely any of this knowledge is embedded and encoded in processes, structures, or documents. Therefore, the knowledge of the full production process was tacit in nature, which was hard to articulate and represents a trade secret owned fully by the artisan. Encultured knowledge was of less significance, as most production operations were based in households or small workshops. Moreover, each craftsman knowledge and skills are unique, which resulted in variations in quality and product differentiation, both dependent on the artisan's level of skill. Merchant capitalists specialized in managing the supply chain and marketing, complementary yet completely separate processes from the production process. Due to the dominance of tacit knowledge, the transfer of knowledge took place through the apprenticeship process. The master artisan takes an apprentice, who would shadow and work under direct supervision. Thus, the process of learning was through intensive tacit knowledge exchange (imitation, mentorship, on-the-job training, trial and error...etc.), and gradual (from a novice to tradesman-in-training to master), which took years before the apprentice reached the level of mastery.

The introduction of machines during Industry 1.0 resulted in the automation of much of the knowledge previously held by craftsmen. For instance, tasks like knotting, cutting, and stitching, once done with simple tools by craftsmen, were gradually replaced by machines. This shift accelerated during the Second Industrial Revolution when machines became more complex, and assembly lines were introduced. Division of labor and time-and-motion studies led to increased specialization in tasks, with employees performing simple, repetitive tasks that complemented the assembly line. As a consequence, much of the knowledge inherent in craftsmen's skills was decoded and substituted by machines. The comprehensive knowledge of the entire production process was now owned by a new class of supervisors and managers [30]. These managers acted as agents of capitalists, overseeing planning, control, direction, coordination, resource allocation, scheduling, and staffing of operations to ensure efficiency, predictability, and consistency [31].

In this context, employees required only a few basic, easily trainable skills, reducing the need for extensive knowledge transfer among workers and making them readily replaceable. The critical knowledge for organizational success was now vested in managers and supervisors, and a significant portion of it was documented in processes and documents, transforming it from personal to organizational knowledge. As a result, capitalists gained greater control over their investments, and organizations operated in a standardized manner, with reduced risk of losing essential knowledge due to employee turnover.

4.2 What are the proposed knowledge management strategies in the twentieth century?

Many scholars proposed various knowledge management strategies with the emergence of the knowledge management concept in the 1990s. Most notable is the work of Hansen et al. who proposed two main strategies: codification and personalization [23]. The codification strategy follows an IT perspective on knowledge management, which aims to logically codify and store information in databases to increase its accessibility and widespread usability. In other words, the focus is to transfer tacit knowledge, which is embedded in employees, to explicit knowledge. The competitive advantage of codification is speed, reliability, efficiency, and quality control – aiming for standardization and competitive pricing.

On the other hand, the personalization strategy follows an HR perspective on knowledge management, which aims to rely on the knowledge embedded in employees, relationships, and managerial styles. Information systems are viewed here as

Codification

- **Economic Model:** high customization with high-profit margins.
- **Knowledge Management Strategy:** Developing networks to flourish tacit knowledge exchange.
- **IT Approach:** Moderate investment in IT solutions to facilitate tacit knowledge exchange.
- **HR Approach:** Hiring highly skilled talent and invest in their training. Reward knowledge sharing.

Personalization

- **Economic Model:** high standardization with low profit margins, focusing on high revenues.
- **Knowledge Management Strategy:** building databases that codify, store, and disseminate knowledge.
- **IT Approach:** High Investment in IT solutions to ensure high dissemination and reuse of knowledge.
- **HR Approach:** Hiring a few experts. Other employees need little experience and are trained to reuse knowledge developed by experts. Rewards knowledge usage and knowledge contribution to databases.

Figure 6.
Major attributes of the codification and personalization strategies (adapted from: [23]).

mere enablers to augment work, while the key factors are employee experience, networking, interaction, knowledge-sharing with others, and building a knowledge-sharing culture. The competitive advantage of personalization is promoting creativity, uniqueness, and flexibility – aiming for customization and allowing higher pricing for differentiation. The following **Figure 6** presents the major attributes of codification and personalization.

In reality, even when one strategy is dominant or primary, the other will act as supportive or secondary. Hansen et al. warned that only one strategy should be dominant, for if management pushed for both, the result might be confusion and failure [23]. This standpoint was criticized by several scholars, stating that it is hard to neglect the desire of organizations to harvest the benefits of both strategies, stressing their equal importance [32]. Thus, some scholars proposed a combination strategy, where decision-makers in organizations support both personalization and codification, utilizing each to the extent that it is useful to the activity, product, and context [19]. Another critique is that Hansen et al. focused on management consulting firms as a study sample, where such duality might not be applicable in other sectors, such as manufacturing.

Another foundational work is Nonaka's and Takeuchi's knowledge spiral model, which aims to increase knowledge sharing and creation within organizations, thus enabling them to innovate products and processes faster and sustaining their competitive advantage [27]. They proposed the SECI process, which stands for socialization, externalization, combination, and internalization. Socialization is when employees share their tacit knowledge and transfer it to others' tacit knowledge, through interaction and mentorship. The receivers of tacit knowledge will embed it through imitation, observation, and practice. This leads to externalization, where tacit knowledge is articulated, that is, transferred into explicit knowledge through dialogs and reflections. This explicit knowledge will be combined into documents and databases, which allows widespread dissemination. Finally, the explicit knowledge will be available for employees to internalize and transfer to their tacit knowledge through acquisition, sense-making, analysis, and reflection, leading them to be creative in generating new concepts and ideas; that is new tacit knowledge. That said, the four stages of the SECI model do not occur in a vacuum. They take place in groups and organizational contexts, referred to as "Ba". Ba includes the mental space (including experiences, values, and ideas), the physical space, and the virtual space (such as databases, platforms, and informational and communication technologies) (**Figure 7**) [33].

Therefore, based on studying the manufacturing sector in Japan, which could be applied to various sectors and national cultures Nonaka and Takeuchi provided a

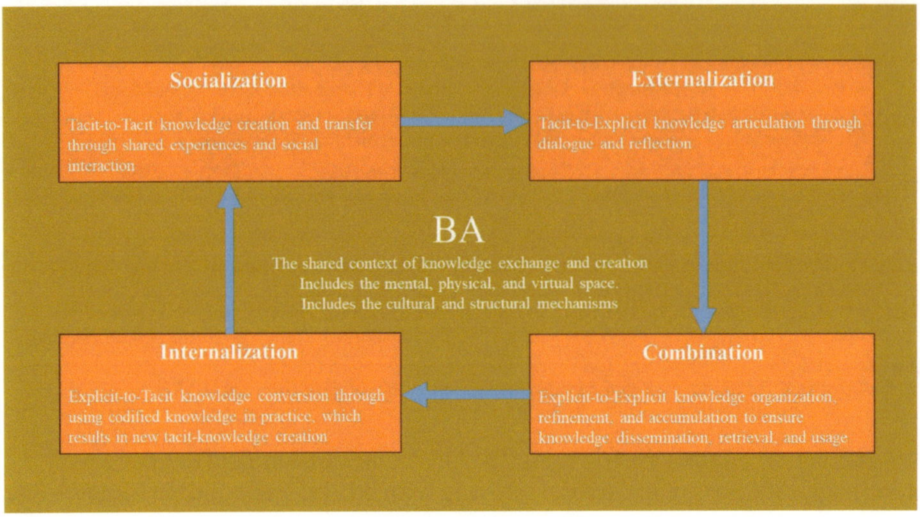

Figure 7.
The SECI model of knowledge creation in organizations (adapted from: [25]).

strategy for how management should manage knowledge to make it more organizational and achieve a learning, creative, and innovative firm [33]. That said, a major critique of this model is that tacit knowledge conversion to explicit is never fully accomplished, as much personal knowledge and knowledge embedded in relationships is hard to articulate and convert, and even the converted knowledge is subject to interpretation [33]. So, although the SECI model provides a framework to formulate a knowledge management strategy and implementation practices, hardly can someone claims its completeness and comprehensiveness in addressing knowledge management activities.

Those are some of the many knowledge management strategies and frameworks that were proposed during the 1990s, which was during the third industrial revolution. Although their relevance is still valid to this date, we will argue that alternative strategies are more suitable for the fourth industrial revolution era, reflecting the substantial technological advancements of the twenty-first century.

5. Knowledge management strategies for industry 4.0

In light of the opportunities and challenges presented by the fourth industrial revolution, organizations must develop a strategic approach to Knowledge Management to harness the advantages and address the risks. The management of knowledge activities and processes is still influenced by two principal dimensions: the technological and the human. AI and CPS are progressively assuming cognitive responsibilities once handled by humans, leading to increased automation. However, it's important to note that AI and CPS also have the potential to enable augmentation, where humans and machines collaborate closely to accomplish tasks. As a result, automation and augmentation appear to represent two contrasting strategic directions for Knowledge Management, especially within the Human Resources dimension. The former seeks to minimize if not entirely replace human involvement, while the latter aims to retain and enhance human performance.

In line with these two dimensions, the industry 5.0 represents a significant shift from the automation and efficiency focus of Industry 4.0 toward a model that integrates human creativity and collaboration with smart technologies. This transition necessitates a nuanced approach to knowledge management, highlighting the importance of human-centric values, sustainability, and resilience. The progression from Industry 4.0 to 5.0 amplifies the importance of these processes but adds layers of complexity and opportunity, particularly in terms of leveraging human-machine collaboration. In Industry 5.0, KM must not only ensure that information flows effectively but also that there is a symbiotic relationship between the cognitive and creative capabilities of humans and the analytical, data-processing powers of AI and machine learning systems. Additionally, the transition from Industry 4.0 to Industry 5.0 is not marked by a clear boundary but rather represents an evolving paradigm.

If the ultimate goal is achieving hyper-automation, which means automating nearly all organizational processes from start to finish, the result is a more efficient, logical, and comprehensive workflow [15]. This can lead to higher levels of quality control and faster production, potentially increasing profitability. However, machines, as they currently stand, have various limitations that prevent them from completely replacing humans. These limitations include areas such as emotional intelligence, comprehension, problem-solving, intuition, creativity, consciousness, and judgment. In essence, current AI solutions are specialized and lack commercialized strong or super AI systems; these are still in the realm of theory and the future. Consequently, existing solutions excel in rule-based decision-making and managing structured and semi-structured tasks. Yet, they fall short when dealing with unstructured, complex, and ambiguous tasks due to their inability to adapt beyond their predefined algorithms.

Alternatively, the augmentation approach suggests harnessing the capabilities of machines while keeping humans in the loop to address the limitations mentioned earlier. However, the allure of automation is hard to resist whenever the opportunity arises to automate a task, offering greater benefits and lower costs. For the time being, humans, working alongside machines, are better equipped to handle tasks that are predicted for strong and super AI. They are better positioned to exercise responsibility, judgment, substantial reasoning, and complex decision-making thanks to their adaptability and interpersonal skills. The following **Figure 8** outlines some advantages of both automation and augmentation, where the strengths of one approach can be seen as the weaknesses of the other, underscoring the inherent contradiction between these two approaches.

Recognizing the distinctions and conflicts between the automation and augmentation strategies, Raisch and Krakowski also emphasized their interconnectedness [15]. They contend that favoring one approach over the other restricts the potential to reap the advantages of both, as each can enhance the capabilities of the other. This interrelationship is highlighted through both the timing and the scope of implementation, which they debated under the following two scales: temporal and spatial.

5.1 Temporal scale

At a certain juncture, management may opt for augmentation when dealing with complex tasks that require the nuanced expertise of professionals, making them challenging to automate. Managers and experts collaborate with data scientists and engage with intelligent systems, where the output of these systems enhances their capabilities and knowledge. They assess the systems' results, make choices based

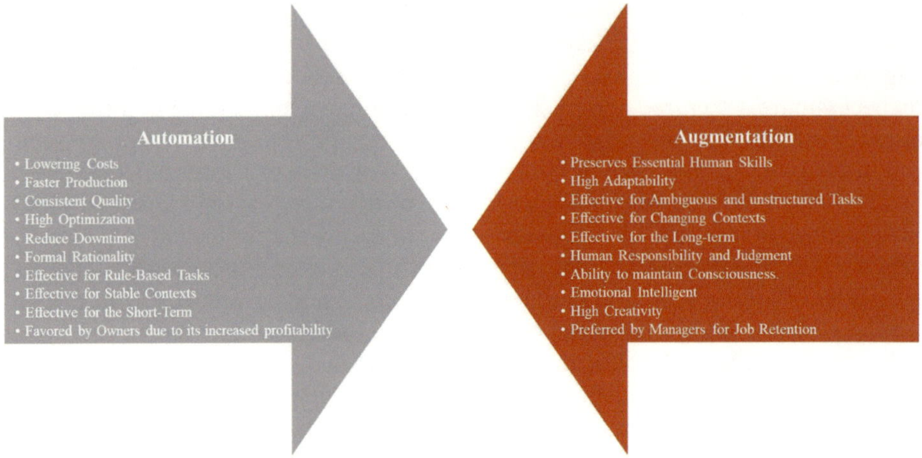

Figure 8.
Major advantages of automation and augmentation.

on their expertise, and compensate for the system's limitations. Over time, the intelligent system learns and refines its output, leading to a transition from augmentation to automation, resulting in improved efficiency, precision, and overall effectiveness.

However, as time progresses, circumstances can evolve, and the intelligent system's output may no longer lead to optimal outcomes. This can be attributed to the limited capacity of systems to adapt to significant contextual changes. At this stage, augmentation is reintroduced to restore optimized results that align with the evolving context. This shift from augmentation to automation and, subsequently, from automation to augmentation forms a cyclical relationship. Therefore, the assertion is that to sustain long-term performance, organizations should effectively manage the periodic transitions between these two approaches.

5.2 Spatial scale

Tasks are interconnected, and when one task is automated, managers and experts engage with the inputs and outcomes of the automated task to carry out other related tasks that come before or after it. This interaction leads to an enhancement of their performance in the adjacent preceding or subsequent tasks. Furthermore, the ongoing collaboration between humans and machines serves to fine-tune the automated outputs, as experts adapt the input tasks based on their assessment of the results.

For instance, the process of problem-solving involves three primary sequential tasks: defining the problem, generating alternative solutions, and choosing the best solution. If automation is applied to the task of generating alternative solutions, decision-makers input the problem definition and constraints into the system and then select from the alternative solutions provided by the system. The interaction between decision-makers and the system empowers them to improve the task of defining the problem and the task of selecting the best solution. Additionally, drawing from the input and output, decision-makers propose adjustments to enhance the efficiency of the automated task of generating alternative solutions.

5.3 The automation-augmentation co-existence

The shift from automation to augmentation and vice versa is conditional to the optimization of the tasks' effectiveness and efficiency. It is also important to highlight that current AI solutions cannot fully replace humans, as they have not reached the point of singularity, which is hard to reach, if ever, in the foreseeable future. Thus, automation will always co-exist with augmentation, where some tasks are easier to automate, and others are optimal to keep augmented. Also, as highlighted before, the cyclical relationship between both is vital to keep optimization and sustain competitive advantage.

5.4 What are the knowledge management strategies in the fourth industrial revolution?

The aforementioned debate leads us to distinctively identify three Knowledge Management strategies. The first takes the approach of automation, aiming to reach hyper-automation to the fullest extent possible. Some Scholars referred to this approach as "Robonomics", where overwhelming production is achieved through robotics, artificial intelligence, and automation technologies [11].

The second strategy recognizes the importance of embracing technological advancements to enhance and amplify human performance. This approach encourages high levels of interaction between humans and machines, constituting a knowledge management strategy labeled as "Cybernetication." Cybernetication seeks to augment human capabilities through artificial intelligence systems and robotics. Some scholars even anticipate that the future development and widespread adoption of general-purpose technologies such as virtual and augmented realities, cobots, cognitive systems, brain-computer interfaces, cybernetic implants, wearable technologies, and genetic modifications will propel a significant leap in augmentation and human-machine interactions, potentially paving the way for the fifth industrial revolution [12, 17].

The choice between hyper-automation and Cybernetication represents a tradeoff in approach. Management decisions may lean toward using AI to reduce human involvement and enhance efficiency, or they may prioritize augmenting human abilities and increasing human-machine interaction. Raisch and Krakowski presented these two approaches as a paradox, highlighting their contradictory yet interconnected and complementary nature, an argument supported by their temporal and spatial scales [15].

A third Knowledge Management strategy emerges, labeled as "DeParadoxication." This strategy aims to resolve the contradictions between the two approaches and effectively manage their interplay and transitions. In other words, under the third Knowledge Management strategy, management seeks to minimize the tension between automation and augmentation by selectively adopting one approach over the other for specific tasks and timeframes. It also manages the transition between these approaches as needed. Moreover, this approach appears to be the most suitable strategy for achieving mass personalization, given its adaptability and efficiency.

The following **Figure 9** illustrates these three strategies within KM 4.0, replacing the strategies prevalent in the twentieth century (codification, personalization, and combination). These strategic alternatives align with the shift from Industry 3.0 to Industry 4.0, reflecting the widespread adoption of Industry 4.0 General-Purpose Technologies.

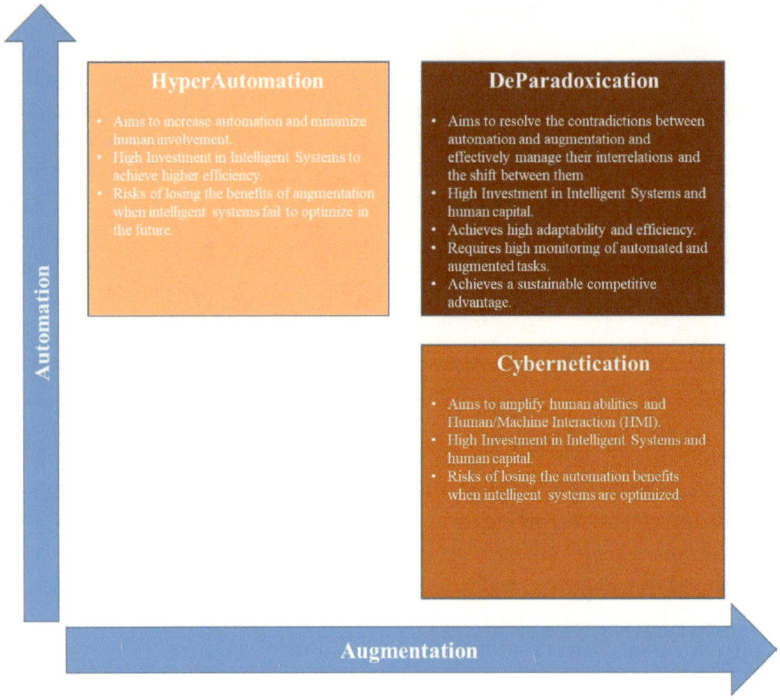

Figure 9.
Industry 4.0 knowledge management strategies: HyperAutomation, Cybernetication, and DeParadoxication.

6. Knowledge leadership

When discussing strategies for managing knowledge, it is essential to emphasize the crucial role of leadership in shaping the vision, goals, and values related to knowledge [33]. "Knowledge leaders", also referred to as "e-leaders", influence others to achieve what needs to be done to manage organizational knowledge. Being in a position of influence and decision-making power, leaders contribute to the cultural and structural contexts to flourish knowledge sharing and creation [34]. Additionally, the increasing frequency and advancements in information technology have placed pressure on leaders to adapt their leadership styles and use their influence to bring about changes in attitudes, behaviors, and performance at all levels, including individuals, groups, and the organization as a whole [35]. Moreover, it's not just that technology impacts leadership; leadership also has a significant influence on how technological solutions are integrated into organizational structures and behaviors, leading to the social construction of technological solutions throughout the change management process [35].

The literature focuses on leadership styles and behaviors that work best to create knowledge-creating and learning organizations, by focusing on influencing individuals, groups, and networks and creating processes and norms to support the creation of tangible and intangible knowledge assets. It should be noted that considering the diverse approaches to knowledge management strategies, the role and style of leadership may differ significantly in each case. Furthermore, these leadership roles may evolve based on the changes required to achieve optimization and competitiveness at different phases of knowledge creation or in response to alterations in knowledge management strategies driven by internal and external contextual factors.

6.1 What is the best leadership style to manage knowledge?

Several organizational factors influence successful digital changes, such as organizational culture, background, external environment, market competition, and technological advancement [36]. Among those, organizational leadership tends to be the most cited factor. There is a lot of debate in the literature on the best leadership style to flourish innovation and ensure the adoption of new technologies. That said, transformational and shared leadership styles are empirically the most effective for IT innovation, adoption, and implementation [34, 37].

In this context, transformational leadership influences employee behaviors and values beyond self-interest to care for organizational well-being, thus increasing the process of knowledge sharing and innovation and minimizing resistance to IT adoption. Shared leadership is also stressed due to the increasing level of complexity, where leadership roles shift based on the situation, making leadership contingent, dynamic, mutual, and emergent [37]. Various leadership styles are not distinctive alternatives, as they could be connected and complimentary to each other. Transformational leaders focus on individuals and groups, intellectually stimulating and inspiring them to be innovative and participative in the process of change [37]. This leads them to own the change initiative and jointly work toward achieving the goals and organizational objectives, thus acting in a shared leadership mode. Moreover, other scholars highlighted the importance of charismatic, distributed, empowering, visionary, and servant leadership styles to support knowledge management initiatives, such as in supporting the knowledge sharing and creation processes and the new IT systems' adoption [34, 36]. Those leadership styles are also not contradictory and they enforce transformational and shared leadership, which are needed to achieve successful innovative and technological changes.

Many scholars focused on the roles, skills, and attributes of knowledge leaders. The most common roles are being visionary and strategic in designing and implementing a knowledge management strategy [34]. This vision is then implemented by influencing employees to adopt it, collaborating, and participating in translating the vision into goals and implementation tactics. Other leadership roles are essential in the process, such as being an effective communicator, change agent, motivator, coach and mentor, learner, facilitator of learning, intellectual stimulator, educator, supporter, role model, and technologist [34]. As for skills, soft skills were mostly stressed in the literature, especially when it comes to networking and communication skills, both face-to-face and through digital media. Moreover, e-leaders should be skilled in high-speed decision-making, and effectively managing disruptive change, connectivity, and teams (both in-person and virtual) [35]. Some common knowledge leaders' attributes are being resilient, creative, initiative, competitive, trustworthy, trusting, humble, ethical, and empathic [34].

Although most of the abilities, skills, and roles are people-oriented, suggesting a similar yet evolutionary track of the trend of leadership studies in the past decades, the new phenomenon is the high inclusivity of digital communication and platforms and the high decentralization and openness of organizations. More so, there is a return to technical skills when it comes to effective leaders. Knowledge leaders should be able to understand and use various digital solutions, but also, need to stay updated with technological advancements, monitoring any that need to be adopted to ensure a sustainable competitive advantage. The combination of mastery of current IT solutions and the ability to be up-to-date with new advancements put the e-leader under the need for lifelong learning of digital and technical skills [35]. Leaders at various levels need to highly coordinate with IT specialists, who are now positioned, more than ever, in a strategic role. This is true whether the technological solutions are leading to more automation, augmentation, or both. The adoption of IT solutions has both technical and human dimensions to ensure its success, and the interaction between both dimensions is inevitable.

6.2 Technological challenges

To remain competitive, organizations must increase their investments in AI and CPS solutions, to enhance automation and augmentation. One significant factor influencing the adoption of these new solutions is their cost. Another crucial consideration is determining which tasks should be automated, and conducting a comprehensive cost-benefit analysis, considering both short-term and long-term implications.

It is imperative to assess how the automation of a specific task will impact other tasks, with a focus on generating value by minimizing costs and/or enhancing differentiation, all while minimizing disruptions and negative side effects [15]. This approach ensures sustainable competitiveness. Furthermore, the availability of high-quality data is a key determining factor, as any algorithm, regardless of its complexity, will be ineffective without access to robust data sources.

Adopting a new solution or upgrading an existing one carries a socio-technical dimension that cannot be underestimated [13]. Several important questions must be addressed, such as:

1. Why is a new IT solution necessary, and how will it impact tasks and productivity?

2. Is the organizational culture adaptable enough to embrace the new solution?

3. What change management techniques are required to minimize resistance and foster acceptance?

4. Do employees possess the necessary complementary and augmented skills? If not, what is the plan for acquiring and developing these skills?

5. Is the current organizational structure and existing procedures compatible with the new solution? If not, what changes are necessary, including potential restructuring of departments and jobs, and adjustments to procedures, to ensure the effective integration of the AI solution?

6.3 Human challenges

Automation and augmentation necessitate significant reskilling efforts, requiring the workforce to acquire new skills, upskill, or even deskill to complement AI solutions effectively. In the context of Industry 4.0, many scholars emphasize the importance of soft skills and abilities since most hard skills can be readily replaced by machines [38]. This assertion holds true, particularly regarding cognitive and social skills, which remain challenging to replicate using automation. Among the most frequently cited irreplaceable skills are leadership, teamwork, collaboration, experimentation, problem framing, complex problem-solving, networking, creativity, abstract and design thinking, interpersonal and emotional intelligence, communication, and mentoring. Furthermore, certain abilities continue to be deemed crucial, such as adaptability, responsibility, the ability to learn, sensemaking, insightfulness and intuition, critical thinking, and integrity. Overall, employees with skills that are easily replaceable by machines face a higher risk of job displacement. The more advanced the technical solutions adopted by a company, the less need there is for a large workforce, with an increased focus on the quality of employees.

However, organizations that lose subject-matter expertise may encounter significant setbacks that could result in a competitive disadvantage, even if they have successfully automated hard skills [15]. It's important to note that if the context changes, hard skills are necessary to adjust AI solutions. Additionally, for augmentation, a deep understanding of how automated tasks function is vital for making necessary adjustments to their inputs and outputs. In essence, human knowledge and hard skills continue to play a critical role in exercising judgment and responsibility since machines are currently incapable of adapting their rules and purpose. Some argue that AI-generic solutions could replace AI-specific solutions, but achieving general intelligence equivalent to human intelligence remains a complex and ongoing experiment.

Therefore, it is essential to maintain a minimum level of human capital with hard skills, especially organization-specific hard skills are not easily acquired on demand due to the time-consuming learning and experience curves. As a result, the number of experts required may decrease due to automation or augmentation, but the level of expertise that must be retained will need to be at a higher level. Some key hard skills that are still in demand include high-level technical expertise (subject-matter knowledge), interpretive and investigative reporting, digital literacy, analytics, and strategy development.

For knowledge leaders, a significant challenge lies in HR planning, encompassing both workforce planning and job design. Striking the right balance is essential, as organizations must retain key, specialized talent while also maintaining functional and numerical flexibility. This necessitates the adoption of various staffing techniques, such as outsourcing, contracting, offshoring, and strategic partnerships. Achieving this balance is critical for maintaining competitiveness while enhancing workforce flexibility and efficiency.

7. Conclusion

This chapter commences with an exploration of the first three industrial revolutions, culminating in an extensive discussion of the fourth industrial revolution. It places a particular emphasis on Artificial Intelligence and Cyber-Physical Systems as the primary General-Purpose Technologies of Industry 4.0. Subsequently, it delves into the concept of knowledge management and provides an overview of how knowledge was managed during the initial two industrial revolutions. The discussion then shifts to major knowledge management strategies that were implemented during Industry 3.0, underlining the necessity for a novel approach to knowledge management in Industry 4.0 due to the emergence and adoption of technological advancements.

Within this context, three distinct knowledge management strategies are proposed: HyperAutomation, Cybernetication, and DeParadoxication. HyperAutomation strives to maximize automation, minimizing human involvement to the greatest extent possible using current technological solutions. However, achieving this goal can be challenging, given the existing limitations of narrow-focused artificial intelligence systems. Future advancements in general-purpose systems, including strong or even super AI, remain theoretical and experimental but hold promise for realizing HyperAutomation.

Conversely, Cybernetication seeks to enhance human capabilities through technological means, such as AI and robotics. Further developments in this domain may lead to even more augmented employees, potentially involving cybernetic implants, wearable technologies, and genetic modifications. Many experts argue that such advancements could usher in the Fifth Industrial Revolution and may come to fruition sooner than the development of strong or super AI systems.

The third strategy, DeParadoxication, focuses on resolving the contradictions between automation and augmentation, effectively managing their interplay and transitions. This strategy, arguably the most complex to manage, due to its highly disruptive nature, necessitates continuous change management, encompassing both structural and cultural adaptation. Nevertheless, it is argued to be the most effective way to sustain a competitive advantage in the current era.

The chapter underscores the critical role of knowledge leaders in orchestrating the change required to embrace new IT solutions. It is suggested that the most effective leadership styles are transformational and distributed, with a focus on highlighting the significant roles, skills, and attributes of effective e-leaders. Additionally, the chapter ends with identifying some of the challenges faced by knowledge leaders in both the IT and HR dimensions, where both dimensions are undeniably interrelated due to the high human-machine interactions required in Industry 4.0.

Author details

Hadi El-Farr[1*] and Kevin Sevag Kertechian[2]

1 Human Resource Management Department, School of Management and Labor Relations, Rutgers University, Piscataway, United States of America

2 ESSCA School of Management, AI and Sustainability Institute, Angers, France

*Address all correspondence to: hadi.elfarr@rutgers.edu

References

[1] Drucker P. The Age of Discontinuity: Guidelines to Our Changing Society. 2nd ed. New York: Routledge; 1992

[2] Nonaka I. The knowledge-creating company. Harvard Business Review. 1991;**69**(6):96-104

[3] Powell WW, Snellman K. The knowledge economy. Annual Review of Sociology. 2004;**30**(1):199-220

[4] World Economic Forum. The Fourth Industrial Revolution, by Klaus Schwab [Online]. Cologny/Geneva: World Economic Forum; 2017. Available from: https://www.weforum.org/about/the-fourth-industrial-revolution-by-klaus-schwab; [Accessed: July 27, 2023]

[5] Schwab K. The Fourth Industrial Revolution. Geneva: World Economic Forum; 2016

[6] Agrawal M, Eloot K, Mancini M, Patel A. Industry 4.0: Reimagining Manufacturing Operations after COVID-19 [Online]. McKinsey & Company; 2020. Available from: https://www.mckinsey.com/capabilities/operations/our-insights/industry-40-reimagining-manufacturing-operations-after-covid-19 [Accessed: July 27, 2023]

[7] Manesh MK, Pellegrini MM, Marzi G, Dabic M. Knowledge Management in the Fourth Industrial Revolution: Mapping the literature and scoping future avenues. IEEE Transactions on Engineering Management. 2021;**68**(1):289-300

[8] Martinelli A, Mina A, Moggi M. The enabling technologies of industry 4.0: Examining the seeds of the fourth industrial revolution. Industrial and Corporate Change. 2021;**30**(1):161-188

[9] Hayat A, Shahare V, Sharma AK, Arora N. Introduction to industry 4.0. In Namasudra S,AK, editor. Blockchain and its Applications in Industry 4.0. Singapore: Springer; 2023. p. 29-59.

[10] Haenlein M, Kaplan A. A brief history of artificial intelligence: On the past, present, and future of artificial intelligence. California Management Review. 2019;**61**(4):5-14

[11] Dolanay SS. Artificial intelligence, smart robots, types of artificial intelligence and a new economic order. In: de Souza GHS, editor. An Overview on Business, Management and Economics Research Vol. 2.: B P International; [online] 2023. p. 138-160

[12] Santhi AR, Muthuswamy P. Industry 5.0 or industry 4.0S? Introduction to industry 4.0 and a peek into the prospective industry 5.0 technologies. International Journal on Interactive Design and Manufacturing. 2023;**17**:947-979

[13] Duan Y, Edwards JS, Dwivedi YK. Artificial intelligence for decision making in the era of big data – Evolution, challenges, and research agenda. International Journal of Information Management. 2019;**48**:63-71

[14] Rao AS, Verweij G. Sizing the Prize: What's the Real Value of AI for your Business and How Can You Capitalize? [online] PricewaterhouseCoopers; 2017. Available from: https://www.pwc.com/gx/en/issues/analytics/assets/pwc-ai-analysis-sizing-the-prize-report.pdf [Accessed: May 5, 2024]

[15] Raisch S, Krakowski S. Artificial intelligence and management: The automation–augmentation paradox.

The Academy of Management Review. 2021;**46**(1):192-210

[16] Baranauskas G. Mass personalization vs. mass customization: Finding variance in semantical meaning and practical implementation between sectors. Social Transformations in Contemporary Society. 2019;**7**:6-15

[17] Narkhede G, Pasi B, Rajhans N, Kulkarni A. Industry 5.0 and the future of sustainable manufacturing: A systematic literature review. Business Strategy & Development. 2023;**6**:704-723

[18] Fenech C, Perkins B. The Deloitte Consumer Review: Made-to-Order: The Rise of Mass Personalization [online]. Deloitte; 2019. Available from: https://www2.deloitte.com/content/dam/Deloitte/ch/Documents/consumer-business/ch-en-consumer-business-made-to-order-consumer-review.pdf [Accessed: May 5, 2024]

[19] El-Farr H. Aligning Human Resource Management to Knowledge Management within the UK Management Consulting Sector. Leeds: University of Leeds; 2011

[20] Neef D. Making the case for knowledge management: The bigger picture. Management Decision. 1999;**37**(1):72-78

[21] Hislop D. Knowledge Management. In: Redman T, Wilkinson A, editors. Contemporary Human Resource Management. Essex: Pearson Education Limited; 2006

[22] Alavi M, Leidner DE. Review: Knowledge management and knowledge management systems: Conceptual foundations and research issues. MIS Quarterly. 2001;**25**(1):107-136

[23] Hansen MT, Nohria N, Tierney TJ. What's your strategy for managing knowledge? Harvard Business Review. 1999;**77**(2):106-187

[24] Anshari M, Syafrudin M, Fitriyani NL. Fourth industrial revolution between knowledge management and digital humanities. Information. 2022;**13**(6):292

[25] Nonaka I. A dynamic theory of organisational knowledge creation. Organisation Science. 1994;**5**(1):14-37

[26] Bhatt GD. Information dynamics, learning and knowledge creation in organizations. The Learning Organization. 2000;**7**(2):89-99

[27] Nonaka I, Takeuchi H. The Knowledge-Creating Company: How Japanese Companies Create the Dynamics of Innovation. Oxford: Oxford University Press; 1995

[28] El-Farr H, Hosseingholizadeh R. Aligning human resource management with knowledge Management for Better Organizational Performance: How human resource practices support knowledge management strategies. In: Wickham M, editor. Current Issues in Knowledge Management. London, UK: IntechOpen; [online] 2019

[29] Tsoukas H, Vladimirou E. What is organizational knowledge? Journal of Management Studies. 2002;**38**(7):973-993

[30] McGrath R. Harvard Business Review [Online]. 2014. Available from: https://hbr.org/2014/07/managements-three-eras-a-brief-history [Accessed: October 31, 2023].

[31] Unyimadu SO. Management and industrial revolution in Europe, United States of America and Japan. Engineering Management International. 1989;**5**:209-218

[32] Edwards JS, Handzic M, Carlsson S, Nissen M. Knowledge management research & practice: Visions and directions. Knowledge Management Research & Practice. 2003;**1**(1):49-60

[33] Kahrens M, Früauff DH. Critical evaluation of Nonaka's SECI model. In: Syed J, Murray PA, Hislop D, Mouzughi Y, editors. The Palgrave Handbook of Knowledge Management. Cham: Palgrave Macmillan; 2018

[34] Hosseingholizadeh R, El-Farr H, Kerman NT, Lotfi H, Ahmadi M, Akhoondi M, et al. A systematic review and synthesis of empirical research on "knowledge leadership": A new insight in the field of knowledge management. International Journal of Information Science and Management. 2022;**20**(4):167-190

[35] Cortellazzo L, Bruni E, Zampieri R. The role of leadership in a digitalized world: A review. Frontiers in Psychology. 2019;**10**:1938

[36] Tseng SM. Investigating the moderating effects of organizational culture and leadership style on IT-adoption and knowledge-sharing intention. Journal of Enterprise Information Management. 2017;**30**(4):583-604

[37] Bunjak L, Bruch H, Matej Č. Context is key: The joint roles of transformational and shared leadership and management innovation in predicting employee IT innovation adoption. International Journal of Information Management. 2022;**66**:102516

[38] Mabe K, Bwalya K. Critical soft skills for information and knowledge management practitioners in the fourth industrial revolution. SA Journal of Information Management. 2022;**24**(1):a1519

Chapter 3

Dissecting the Paradox of Progress: The Socioeconomic Implications of Artificial Intelligence

Kevin Sevag Kertechian and Hadi El-Farr

Abstract

The rapid ascent of artificial intelligence (AI) and other general-purpose technologies has marked the advent of the fourth industrial revolution, triggering substantial transformations in business practices and productivity potential. While these emerging technologies offer numerous benefits, they also present a range of threats, concerns, and challenges. This chapter aims to investigate the dark side of the fourth industrial revolution, based on the available literature. One major concern revolves around employment, encompassing the potential rise in unemployment rates and the emergence of structural unemployment. The set of skills needed for the changing nature of work is significantly different, thus there is a need for rapid reskilling and deskilling to ensure the future employability of the existing workforce. Furthermore, high dependence on machines might lead to major ethical concerns, including, but not limited to, breaches of privacy and discrimination. More so, high unemployment might lead to further social and income inequalities, relegating many to the lower class and decreasing their purchasing power, while placing few in the upper class.

Keywords: artificial intelligence, fourth industrial revolution, discrimination, income inequalities, unemployment

1. Introduction

According to a survey conducted by McKinsey in 2022, there has been a remarkable surge in the adoption rate of artificial intelligence (AI). In 2017, a mere 20% of the respondents reported incorporating AI in at least one business area. However, this figure has more than doubled since then, currently standing in 2022 at 50% [1].

Undoubtedly, AI is poised to become the dominant force in the business landscape in the foreseeable future. AI has emerged as a highly disruptive innovation, it offers vast and unparalleled possibilities for transformative advancements and substantial enhancements across numerous industries [2]. Consequently, an imperative need arises for a meticulous examination of the ramifications of AI across a wide spectrum of organizational hierarchies and societal domains. Equally crucial is the thorough identification and comprehension of the prevailing downsides inherent to AI, including but not limited to the potential reduction in employment opportunities and the emergence of ethical dilemmas (i.e. socioeconomic factors) [3].

Socioeconomic factors are key elements that significantly impact individuals, communities, and societies. These factors shape various aspects of life, including opportunities, well-being, and development. They encompass social and economic conditions that define the fabric of societies, influencing areas such as education, employment, income distribution, healthcare, housing, social mobility, equity, economic development, and environmental sustainability. By understanding and analyzing these factors, we gain valuable insights into the intricate dynamics that affect people's lives and society. This chapter will center on AI and its impact on various work-related factors, including unemployment, wage disparities, and discriminatory practices.

The development of AI occurs within the context of what Klaus Schwab suggests as the emergence of the fourth industrial revolution (4IR) [4]. This ongoing revolution has led to the convergence of multiple interrelated digital technologies, facilitated by remarkable advancements in computing power and the cost-effective networking of objects. This convergence, combined with the massive volumes of data being generated, catalyzes the rapid growth of AI technologies. As a result, the automation of numerous complex tasks has become possible.

The objective of this chapter is to shed light on the negative aspects that AI brings to various socioeconomic domains. To achieve this, we conducted a comprehensive review of the literature to present a broader perspective on the potential landscape of AI and its adverse consequences on different socioeconomic factors. It is crucial to address these negative effects, as previous studies have predominantly emphasized the positive impact of AI [5–8], leaving the examination of its negative aspects on socioeconomic factors relatively unexplored.

2. The fourth industrial revolution

Modern history has witnessed three influential industrial revolutions that have had a profound impact on our society [9]. The initial revolution (1760), characterized by the utilization of water and steam power, revolutionized mechanical production. One notable example of this revolution is the development of the steam engine by James Watt, which paved the way for advancements in transportation, manufacturing, and agriculture. The second industrial revolution (1870) emerged with the widespread adoption of electricity and the implementation of mass manufacturing techniques through the division of labor. This period saw remarkable innovations, such as the assembly line introduced by Henry Ford, which revolutionized the automotive industry and accelerated production rates. The third industrial revolution (1969), driven by the integration of information communications technology (ICT) and electronics, ushered in an era of customized and specialized manufacturing processes. One significant example of this revolution is the rise of 3D printing, enabling the production of intricate and tailor-made products with reduced costs and increased efficiency [10]. These industrial revolutions have not only transformed the manufacturing landscape but have also had profound societal implications, shaping economies, lifestyles, and global interconnectedness [9, 11]. They serve as milestones in our history, marking significant shifts in technological advancements and paving the way for further progress in various sectors of the economy.

The fourth industrial revolution is now underway, building upon the digital revolution of the past century. It is characterized by the convergence of technologies that blur the boundaries between the physical, digital, and biological realms. This ongoing transformation represents not merely an extension of the third industrial revolution, but rather a distinct and separate phase, driven by three key factors: velocity, scope, and systemic impact [12]. The velocity of progress in the fourth industrial revolution surpasses anything seen in history. Unlike previous industrial revolutions that followed a linear trajectory, this revolution is unfolding at an exponential pace. Its impact extends far beyond individual industries, disrupting and reshaping virtually every sector worldwide. The breadth and depth of these changes herald a complete transformation of entire systems of production, management, and governance [4]. However, caution is advised. As Schwab aptly emphasizes, the fourth industrial revolution embodies a realm of boundless promises intertwined with an array of potential perils [4].

In his 1907 book "L'évolution créatrice", Bergson astutely pointed out that "intelligence... is the faculty of making artificial objects, especially tools to make tools, and to vary its production indefinitely" [13]. Taking everything into account, it can be argued that humans were inherently destined to develop artificial intelligence, as we are what Bergson referred to as *homo faber*. Similarly, Benjamin Franklin used the term "toolmaking animals" to describe the human condition. Sooner or later, AI would have inevitably emerged, although neither Bergson nor Benjamin Franklin could have envisioned the remarkable achievements of contemporary AI.

In the context of the fourth industrial revolution, artificial intelligence emerges as the leading force, offering a multitude of possibilities. While it is important to recognize the presence of other general-purpose technologies (GPTs) in Industry 4.0, such as big data, the Internet of Things (IoT), machine learning, and cyber-physical systems [13, 14], our primary focus in this chapter is on AI. It is worth noting that Industry 4.0 refers to the manufacturing and production systems established during a period dominated by the fourth industrial revolution, and although Industry 4.0 and 4IR are not synonymous, they are complementary as Industry 4.0 is a part of the broader 4IR [13]. Generally speaking, AI is defined as "the knowledge and techniques developed to make machines "intelligent," that is to say able to function appropriately also through foresight in their environment of the application" [15]. Alternatively, AI can be described as a multifaceted interplay with humans, encompassing four key characteristics [13]:

1. Standards: AI possesses advantages over humans in certain areas, allowing it to cover a broader range of tasks, particularly evident in sectors like production.

2. Substitution: AI serves as a complete replacement for human tasks, particularly evident in the automation of low-skilled jobs.

3. Superiority: human intelligence, including emotional intelligence such as empathy, still surpasses AI because these traits are intricate and challenging to replicate.

4. Synthesis: humans and AI collaborate harmoniously, combining their strengths to yield enhanced business outcomes.

In the realm of human resource management (HRM), the emergence of artificial intelligence (AI) has proven to be a game-changer, significantly boosting efficiency and effectiveness [14]. Rather than viewing AI as a replacement for human interaction, it should be seen as a strategic tool that enhances it [16]. One notable example is the integration of smart chatbots, which can provide invaluable support in making strategic HRM decisions [17]. By leveraging AI technologies strategically, organizations can revolutionize their HR practices, streamline processes, and unlock new possibilities for success.

The upcoming section will examine the influence of AI on individuals, initially by exploring its impact on HRM in organizations and subsequently by taking a broader perspective to analyze how AI affects socioeconomic factors.

3. AI impact on human resources

3.1 Artificial intelligence and impacts in HRM

The HR function within organizations holds a pivotal role that extends far beyond mere administrative tasks. In today's context, HR is viewed as a strategic business partner, tasked with ensuring an organization's success and competitive edge through its workforce. However, the advent of AI has significantly disrupted this traditional paradigm. As tasks that were once performed exclusively by humans are now being efficiently completed by AI, the HR function must adapt to this transformation to remain effective in its mission of providing a skilled and equipped workforce.

The field of artificial intelligence offers a vast array of possibilities, and significant advancements have already been made in various domains, such as video games [14], vehicles [12], and content generation [15]. Beyond just a few areas, AI can be likened to a true "tidal wave" in the context of the fourth industrial revolution, exerting its influence on every aspect of our lives, both near and far [16]. Hence, a more nuanced perspective emerges regarding the impact of AI in human resource management (HRM).

The utilization of AI in HRM is situated within a broader framework known as "algorithmic management," which facilitates the implementation of "people analytics" [17]. People analytics, a practice adopted by organizations globally, involves leveraging employee-related data to enhance workforce management [18]. Through the integration of AI, decision-making processes in HRM have been elevated by leveraging people analytics, leading to an intensified approach known as learning analytics. This approach entails continuous analysis of human tasks within organizations to identify patterns and make predictions [19, 20]. It is safe to say that both scholars and practitioners in the field of AI in management anticipate significantly more positive organizational outcomes from AI than negative ones [21].

Several recent studies have highlighted significant limitations in the impact of decision-making processes within work settings, especially in the realm of HRM functions that directly influence individuals' socioeconomic facets, such as job promotions and employment prospects.

In their study on AI and decision-making, Bankins et al. [22] discovered that AI is generally perceived as an inadequate decision-maker when the outcome is negative. Participants specifically cited AI's reliance on incorrect or irrelevant data, its lack of respect or ability to express respect/disrespect, its deficiency in emotional intelligence, and its perceived incompetence in making decisions [22]. However, when AI produced a positive outcome, regardless of whether it contradicted a negative outcome from a human or another AI decision, participants were more inclined to trust it and had higher perceptions of interactional justice [22]. In their $2 \times 2 \times 6$ design, Bankins et al. [22] did not find any significant differences among the six evaluated HRM functions, which included recruitment and selection, training, performance management, work

DOI: http://dx.doi.org/10.5772/intechopen.1004872

allocation, firing, and promotion. These results are crucial as they offer more insights into the theory of machines [23], which pertains to how people perceive the distinctions between human and algorithmic judgments in terms of input, process, and output [23].

In their systematic literature review, Giermindl et al. [21] raised concerns among scholars and practitioners regarding the limitations of people analytics within the realm of AI and human-algorithmic management. They emphasized that people analytics should not be seen as a one-size-fits-all solution for improved management. Instead, they acknowledged the shift toward AI-driven people-centered analytics but cautioned that it currently creates an illusion of control by providing a false sense of certainty and reductionism through the erroneous linking of unrelated events. Giermindl et al.'s [21] research also revealed that the extensive amount of data gathered and analyzed by AI and algorithms tends to reinforce a self-fulfilling prophecy rather than focusing on employee competencies. Furthermore, this reliance on past data to predict future events results in a "profound deference to precedent" [24], making the deciphering of gathered data increasingly challenging, even for specialists.

Moreover, people analytics significantly diminishes employee autonomy, creativity, and decision-making latitude, leading to "reactive chains of action" instead of self-reliant and self-organized behavior aligned with employees' self-determination [21]. Over time, this erosion of trust among employees and in their decision-making abilities becomes increasingly apparent as they feel socially pressured to "listen" to machines, gradually leading to a form of digital Taylorism, where creative and intellectual tasks are subjected to the same rigid processes as routine work [25]. Nowadays algorithmic management is applied in HRM for resume screening [26], assessing the fit between employees and tasks [27], establishing performance management [28], and dealing with compensation [29]. Problems can arise within these processes such as discrimination [30, 31], due to the reinforcement of biases that in turn foster inequalities [32].

Research has shown that AI-based hiring tools may inadvertently discriminate against certain demographic groups. For example, as reported by Dastin [33], Amazon's AI recruitment tool displayed gender bias, penalizing resumes that included terms commonly used by women. Similarly, a study by Obermeyer et al. [34] revealed that an AI-based algorithm used in healthcare was racially biased, leading to lower care recommendations for Black patients compared to white patients with the same level of health. The issue of discrimination in AI extends beyond hiring. For instance, AI-driven performance evaluation systems might inadvertently reward or penalize employees based on factors unrelated to their actual performance. This can have adverse effects on employee morale, engagement, and career advancement opportunities.

From the HR perspective, there is notable resistance among employees toward AI and algorithmic management in general [35, 36]. This resistance stems from employees' inherent distrust toward AI, as its rapid integration into various industries has disrupted established working routines [37, 38]. As a result, employees may resort to deviant behaviors, such as knowledge hiding [39], as a means of coping. Unfortunately, this resistance and disruption also take a toll on employees' overall well-being [40, 41]. Recognizing and addressing these concerns is crucial for fostering a harmonious and productive work environment.

4. AI socioeconomic impacts

As noted by Giermindl et al. [21], basing hiring decisions solely on past data has resulted in the formation of groups composed of individuals from similar social backgrounds. This phenomenon, known as homosocial reproduction, directly promotes homophily and contributes to the emergence of discriminatory practices. The decision-making process is highly biased, further exacerbating these issues [29, 42]. The increasing presence of algorithms in the hiring process poses an even greater risk of discrimination. Similarly, we found in the literature that AI-based surveillance technologies can disproportionately target and marginalize certain communities, leading to privacy concerns and potential discrimination. For example, facial recognition systems have been criticized for their higher error rates on individuals with darker skin tones, leading to potential adverse consequences for marginalized communities [43].

As algorithms become more omnipresent, the aforementioned tendencies are expected to intensify. Consequently, social and economic categorization will be reinforced, exacerbating overall inequality and leading to increased social and economic isolation for those who are already marginalized [24, 29, 44]. In the same vein, the digital divide can result in marginalized communities having limited access to AI technologies and the opportunities they provide. Lack of access to AI-driven services and resources can further marginalize already disadvantaged individuals [45].

The widespread adoption of AI technologies in various domains has raised significant privacy concerns. AI systems often require vast amounts of data to train and improve their performance, and this data can contain sensitive personal information. This raises potential risks of data breaches, unauthorized access, and misuse of personal data. One notable area of concern is AI-powered surveillance technologies. Facial recognition systems, for example, can capture and analyze people's faces in real-time, leading to concerns about privacy and surveillance. A study by Kroll et al. [46] highlighted that facial recognition systems can suffer from racial and gender bias, potentially exacerbating existing privacy and discrimination issues. AI-powered personal assistants, like virtual voice assistants, have also raised privacy concerns. These systems typically process voice recordings to improve their performance, but this data collection can raise questions about user privacy and data retention policies [47]. Nonetheless, AI-driven cybersecurity systems may raise privacy concerns as they often process vast amounts of data, including personal information, for threat analysis. It is essential to ensure that privacy regulations are upheld while using AI in cybersecurity [48], therefore, keeping safe individual-level information is considered a key element [49].

The rapid computerization witnessed at the turn of the twenty-first century has exacerbated wage inequality, creating a divide between those who have embraced technology and those who have not [50, 51]. A similar trend is expected to emerge with the rise of Artificial Intelligence [52]. In a 2016 paper by Brougham and Haar, they introduced the concept of "Smart Technology, Artificial Intelligence, Robotics, and Algorithms" (STARA), estimating that by 2025, one-third of existing jobs could be replaced by STARA. While the previous discussion focused on the impact of AI and algorithmic management on HRM professionals and employees, it is crucial to recognize that individuals' social lives will be greatly affected. Surviving and thriving in the fourth industrial revolution (4IR) era will require a necessary readjustment. This leads us to ponder whether AI will surpass humans in daily tasks to the extent that a significant portion of the workforce will become obsolete, or if alternative solutions can be envisioned to complement the existing workforce. A significant illustration of potential employment disparities arises from the replacement of skilled and unskilled jobs, which could lead to increased unemployment rates [53]. Also, according to Su [54], AI will be a major contributor to structural unemployment, which refers to a type of unemployment that arises from a mismatch between the skills and qualifications of job seekers and the requirements of available job opportunities within an economy [55].

The previous three industrial revolutions provide some evidence of shifting employment patterns. Initially, the farming sector dominated, but with the advent of the third industrial revolution, there was a notable transition toward the service industry. As low-skilled jobs gradually disappeared, there was a significant surge in management and clerical positions [56]. However, the creation of new jobs to compensate for those currently being displaced by the fourth industrial revolution (4IR) and the omnipresence of AI is no longer a natural process as it was in the past. Scholars are expressing more pessimism, foreseeing a potential intensification of inequalities among workers [57]. This pessimistic outlook is supported by recent studies indicating that the automation of tasks could primarily eliminate lower-skilled jobs, with new jobs emerging predominantly in the technology sector [52, 58]. Similarly, certain jobs have become declassified or faded out as they were once considered high-skilled, but with the introduction of AI, human intervention has gradually become redundant over time [59].

It is crucial to recognize the challenges posed by these changes in the job market [60] (e.g. automation technologies as a substitute for human intervention) and address them proactively. Rather than relying on automatic job creation, deliberate efforts are required to reskill and upskill the workforce, ensuring that individuals can transition into the new roles demanded by the evolving economy. Thus, we align with Autor who believes that "AI will change the labor market, but not in the way Musk and Hinton believe. Instead, it will reshape the value and nature of human expertise" [61]. As Artificial Intelligence (AI) develops alongside the 4IR, often seen as a major change in services described by Baldwin, experts agree on a common transformation process that could benefit the job market. The first step starts a chain of changes, leading to a shake-up phase. Then, the third step deals with possible negative reactions or unexpected results of AI. Despite these challenges, with strong and well-thought-out rules, we can expect good results in the end [62, 63]. Therefore, organizations and practitioners can adopt AI in various ways that enhance their workforce's value and minimize the potential negative impacts of AI.

Practically speaking, initiatives should focus on providing accessible and comprehensive training programs that equip workers with the necessary skills to thrive in the technology-driven landscape of the 4IR. In the context of the 4IR, the future workforce must possess specific skills to thrive in the evolving landscape. These skills are crucial for individuals to adapt and excel in a rapidly changing environment [64]. First and foremost, analytical thinking and innovation will be paramount. The ability to analyze complex information, think critically, and generate innovative solutions will differentiate successful professionals from their counterparts. This skill set enables individuals to navigate the complexities of the modern workplace and identify new opportunities for growth and improvement. The second essential skill is active learning and learning strategies. As technology continues to advance at an unprecedented rate, the acquisition of new knowledge and the ability to learn continuously becomes crucial. Embracing a mindset of lifelong learning and developing effective learning strategies will empower individuals to stay ahead of the curve and remain adaptable in the face of technological advancements. Lastly, complex problem-solving skills will be in high demand. The fourth industrial revolution brings forth a multitude of intricate challenges that require creative and systematic problem-solving approaches. Individuals who can tackle complex problems by breaking them down into manageable components, analyzing various perspectives, and generating innovative solutions will be highly sought after.

Reskilling and upskilling will play a pivotal role in shaping the future of the workforce in the coming years. Reskilling involves a complete transition to a new set of skills required for a different occupation or industry, while upskilling refers to updating an employee's skill set to address new occupational challenges and demands [65]. According to the Future Jobs Report by the World Economic Forum, around 50% of workers will be affected by reskilling by 2025. Additionally, a 2016 report from the World Economic Forum stated that 65% of today's primary school students will work in jobs that do not yet exist. Furthermore, it is projected that 14% of the

Government body	Type of policy	Date	Objective
European Union*	AI act	April 2021	This act aimed to regulate AI systems' development, deployment, and use across the EU member states. It focused on high-risk AI applications, such as those used in critical infrastructure, healthcare, and law enforcement, and required developers to follow specific requirements to ensure the safety, transparency, and ethical use of AI technologies.
United States of America**	Executive Order on AI	February 2019	The United States government issued an executive order called "Maintaining American Leadership in Artificial Intelligence." The order aimed to enhance AI research and development in the country and promote responsible AI practices. The order also directed federal agencies to prioritize AI funding and incorporate AI considerations into their strategies.
Canada***	Directive on Automated Decision-Making	April 2020	The directive required federal agencies to implement specific practices when using automated decision-making systems, including AI. It emphasized the importance of transparency, accountability, and human oversight in AI systems to avoid biases and ensure sustainable AI practices.
United Nations****	AI for good initiative		The United Nations launched the "AI for Good" initiative to encourage the use of AI technologies for positive societal impact and sustainable development. This initiative brings together stakeholders from governments, academia, industry, and civil society to collaborate on projects that leverage AI for achieving the UN's Sustainable Development Goals.
Singapore*****	Model AI Governance Framework	January 2019	Singapore's government published the Model AI Governance Framework to guide organizations in developing and deploying AI technologies. The framework outlines key principles, such as fairness, accountability, and transparency, to promote responsible and sustainable AI practices in the country.

**Artificial Intelligence Act, COM/2021/206 final—2021/0106 (COD).*
***Executive Order 13859 of February 11, 2019—Maintaining American Leadership in AI.*
****Directive on Automated Decision-Making, Treasury Board of Canada Secretariat, April 2020.*
*****AI for Good, United Nations.*
******Model AI Governance Framework, Personal Data Protection Commission.*

Table 1.
Example of government policies toward a sustainable AI practice.

global workforce will need to change their occupation due to the influence of AI [65]. This transition to new technologies follows a historical pattern observed during the shift from agriculture to assembly lines. However, the current shift toward AI integration is likely to impact the working class more significantly, potentially exacerbating the gap between blue-collar and white-collar workers. Therefore, education and organizations have crucial roles in facilitating the reskilling and upskilling processes. Education institutions will need to provide updated skills to prepare the next generation of workers for the creation of new jobs in the coming years, which will require a fresh set of skills [66].

It is obvious that governments around the world will have a role to play in establishing policies around a more sustainable AI practice. Indeed, governments recognized the need to regulate AI technologies to ensure responsible, ethical, and sustainable development and deployment. The focus was on addressing potential risks and ensuring that AI applications align with societal values, human rights, and environmental concerns. **Table 1** provides an overview of these regulatory processes:

Simultaneously, organizations must take responsibility for providing necessary training to the existing workforce [67]. By acknowledging the potential inequalities and actively working toward inclusive strategies, we can strive for a future where the benefits of technological advancements are distributed more equitably. Collaboration between policymakers, industry leaders, and educational institutions is vital to facilitate a smooth transition, empower workers, and build a resilient workforce capable of embracing the opportunities presented by the 4IR.

In response to these multiple concerns, industry experts have joined forces to deliberate and propose essential measures for effectively navigating the transition toward the disruptive technologies offered by the fourth industrial revolution.

5. Minimizing AI negative impacts

In March 2023, companies specializing in AI embarked on a scheduled pause to deliberate on ethical concerns surrounding AI and call for regulations governing its use. On the Future of Life website, an insightful statement is made: "Advanced AI could represent a profound change in the history of life on Earth, and should be planned for and managed with commensurate care and resources." This thought-provoking premise serves as the foundation for an open letter that has garnered an impressive 33,002 signatures of important stakeholders as of July 10th, 2023, signifying the widespread concerns and urgent call for regulations surrounding AI due to the prevailing level of distrust. Among the signatories are renewed CEOs and scientists in the field of AI such as:

- Anthony Aguirre, University of California, Santa Cruz, Executive Director of Future of Life Institute.

- Yoshua Bengio, Founder and Scientific Director at Mila, Professor at the University of Montreal.

- Chris Larsen, Co-Founder, Ripple.

- Emad Mostaque, CEO, Stability AI.

- Elon Musk, CEO of SpaceX, Tesla & Twitter.
- Stuart Russell, Berkeley, Professor of Computer Science, Center for Intelligent Systems.
- Jaan Tallinn, Co-Founder of Skype, Centre for the Study of Existential Risk, Future of Life Institute.
- Max Tegmark, MIT Center for Artificial Intelligence & Fundamental Interactions.
- Steve Wozniak, Co-founder, Apple.

Not only are leaders in the field highlighting the potential adverse impacts of AI, but they are particularly emphasizing the looming danger of uncontrolled harmful effects: "Powerful AI systems should be developed only once we are confident that their effects will be positive, and their risks will be manageable." The Asilomar AI principles offer governance mechanisms that have been identified at the Beneficial AI 2017 conference and it focused on: research issues (**Table 2**), ethical values (**Table 3**), and long-term issues (**Table 4**).

The AI research goal is to create beneficial intelligence, not undirected. Funding should support research on its beneficial use, addressing key areas: robust AI systems, managing automation's impact, updating legal systems, and defining AI's values. The constructive exchange between researchers and policy-makers is crucial, fostering cooperation, trust, and transparency. Teams must cooperate to ensure safety standards.

Ethics and values in AI entail prioritizing safety and security throughout AI's operational lifetime. Transparency is essential, in explaining AI-caused harm and judicial decisions involving AI. Designers have a responsibility to align AI goals with human values while safeguarding privacy and ensuring shared benefits. Human control over AI decisions is vital to prevent undermining societal processes. An AI arms race, especially with lethal autonomous weapons, should be avoided.

In the development of AI, caution is necessary regarding assumptions about future capabilities. Advanced AI could have profound implications for life on Earth,

Scope	Domain	Solution
Research issues	Research goal	The goal of AI research should be to create not undirected intelligence, but beneficial intelligence.
	Research funding	Investments in AI should be accompanied by funding for research on ensuring its beneficial use ... in computer science, economics, law, ethics, and social studies.
	Science-policy link	There should be constructive and healthy exchanges between AI researchers and policymakers.
	Research culture	A culture of cooperation, trust, and transparency should be fostered among researchers and developers of AI.
	Race avoidance	Teams developing AI systems should actively cooperate to avoid corner-cutting safety standards.

Source: AI Principles—Future of Life Institute.

Table 2.
Research issues and AI principles for governance from the Future of Life Institute.

Scope	Domain	Solution
Ethical and values	Safety	AI systems should be safe and secure throughout their operational lifetime, and verifiably so where applicable and feasible.
	Failure transparency	If an AI system causes harm, it should be possible to ascertain why.
	Judicial transparency	Any involvement by an autonomous system in judicial decision-making should provide a satisfactory explanation auditable by a competent human authority.
	Responsibility	Designers and builders of advanced AI systems are stakeholders in the moral implications of their use, misuse, and actions, with a responsibility and opportunity to shape those implications.
	Value alignment	Highly autonomous AI systems should be designed so that their goals and behaviors can be assured to align with human values throughout their operation.
	Human values	AI systems should be designed and operated to be compatible with ideals of human dignity, rights, freedoms, and cultural diversity.
	Personal privacy	People should have the right to access, manage, and control the data they generate, given AI systems' power to analyze and utilize that data.
	Liberty and privacy	The application of AI to personal data must not unreasonably curtail people's real or perceived liberty.
	Shared benefit	AI technologies should benefit and empower as many people as possible.
	Shared prosperity	The economic prosperity created by AI should be shared broadly, to benefit all of humanity.
	Human control	Humans should choose how and whether to delegate decisions to AI systems, to accomplish human-chosen objectives.
	Non-subversion	The power conferred by control of highly advanced AI systems should respect and improve, rather than subvert, the social and civic processes on which the health of society depends.
	AI arms race	An arms race for lethal autonomous weapons should be avoided.

Source: AI Principles—Future of Life Institute.

Table 3.
Ethical values and AI principles for governance from the Future of Life Institute.

Scope	Domain	Solution
Long-term issues	Capability caution	There being no consensus, we should avoid strong assumptions regarding upper limits on future AI capabilities.
	Importance	Advanced AI could represent a profound change in the history of life on Earth, and should be planned for and managed with commensurate care and resources.
	Risks	Risks posed by AI systems, especially catastrophic or existential risks, must be subject to planning and mitigation efforts commensurate with their expected impact.
	Recursive self-improvement	AI systems designed to recursively self-improve or self-replicate in a manner that could lead to rapidly increasing quality or quantity must be subject to strict safety and control measures.
	Common good	Superintelligence should only be developed in the service of widely shared ethical ideals and for the benefit of all humanity rather than one state or organization.

Source: AI Principles—Future of Life Institute.

Table 4.
Long-term issues and AI principles for governance from the Future of Life Institute.

requiring careful planning and allocation of resources. Mitigating risks, especially catastrophic ones is vital and should match the potential impact. AI systems with recursive self-improvement capabilities must adhere to strict safety measures. Superintelligence should serve shared ethical ideals and benefit all of humanity, rather than being controlled by a single state or organization.

6. Conclusion

The rapid ascent of AI and other general-purpose technologies has marked the advent of the fourth industrial revolution, triggering substantial transformations in business practices and productivity potential. While these emerging technologies offer numerous benefits, they also present a range of threats, concerns, and challenges. This chapter has delved into the dark side of the fourth industrial revolution, exploring its negative implications based on the available literature.

One major concern revolves around employment, encompassing the potential rise in unemployment rates and the emergence of structural unemployment. As the nature of work changes, there is a need for rapid reskilling and upskilling to ensure the future employability of the existing workforce. Moreover, the high dependence on machines raises major ethical concerns, including privacy breaches and discrimination. The impact of AI on socioeconomic factors is also worrisome, as it can exacerbate social and income inequalities, further dividing society into different socioeconomic classes. Also, the development of AI and its integration into human resource management (HRM) has brought both opportunities and challenges. Algorithmic management and people analytics have the potential to enhance HR practices, but they also raise concerns regarding decision-making fairness, employee autonomy, and potential discrimination. Resistance from employees toward AI and algorithmic management further complicates the adoption and implementation process. The socioeconomic impacts of AI go beyond HRM, affecting various domains such as hiring practices and economic inequalities. Homosocial reproduction and biased decision-making perpetuate discrimination and reinforce social and economic categorization. The widening gap between technology-driven jobs and the disappearance of lower-skilled positions and fading jobs pose significant challenges, necessitating proactive measures to reskill and upskill the workforce. Education institutions and organizations have vital roles to play in facilitating the necessary training and skill development required to thrive in the technology-driven landscape.

By addressing the negative effects of AI and embracing inclusive strategies, we can strive for a future where the benefits of technological advancements are distributed more equitably. However, the uncontrolled and unregulated use of AI poses significant risks. Leaders in the field, along with stakeholders (e.g. governments) emphasize the importance of responsible AI development and the need for governance mechanisms to ensure positive outcomes and manage potential harms. These include considerations of safety, failure transparency, human values, shared prosperity, and the avoidance of AI arms races. Thus, navigating the challenges and maximizing the benefits of AI in the fourth industrial revolution requires a comprehensive approach. It demands collaboration among policymakers, industry leaders, educational institutions, governments, and society as a whole. By addressing concerns, promoting reskilling and upskilling, and implementing ethical frameworks, we can strive for a future where AI enhances the well-being of individuals and society as a whole, leading to a more inclusive and equitable socioeconomic landscape.

DOI: http://dx.doi.org/10.5772/intechopen.1004872

Author details

Kevin Sevag Kertechian[1]* and Hadi El-Farr[2]

1 ESSCA School of Management, Member of the AI and Sustainability Institute, Angers, Angers, France

2 Human Resource Management Department, School of Management and Labor Relations, Rutgers University, Piscataway, United States of America

*Address all correspondence to: kevin.kertechian@gmail.com

References

[1] McKinsey. The state of AI 2022-and a half decade in review. 2023 [En ligne]. Disponible sur: https://www.mckinsey.com/capabilities/quantumblack/our-insights/the-state-of-ai-in-2022-and-a-half-decade-in-review#/

[2] Cheng X, Lin X, Shen X-L, Zarifis A, Mou J. The dark sides of AI. Electronic Markets. 2022;**32**(1):11-15. DOI: 10.1007/s12525-022-00531-5

[3] Q. Ai, The Pros and Cons of Artificial Intelligence. 2022 [En ligne]. Disponible sur: https://www.forbes.com/sites/qai/2022/12/01/the-pros-and-cons-of-artificial-intelligence/?sh=1cb8010a4703

[4] Schwab K. The Fourth Industrial Revolution. New York, USA: Crown; 2017

[5] Tomašev N et al. AI for social good: Unlocking the opportunity for positive impact. Nature Communications. 2020;**11**(1):Art. n° 1. DOI: 10.1038/s41467-020-15871-z

[6] Vinuesa R et al. The role of artificial intelligence in achieving the sustainable development goals. Nature Communications. 2020;**11**(1):Art. n° 1. DOI: 10.1038/s41467-019-14108-y

[7] Braganza A, Chen W, Canhoto A, Sap S. Productive employment and decent work: The impact of AI adoption on psychological contracts, job engagement and employee trust. Journal of Business Research. 2021;**131**:485-494. DOI: 10.1016/j.jbusres.2020.08.018

[8] García-Micó TG, Laukyte M. Gender, health, and AI: How using AI to empower women could positively impact the sustainable development goals. In: Mazzi F, Floridi L, editors. The Ethics of Artificial Intelligence for the Sustainable Development Goals, Philosophical Studies Series. Cham: Springer International Publishing; 2023. pp. 291-304. DOI: 10.1007/978-3-031-21147-8_16

[9] Anshari M, Hamdan M. Understanding knowledge management and upskilling in Fourth Industrial Revolution: Transformational shift and SECI model. VINE Journal of Information and Knowledge Management Systems. 2022;**52**(3):373-393. DOI: 10.1108/VJIKMS-09-2021-0203

[10] Davis N. What is the fourth industrial revolution? World Economic Forum [En ligne]. Disponible sur: https://alejandroarbelaez.com/wp-content/uploads/2020/10/What-is-the-fourth-industrial-revolution-WEF.pdf

[11] Rainnie A, Dean M. Industry 4.0 and the future of quality work in the global digital economy. Labour and Industry: A Journal of the Social and Economic Relations of Work. 2020;**30**(1):16-33. DOI: 10.1080/10301763.2019.1697598

[12] Xu M, David JM, Kim SH. The fourth industrial revolution: Opportunities and challenges. International Journal of Financial Research. 2018;**9**(2):90. DOI: 10.5430/ijfr.v9n2p90

[13] Lichtenthaler U. Substitute or synthesis: The interplay between human and artificial intelligence. Research-Technology Management. 2018;**61**(5):12-14. DOI: 10.1080/08956308.2018.1495962

[14] LeCun Y, Bengio Y, Hinton G. Deep learning. Nature. 2015;**521**(7553):Art. 7553. DOI: 10.1038/nature14539

[15] Martinelli A, Mina A, Moggi M. The enabling technologies of industry

4.0: Examining the seeds of the fourth industrial revolution. Industrial and Corporate Change. 2021;**30**(1):161-188. DOI: 10.1093/icc/dtaa060

[16] Kurian N, Cherian JM, Sudharson NA, Varghese KG, Wadhwa S. AI is now everywhere. British Dental Journal. 2023;**234**(2):72-72

[17] Gal U, Jensen TB, Stein M-K. Breaking the vicious cycle of algorithmic management: A virtue ethics approach to people analytics. Information and Organization. 2020;**30**(2):100301. DOI: 10.1016/j.infoandorg.2020.100301

[18] Fernandez V, Gallardo-Gallardo E. Tackling the HR digitalization challenge: Key factors and barriers to HR analytics adoption. Competitiveness Review: An International Business Journal. 2020;**31**(1):162-187. DOI: 10.1108/CR-12-2019-0163

[19] Cappelli P. Data science can't fix hiring (yet). Harvard Business Review. 2019;**1** [En ligne]. Disponible sur: https://hbr.org/2019/05/data-science-cant-fix-hiring-yet

[20] von Krogh G. Artificial intelligence in organizations: New opportunities for phenomenon-based theorizing. Academy of Management Discoveries. 2018;**4**(4):404-409. DOI: 10.5465/amd.2018.0084

[21] Giermindl LM, Strich F, Christ O, Leicht-Deobald U, Redzepi A. The dark sides of people analytics: Reviewing the perils for organisations and employees. European Journal of Information Systems. 2022;**31**(3):410-435. DOI: 10.1080/0960085X.2021.1927213

[22] Bankins S, Formosa P, Griep Y, Richards D. AI decision making with dignity? Contrasting workers' justice perceptions of human and AI decision making in a human resource management context. Information Systems Frontiers. 2022;**24**(3):857-875. DOI: 10.1007/s10796-021-10223-8

[23] Logg JM, Minson JA, Moore DA. Algorithm appreciation: People prefer algorithmic to human judgment. Organizational Behavior and Human Decision Processes. 2019;**151**:90-103. DOI: 10.1016/j.obhdp.2018.12.005

[24] Barocas S, Hood S, Ziewitz M. Governing algorithms: A provocation piece. Malte Ziewitz: SSRN Electronic Journal. 2013. DOI: 10.2139/ssrn.2245322

[25] Holford WD. The future of human creative knowledge work within the digital economy. Futures. 2019;**105**:143-154. DOI: 10.1016/j.futures.2018.10.002. Available from: Governing Algorithms: A Provocation Piece by Solon Barocas, Sophie Hood, Malte Ziewitz :: SSRN

[26] Cheng MM, Hackett RD. A critical review of algorithms in HRM: Definition, theory, and practice. Human Resource Management Review. 2021;**31**(1):100698

[27] Rosenblat A, Stark L. Algorithmic labor and information asymmetries: A case study of uber's drivers. International Journal of Communication. 30 July 2016;**10**:27. DOI: 10.2139/ssrn.2686227. Available from: https://ssrn.com/abstract=2686227

[28] Jarrahi MH, Sutherland W. Algorithmic management and algorithmic competencies: Understanding and appropriating algorithms in gig work. In: Information in Contemporary Society: 14th International Conference, iConference 2019, March 31–April 3, 2019, Proceedings 14. Vol. 2019. Washington, DC, USA: Springer; 2019. pp. 578-589

[29] Kellogg KC, Valentine MA, Christin A. Algorithms at work: The new contested terrain of control. Academy of Management Annals. 2020;**14**(1):366-410. DOI: 10.5465/annals.2018.0174

[30] Lamers L, Meijerink J, Jansen G, Boon M. A capability approach to worker dignity under algorithmic management. Ethics and Information Technology. 2022;**24**(1):10

[31] Rodgers W, Murray JM, Stefanidis A, Degbey WY, Tarba SY. An artificial intelligence algorithmic approach to ethical decision-making in human resource management processes. Human Resource Management Review. 2023;**33**(1):100925. DOI: 10.1016/j.hrmr.2022.100925

[32] Selbst AD, Boyd D, Friedler SA, Venkatasubramanian S, Vertesi J. Fairness and Abstraction in Sociotechnical Systems. In: Proceedings of the Conference on Fairness, Accountability, and Transparency. Atlanta, GA, USA: ACM; 2019. pp. 59-68. DOI: 10.1145/3287560.3287598

[33] Dastin J. Amazon's surveillance culture is "breaking" its workers, Huck. 2023 [En ligne]. Disponible sur: https://www.huckmag.com/article/speaking-to-amazon-uk-workers-on-the-picket-lines-in-coventry-2023

[34] Obermeyer Z, Powers B, Vogeli C, Mullainathan S. Dissecting racial bias in an algorithm used to manage the health of populations. Science. 2019;**366**(6464):447-453. DOI: 10.1126/science.aax2342

[35] Kordzadeh N, Ghasemaghaei M. Algorithmic bias: Review, synthesis, and future research directions. European Journal of Information Systems. 2022;**31**(3):388-409. DOI: 10.1080/0960085X.2021.1927212

[36] Wang J, Zhang X, Zhang LJ. Effects of teacher engagement on students' achievement in an online english as a foreign language classroom: The mediating role of autonomous motivation and positive emotions. Frontiers in Psychology. 2022;**13**:950652. DOI: 10.3389/fpsyg.2022.950652

[37] Ferrari F, Graham M. Fissures in algorithmic power: Platforms, code, and contestation. Cultural Studies. 2021;**35**(4-5):814-832. DOI: 10.1080/09502386.2021.1895250

[38] Goods C, Veen A, Barratt T. "Is your gig any good?" Analysing job quality in the Australian platform-based food-delivery sector. Journal of Industrial Relations. 2019;**61**(4):502-527. DOI: 10.1177/0022185618817069

[39] Di Vaio A, Hasan S, Palladino R, Profita F, Mejri I. Understanding knowledge hiding in business organizations: A bibliometric analysis of research trends, 1988-2020. Journal of Business Research. 2021;**134**:560-573. DOI: 10.1016/j.jbusres.2021.05.040

[40] Baiocco S, Fernandez-Macías E, Rani U, Pesole A. The algorithmic management of work and its implications in different contexts. JRC Working Papers on Labour, Education and Technology 2022-02, Joint Research Centre (Seville site). Available from: https://ideas.repec.org/p/ipt/laedte/202202.html

[41] Parent-Rocheleau X, Parker SK. Algorithms as work designers: How algorithmic management influences the design of jobs. Human Resource Management Review. 2022;**32**(3):100838. DOI: 10.1016/j.hrmr.2021.100838

[42] Hamilton RH, Sodeman WA. The questions we ask: Opportunities and challenges for using big data analytics

to strategically manage human capital resources. Business Horizons. 2020;**63**(1):85-95. DOI: 10.1016/j.bushor.2019.10.001

[43] Buolamwini J, Gebru T. Gender shades: Intersectional accuracy disparities in commercial gender classification. In: Conference on Fairness, Accountability and Transparency. New York, USA: PMLR; 2018. pp. 77-91

[44] Simbeck K. HR analytics and ethics. IBM Journal of Research and Development. 2019;**63**(4/5):9:1-9:12. DOI: 10.1147/JRD.2019.2915067

[45] Yuan X, Bennett Gayle D, Knight T, Dubois E. Adoption of artificial intelligence technologies by often marginalized populations. In: Yuan X, Wu D, Gayle DB, editors. Social Vulnerability to COVID-19: Impacts of Technology Adoption and Information Behavior, Synthesis Lectures on Information Concepts, Retrieval, and Services. Cham: Springer International Publishing; 2023. pp. 31-49. DOI: 10.1007/978-3-031-06897-3_3

[46] Kroll JA, Huey J, Barocas S, Felten EW, Reidenberg, Joel R, et al. Accountable Algorithms (March 2, 2016). University of Pennsylvania Law Review, Vol. 165, 2017 Forthcoming, Fordham Law Legal Studies Research Paper No. 2765268. Available from: https://ssrn.com/abstract=2765268

[47] Chung H, Iorga M, Voas J, Lee S. Alexa, Can I Trust You? Computer. 2017;**50**:100-104. DOI: 10.1109/MC.2017.3571053

[48] Mittelstadt BD, Allo P, Taddeo M, Wachter S, Floridi L. The ethics of algorithms: Mapping the debate. Big Data & Society. 2016;**3**(2):2053951716679679

[49] McMahan HB, Moore E, Ramage D, Hampson S, Arcas BAY. Communication-efficient learning of deep networks from decentralized data. arXiv. 2023;**54**:1273-1282. DOI: 10.48550/arXiv.1602.05629

[50] Krueger AB. How computers have changed the wage structure: Evidence from microdata, 1984-1989. Quarterly Journal of Economics. 1993;**108**(1):33-60

[51] Autor DH, Dorn D. The growth of low-skill service jobs and the polarization of the US labor market. American Economic Review. 2013;**103**(5):1553-1597. DOI: 10.1257/aer.103.5.1553

[52] Frey CB, Osborne MA. The future of employment: How susceptible are jobs to computerisation? Technological Forecasting and Social Change. 2017;**114**:254-280

[53] Santiago LE. The industries of the future in Mexico: Local and non-local effects in the localization of "knowledge-intensive services". Growth Change. 2020;**51**(2):584-606

[54] Su G. Unemployment in the AI age. AI Matters. 2018;**3**(4):35-43. DOI: 10.1145/3175502.3175511

[55] Blanchard OJ, Summers LH. Hysteresis and the European unemployment problem. NBER Macroeconomics Annual. 1986;**1**:15-78

[56] Gray R. Taking technology to task: The skill content of technological change in early twentieth century United States. Explorations in Economic History. 2013;**50**(3):351-367. DOI: 10.1016/j.eeh.2013.04.002

[57] Rathi A. Stephen Hawking: Robots aren't just taking our jobs, they're making society more unequal , Quartz. 2023. [En ligne]. Disponible sur: https://qz.com/520907/

stephen-hawking-robots-arent-just-taking-our-jobs-theyre-making-society-more-unequal

[58] Brougham D, Haar J. Smart Technology, Artificial Intelligence, Robotics, and Algorithms (STARA): Employees' perceptions of our future workplace. Journal of Management & Organization. 2018;**24**(2):239-257. DOI: 10.1017/jmo.2016.55

[59] Webb M. The impact of artificial intelligence on the labor market. SSRN Electronic Journal. 2019. DOI: 10.2139/ssrn.3482150. Available from: https://papers.ssrn.com/sol3/papers.cfm?abstract_id=3482150

[60] D. Acemoglu P. Restrepo, The Wrong Kind of AI? Artificial Intelligence and the Future of Labor Demand 2020. [En ligne]. Disponible sur: https://www.nber.org/system/files/working_papers/w25682/w25682.pdf

[61] Autor DH. Applying AI to rebuild middle class jobs. SSRN Electronic Journal. 2024: w32140. DOI: 10.2139/ssrn.4722981. Available from: https://papers.ssrn.com/sol3/papers.cfm?abstract_id=4722981

[62] Baldwin R. The Globotics Upheaval: Globalization, Robotics, and the Future of Work. Oxford, UK: Oxford University Press; 2019

[63] Agrawal A, Gans J, Goldfarb A. Power and Prediction: The Disruptive Economics of Artificial Intelligence. Harvard, USA: Harvard Business Press; 2022

[64] Li L. Reskilling and upskilling the future-ready workforce for Industry 4.0 and beyond. Information Systems Frontiers. 2022. Available from: https://link.springer.com/article/10.1007/s10796-022-10308-y

[65] Morandini S, Fraboni F, De Angelis M, Puzzo G, Giusino D, Pietrantoni L. The impact of artificial intelligence on workers' skills: Upskilling and reskilling in organisations. Informing Science Institute. 2023;**26**:39

[66] Puzzo G, Fraboni F, Pietrantoni L. Artificial intelligence and professional transformation: Research questions in work psychology. Rivista Italiana di Ergonomia. 2020;**21**:43-60

[67] Jaiswal A, Arun CJ, Varma A. Rebooting employees: Upskilling for artificial intelligence in multinational corporations. The International Journal of Human Resource Management. 2022;**33**(6):1179-1208

Chapter 4

Behold the Fourth Industrial Revolution and How to Keep Pace with Workplace Competencies in an Ever-Changing World of Work!

Joseph Mukuni

Abstract

In recent years, the workplace has been changing constantly in terms of the nature of work and the processes, tools, and competencies required to support sustainable productivity and competitiveness of enterprises. The factors responsible for this change include massive technological innovations, demographic changes, and unforeseen circumstances such as the COVID-19 pandemic. These changes in work have exacerbated the alignment of skills supply and demand, putting pressure on providers of education and training to reform their curriculum content to include the in-demand technical and socioemotional competencies and the signature pedagogies best suited for the ever-changing curriculum content. This chapter identifies the Fourth Industrial Revolution with its attendant digital innovations as one of the key causes of change and proposes some pedagogical approaches to the teaching and learning of in-demand skills. The suggested pedagogies shift the burden of skills acquisition from the instructor to the learner through learner-centered methodologies that prepare students for lifelong learning, problem-solving, and interdisciplinary collaborative searches for solutions to unforeseen challenges associated with the Fourth Industrial Revolution innovations.

Keywords: digital skills, employability skills, portable skills, workforce, workplace

1. Introduction

It can be argued that one of the major purposes of education is to prepare young people for the world after school by giving them the knowledge and skills that will enable them to be effective participants in the socioeconomic activities of their nations. It is important, therefore, that schools and colleges align their curricula to the competencies matching their nations' socioeconomic activities. The socioeconomic activities for which schools and colleges should prepare students beyond schooling include working productively in formal or self-employment in the world of work. The goal of aligning curricula to the world of work is, however, easier said than done because of the nature of the gap between what is taught in schools and colleges and what is needed in the workforce.

The challenges of minimizing the gap between the content of curriculum and the knowledge and skills demanded by industry and commerce include the difficulty of keeping pace with the rate of change on the demand side of education and training. The world of work is continuously in a state of flux, leading to constant adaptations and modifications of skill mixes in the repertoire of the workforce. The factors contributing to changes in work processes and their matching competencies include technological advancements, demographic changes, and unforeseen factors such as the onset of COVID-19 recently witnessed by the world. Some scholars have associated the changes in the workplace with the advent of the Fourth Industrial Revolution characterized by continuous adaptation and optimization of cyber-physical systems and the process required to operate and maintain them [1–4]. These changes and uncertainties in the workplace milieu put pressure on education systems desiring to be demand-responsive. This is because schools and colleges need to keep modifying curricula, reequipping learning stations, and retraining their staff to keep pace with the workplace changes and to maintain relevance and effectiveness in their role as suppliers of knowledge, skills, and dispositions needed by the workforce.

This chapter discusses the push factors of workplace change and proposes some pedagogical approaches to the teaching and learning of in-demand skills. The suggested pedagogies, which are suitable for teaching science, technology, engineering, and mathematics (STEM), shift the burden of skills acquisition from the instructor to the learner through learner-centered methodologies that prepare students for lifelong learning, problem-solving, and interdisciplinary collaborative searches for solutions to unforeseen challenges associated with the Fourth Industrial Revolution innovations. This chapter also proposes that the preparation of STEM-smart workforce should start at the primary school level rather than in later stages of education.

2. Push factors of workplace change

The world of work has witnessed technological changes since the onset of the First Industrial Revolution in the 1800s, with promises of joy to owners of capital and anxiety to the workforce. Owners of capital have welcomed technological advancements, expecting maximization of profits through mass production and a significant drop in labor costs and problems associated with industrial relations. The workforce, on the other hand, has felt threatened by the possibility of job insecurity, fearing that machines would take over work done by human beings. This section discusses the impact of technology on work, demographic factors affecting work in the changing world, and the impact of unforeseen change factors as witnessed recently when the world experienced the devastating COVID-19 pandemic.

2.1 Impact of technology on work

The nature of work has been changing because of several factors, including technological advancements, demographic shifts, and unforeseen circumstances [1]. Technological advancements have been driven by the desire to do less (e.g., by simply pushing a button), with little resources (e.g., fewer workers and a smaller wage bill), and to achieve more (e.g., mass production and greater profits). For instance, the First Industrial Revolution changed the nature of work significantly. The application of machines to manufacturing processes in the mid-to-late 1700s led to mass production of goods, a rise in the number of factories, and an increase in employment opportunities since machines needed operators and the mushrooming factories needed managers and workers. To contribute meaningfully to production and distribution of products and services in a changed world of work, the workforce needed a different set of skills from the agrarian skill sets that had characterized labor requirements before the Industrial Revolution.

The Second Industrial Revolution, like the one before it, had equally an impact on work because of the invention of electrical power, which enhanced mass production [5]. Enhanced mass production necessitated the reengineering of production lines for efficiency. One significant innovation was the change in the organization of work and chunking of tasks. As Beck [5] noted:

> *An improvement in production was the introduction of the assembly line by Henry Ford in 1914. On an assembly line, the complex job of assembling many parts into a finished product was broken down into a series of small tasks. It sped up production and reduced costs as each worker was only required to install one or two parts at their position on the assembly line. Ford would use the assembly line to speed up the production of automobiles in his factory in Highland Park, Michigan.*

The Third Industrial Revolution, according to Schwab [4], will be remembered for the use of electronics and information technology to automate work. The impact of the Third Industrial Revolution on work includes digitalization of work processes, which has brought about the importance of digital skills in workers' repertoire of competences [6, 7]. Today, most jobs are dependent on computers for planning, processing, and storing work, and dissemination of information, to the extent that it is difficult to imagine how work was done before the computer became a common feature at workplaces.

In 2016, Klaus Schwab, founder, and executive chairman of the World Economic Forum, announced the onset of the Fourth Industrial Revolution. He said:

> *We stand on the brink of a technological revolution that will fundamentally alter the way we live, work, and relate to one another. In its scale, scope, and complexity, the transformation will be unlike anything humankind has experienced before. We do not yet know just how it will unfold, but one thing is clear: the response to it must be integrated and comprehensive, involving all stakeholders of the global polity, from the public and private sectors to academia and civil society [4].*

The first three Industrial Revolutions changed the face of the workplace and significantly contributed to socioeconomic development through scientific innovations such as steam engines, electricity, and electronics. The Fourth Industrial Revolution has revolutionized the workplace further through advancements in digital innovations as exemplified by robotics, quantum computing, artificial intelligence (AI), materials science, virtual reality, three-dimensional (3D) printers, intelligent manufacturing, energy storage, the Internet of Things (IoT), genetic engineering, and biotechnology [2, 3]. A term associated with increased use of technology for purposes of work is digitalization of the workplace. Workplace digitization has been explained by Sheng et al. [8] as "electronic tools, automatic systems, technological devices, and resources that generate, process, or store information in the form of binary code" (p. 198). This digitalization trend has made it almost imperative for workers to have digital skills because most jobs require use of computers and digital knowledge and skills to operate computer-controlled machines [9].

The advent of the Fourth Industrial Revolution has not been without anxiety among some workers. The advancements in electronics and digital tools have raised fears about an expected negative impact on the labor market. For example, it has been noted that:

> *Most observers seem to agree that job destruction is likely to accelerate under the impression of current technological changes. In contrast, little is known about the potential for the creation of new jobs. For such new jobs to appear, many comment on the need for new markets to be developed and regulated, in particular in the green economy, care and personal services sectors, or an augmented public sector in areas where currently no profitable activities exist. The fear is that this process might not happen fast enough. Therefore, the number of jobs might fall faster than the global labour force when existing jobs are substituted by automation and other systems operated by artificial intelligence. In other words, machines, robots and computers will increasingly have an absolute advantage over labour and not only a comparative one ([10], p. 8).*

One study [9] reported from a review of literature that the use of robots at workplaces has led to the replacement of 1.6 manufacturing workers per robot and that by 2030, robots will, worldwide, displace 20 million manufacturing jobs. There seems to be a legitimate concern about some serious unintended consequences of the Fourth Industrial Revolution, despite the good intentions of advancements in technology. These concerns affect the morale and productivity of the workforce and should be catered for, along with the rest of the employability skills, when drawing up the list of competences that need to be addressed in the education and training of workers in response to the impact of the Fourth Industrial Revolution.

2.2 Demographic challenges

Concerns about the possibility of technology having an absolute advantage over human beings at workplaces, and the changed nature of competences that workers in the Fourth Industrial Revolution must have for them to contribute effectively to productivity and to maintain their jobs despite advancements in technological tools, are topics worthy of note by workforce development practitioners. To be added to these trending topics is the issue of workforce demographic challenges relating to technology use, particularly with reference to older workers. Some studies have found that older workers generally have difficulties with the use of technology [11, 12], especially older workers of color who have little or no access to computers at home.

The challenges of lack of or little use of computers among older workers do not apply to all older workers. Some older workers are computer literate [12]. This, however, does not belittle the impact of digitalization on older workers. Because of workplace digitalization, some older workers have had to make a serious decision about whether to retire early or to acquire the digital skills needed for their jobs [13].

The discourse about demography and digital skills is not only about the older workers' digital competences or lack of savviness. Young workers too are impacted by the skill demands of the Fourth Industrial Revolution. The myth that all young people, as digital natives, are computer literate has been debunked [14]. Studies have shown that a significant number of young people, particularly those from underprivileged homes, either lack the needed digital competences or have difficulties with applying their digital knowledge and skills to real-world work situations [15, 16]. Furthermore, studies have shown that young people's use of social media can cause harm to them, including cyberbullying, invasion of privacy, identity theft, social isolation, and mental health issues [17–20]. These serious side effects can be mitigated by providing workforce development that includes not only digital literacy skills but also strategies for coping with (or preventing) the risks associated with digital tools and social media platforms.

2.3 Unforeseen challenges

The onset of the COVID-19 pandemic recently taught the world of work to be aware that no matter how much workforce development programs may prepare workers for their tasks and life at work, nature has the final word. Quite unexpectedly, the COVID-19 pandemic befell the world and dealt a serious blow not only to the workforce but also to the nature of work across the globe [21–24]. The impact on the workforce included sickness, death, mental health issues, job insecurity, burnout, and stressful exhaustion [22, 25–27].

Thanks to COVID-19, the nature of work has changed, arguably forever. For instance, the boundary between work and home has practically disappeared because of the shift to remote work [26]. Performance of work is no longer restricted to a workstation in a specific locality. Most jobs are now done remotely. Because of this work-at-home trend, the pandemic has accelerated the Fourth Industrial Revolution by forcing workplaces to adopt virtual platforms and digital tools best suited for remote work [28] to avoid total shutdowns. In a sense, the timing of the Fourth Industrial Revolution can be seen as a blessing in disguise. One can hardly imagine how much greater the impact of COVID-19 would have been without the advancements in digital technologies characterizing the Fourth Industrial Revolution.

3. Pedagogical implications

Just as the First Industrial Revolution had an impact on schooling as we know it today [27], the Fourth Industrial Revolution has educational implications. Before the Industrial Revolution of the 1800s, schooling was mainly for the privileged few who were being prepared for white collar jobs. With the mushrooming of factories resulting from the First Industrial Revolution, factory owners needed skilled labor, which was in low supply, and this led to the proliferation of vocational education and training in the school systems [28]. Initially, the vocational schools were private because:

> *As a logical outgrowth of the Industrial Revolution and the subsequent specialized worker, many industries attempted to give their workers training in order to increase efficiency and thus increase their productivity. Therefore, many industries set up factory schools and one of the first was that of Hue and Company of New York City which, in 1872, set up a plant school for the purpose of training apprentices in the skilled trades and in particular the machinist trade ([29], p. 10).*

The need that was felt in the 1800s to have human capital that would contribute to efficiency and therefore productivity leveraging the advancements in technology is again emerging in the wake of the Fourth Industrial Revolution.

The pedagogical implications of the Fourth Industrial Revolution evolve around two questions: (a) *Curriculum content:* What knowledge, skills, and dispositions should workforce development institutions emphasize to respond to the needs of the changing nature of work? (b) *Pedagogical approaches:* What are the best pedagogical approaches for workforce development in the era of the Fourth Industrial Revolution?

3.1 Curriculum content

Much has been written about the workforce competences demanded in the world of work, given the fast-changing nature of work driven by technological advancements. As far back as 2010, an academician had perceptively foretold the complexity and unpredictable nature of work in the future:

> *The process of managing decisions and solving social scientific problems in contemporary democracies is growing ever more complex. At least 70% of U.S. jobs now require specialized knowledge and skills, as compared to only 5% at the dawn of the century... Furthermore, the nature of work will continue to change ever more rapidly... Thus the new mission of schools is to prepare students to work at jobs that do not exist, creating ideas and solutions for products and problems that have not yet been identified, using technologies that have not yet been invented ([30], p. 2).*

That future which Darling-Hammond [30] foretold has now come and is still unfolding. As she predicted, the workforce is faced with the challenge of coping with tasks and technologies for which no schooling ever prepared them to handle. Little wonder that the general conversation about Fourth Industrial Revolution skills [31–38] seems to focus more on portable employability skills such as the following in addition to technical digital skills:

- Problem-solving skills
- Creativity and originality
- Stress tolerance and flexibility
- Critical thinking skills
- Emotional intelligence
- Judgment and decision-making
- Cognitive flexibility
- Communication skills
- Cognitive load management
- Computational thinking
- Technology design and programming skills

- Lifelong learning skills
- Cross-cultural competency
- Virtual collaboration skills

These skills are portable across disciplines because they are generic. Workers who have these skills are likely to cope with the ever-changing nature of work and the new technologies that drive the work because they will have the right attitude toward change, the resilience to withstand confusing and ambiguous work situations, the cognitive aptitude to learn new skills, the communication and people skills needed to enable them to interact with other people despite the tendency of technology to promote isolation and individualism, and the preparedness and ability to solve problems arising from the nature of machines, tasks, and the social or physical environment at the workplace.

3.2 Pedagogical approaches

One educational phrase that came into popular usage during the era of the most recent industrial revolutions is STEM, or in full, Science, Technology, Engineering, and Mathematics. In searching for the pedagogies best suited for the Fourth Industrial Revolution, we should therefore look at STEM pedagogy.

There are several features that define STEM signature pedagogy. Key among them are student-centered methodologies, promoting problem-solving, encouraging teamwork, fostering critical thinking, and learning by doing. These features are seen in the following STEM approaches to teaching and learning:

a. *Problem-Based Learning (PBL):* Savery [39] described PBL as "an instructional (and curricular) learner-centered approach that empowers learners to conduct research, integrate theory and practice, and apply knowledge and skills to develop a viable solution to a defined problem. Critical to the success of the approach is the selection of ill-structured problems (often interdisciplinary) and a tutor who guides the learning process and conducts a thorough debriefing at the conclusion of the learning experience" (p12). In this approach, students are given a real-world problem to solve. Working in pairs or groups, students analyze the problem and come up with solutions. This process makes them engage and develop higher-order cognitive skills, critical thinking, creativity, and teamwork skills. The teacher's role is not that of a dispenser of knowledge but a provider of authentic tasks and scaffolding while observing and monitoring students as they work.

b. *Inquiry-Based Learning (IBL).* According to Pedaste et al. [40], IBL is "an educational strategy in which students follow methods and practices similar to those of professional scientists in order to construct knowledge" (p. 48). In this method, learning starts with students raising a question to be investigated. Then they conduct an experiment using the right tools and procedures and observe the results. This is followed by information synthesis or report writing after which students share their findings with the rest of the class. The last stage in this process is reflection, which enables students to look back at what they have done and learned during the inquiry.

c. *Project-Based Learning (PjBL):* PjBL has been described [41] as "an inquiry-based instructional method that engages learners in knowledge construction by having them accomplish meaningful projects and develop real-world product" (p. 2). In PjBL, students may work individually or in groups to create a real-world product. They have the autonomy to choose the procedure for developing a solution to an authentic problem. The teacher plays the facilitation role that encourages students to discover on their own what works and what does not work in coming up with a real-world product. This helps students to develop creative skills that are needed in the innovative era of the Fourth Industrial Revolution.

d. *Challenged-Based Learning (CBL):* "Challenge Based Learning is an engaging multidisciplinary approach to teaching and learning that encourages students to leverage the technology they use in their daily lives to solve real-world problems. Challenge Based Learning is collaborative and hands-on, asking students to work with peers, teachers, and experts in their communities and around the world to ask good questions, develop deeper subject area knowledge, accept and solve challenges, take action, and share their experience" ([42], p. 1). In this approach, students select a challenge and the method, materials, and tools that they will use to overcome the challenge. This approach builds on the other approaches mentioned above. Its benefits include development of critical thinking skills, problem-solving skills, creativity skills, and collaborative skills. Interdisciplinary collaboration mimics the real-world practice in which experts work across disciplinary boundaries to complete tasks.

All the approaches discussed above are based on student-centered methodologies in which students are in charge of their own learning. This prepares them for future workforce situations that require them to be lifelong learners.

3.3 STEM talent pipeline

It is generally agreed that investing in STEM in any country is important because STEM is a key element in promoting scientific innovations and carrying out the industrial tasks whose processes have been transformed by recent inventions [43, 44]. What is not mutually understood is the need to start this investment at primary school level instead of later stages of education (secondary school level and higher education) where some policymakers tend to focus. Primary school education is unarguably a foundational building block upon which the rest of the formal education process rests. Investment in STEM should, therefore, begin at the primary school level, leveraging the characteristics of early child development that present opportunities for laying a foundation for STEM education. By nature, primary school children are curious and want to discover the workings of the natural world. This curiosity and motivation to explore the world around them should provide a natural starting point for STEM education and awaken a sustained interest in STEM all through secondary school and college, leading to an increased supply of STEM talent in the workforce.

There are, however, some factors that work against initiating STEM education at primary school level [45]. The key constraint is insufficient funding for retraining of teachers in STEM signature pedagogies and for supply of the necessary teaching/learning materials. The other major constraint is the attitude of teachers who view STEM as an unwanted challenge to their comfort zones and old ways of doing things. These challenges are surmountable and the reward for overcoming them is the

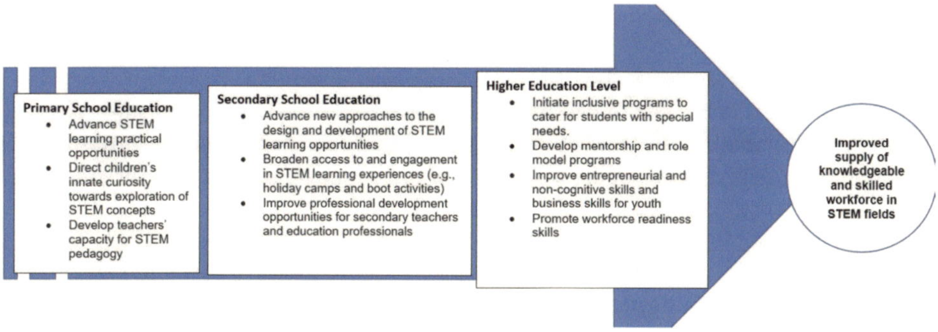

Figure 1.
Science, technology, engineering, and mathematics (STEM) pipeline flow from primary school to the world of work.

existence of an innovative STEM-educated workforce comprising movers and shakers needed for supporting innovations of the Fourth Industrial Revolution.

The diagram given in **Figure 1** describes the STEM talent pipeline from primary school to the world of work.

3.3.1 Primary school education

The primary school level lays the foundation on which the rest of the levels of education are built. It is therefore important that the seeds of STEM be planted at this level. Activities for promoting STEM at this level should include:

- Advancing STEM learning in practical opportunities for students to see applications of science, technology, engineering, and mathematics in everyday life, including children's games.
- Directing children's innate curiosity toward exploration of STEM concepts using games.
- Developing teachers' capacity for STEM pedagogy through exposure to STEM pedagogies during preservice teacher education and in-service programs.

3.3.2 Secondary school education

Promotion of STEM at the secondary school level should build on the foundation laid at the primary school level. Activities for encouraging and nurturing motivation for STEM at this level should include the following activities:

- Advancing new approaches to the design and development of STEM learning opportunities.
- Broadening access to and engagement in STEM learning experiences (e.g., holiday camps and boot activities).
- Improving professional development opportunities for secondary teachers to enhance their theoretical knowledge of STEM pedagogies and their capacity to translate theory into practice in classrooms, laboratories, and experiential learning sites.

3.3.3 Higher education level

At higher education level, the following strategies should be applied:

- Developing mentorship and role model programs by inviting subject matter experts from industry to give talks to students and to establish mentorships with students.

- Improving entrepreneurial and noncognitive skills and business skills through, for example, encouraging students to establish student-led businesses under the guidance of businesspersons/entrepreneurs.

- Promoting workforce readiness skills through internships and research projects that require students to investigate the employability skills (both soft skills and hard skills) demanded by industries.

- Supporting professional development for STEM teachers at primary and secondary school level.

4. Conclusion

The world of work is constantly changing, making it necessary for workforce developers in schools and colleges to review the content and pedagogy of knowledge, skill, and attitude development periodically for learning institutions to remain relevant to the demand side of education and training. This chapter has explored the factors that have in recent years contributed to changes in work processes and their matching competencies. These factors include technological advancements, demographic changes, and unforeseen factors such as the onset of COVID-19 which was recently witnessed by the world. Some scholars [1–4] have associated the changes in the workplace with the advent of the Fourth Industrial Revolution characterized by continuous adaptation and optimization of cyber-physical systems and the process required to operate and maintain them. In response to these factors of change, this chapter has proposed a pedagogical approach to workforce development. The proposal is that suppliers of knowledge, skills, and dispositions should adopt student-centered methods that have characterized STEM signature pedagogies, such Problem-Based Learning, Project-Based Learning, Inquiry-Based Learning, and Challenge-Based Learning. These approaches promote the development of employability skills (such as problem-solving, critical thinking, teamwork, and creativity) which are in demand in workplaces during the era of the Fourth Industrial Revolution. This proposal for changing the traditional teacher-centered pedagogical approaches to student-centered methodologies entails systemic changes among training providers, including periodic professional development, adequate funding for equipment and materials, strengthening quality assurance, establishing strategic linkages with industries, and rewarding instructional best practices in ways that are meaningful to teachers.

Author details

Joseph Mukuni
Virginia Tech, Blacksburg, USA

*Address all correspondence to: mjoseph7@vt.edu

References

[1] Isabirye N, Twinomurinzi H, Rammitlwa T. Operationalizing the future of work to measure job susceptibility. In: Proceedings of NEMISA Summit and Colloquium. Vol. 4. Manchester, UK: EasyChair; 24 Nov 2022. pp. 42-56

[2] Jin BE, Shin DC. The power of 4th industrial revolution in the fashion industry: What, why, and how has the industry changed? Fashion and Textiles. 2021;**8**(1):1-25

[3] McGinnis D. What Is the Fourth Industrial Revolution. San Francisco, CA: Salesforce Blog; Oct 2018

[4] Schwab K. The Fourth Industrial Revolution. Cologny/Geneva: World Economic Forum; 3 Jan 2017

[5] Beck E. First Industrial Revolution Vs Second Industrial Revolution. San Francisco, CA: History Crunch; 2016. Available from: https://www.historycrunch.com/first-industrial-revolution-vs-second-industrial-revolution.html#/

[6] Hecker I, Briggs A. Overlooked and Under-Connected: Exploring Disparities in Digital Skill Levels among Older Youth of Color in the US. Washington, DC: Urban Institute; 2021

[7] Muro M, Liu S, Whiton J, Kulkarni S. Digitalization and the American Workforce. Washington, DC: The Brookings Institution; 2017

[8] Sheng N, Fang Y, Shao Y, Alterman V, Wang M. The impacts of digital technologies on successful aging in non-work and work domains: An organizing taxonomy. Work, Aging and Retirement. 2022;**8**(2):198-207

[9] Butrica BA, Mudrazija S. Skills-Based Hiring and Older Workers. Washington, DC: Urban Institute; 2022

[10] Balliester T, Elsheikhi A. The future of work: A literature review. ILO Research Department Working Paper. 2018;**29**:1-54

[11] De Koning J, Gelderblom A. ICT and older workers: no unwrinkled relationship. International Journal of Manpower. 2006;**27**(5):467-490

[12] Hecker I, Spaulding S, Kuehn D. Digital skills and older workers. Urban Institute. 2021;**2021**:1-24

[13] Komp-Leukkunen K, Sarasma J. Social sustainability in aging populations: A systematic literature review. Gerontologist. 1 Aug 2023:gnad097. DOI: 10.1093/geront/gnad097. Epub ahead of print. PMID: 37526564

[14] Livingstone S, Mascheroni G, Stoilova M. The outcomes of gaining digital skills for young people's lives and wellbeing: A systematic evidence review. New Media & Society. 2023;**25**(5):1176-1202

[15] Helsper EJ, Eynon R. Digital natives: Where is the evidence? British Educational Research Journal. 2010;**36**(3):503-520

[16] Helsper EJ, Schneider LS, van Deursen AJ. The Youth Digital Skills Indicator. Leuven: KU Leuven, ySKILLS; 2020

[17] Juszczyk S. Fields of impact of social media on youth–methodological implications. Acta Technologica Dubnicae. 2015;**5**(2):80-86

[18] Hantrais L, Allin P, Kritikos M, Sogomonjan M, Anand PB, Livingstone S, et al. Covid-19 and the digital revolution. Contemporary Social Science. 2021;**16**(2):256-270

[19] Vissenberg J, d'Haenens L, Livingstone S. Digital literacy and online resilience as facilitators of young people's well-being? European Psychologist. 2022;**27**(2):76-85

[20] Kaushik M, Guleria N. The impact of pandemic COVID-19 in workplace. European Journal of Business and Management. 2020;12(15):1-0.

[21] Rachmawati R, Mei ET, Nurani IW, Ghiffari RA, Rohmah AA, Sejati MA. Innovation in coping with the COVID-19 pandemic: The best practices from five smart cities in Indonesia. Sustainability. 2021;**13**(21):12072

[22] Tshabalala M, Beharry-Ramraj A. Examining the 4th industrial revolution and South Africa youth entrepreneurship linkage to Covid 19: Opportunities and challenges. Gender and Behaviour. 2021;**19**(1):17204-17218

[23] Abramson A. Burnout and stress are everywhere. Monitor on Psychology. 2022;**53**(1):72-73

[24] Lyttelton T, Zang E. Occupations and sickness-related absences during the COVID-19 pandemic. Journal of Health and Social Behavior. 2022;**63**(1):19-36

[25] Maslach C, Leiter MP. COVID changed the world of work forever. Scientific American. 1 Mar 2022;**326**(3)

[26] Bussin MH, Swart-Opperman C. COVID-19: Considering impacts to employees and the workplace. SA Journal of Human Resource Management. 2021;**19**:5

[27] Schrager A. The Modern Education System was Designed to Teach Future Factory Workers to be "Punctual, Docile, and Sober". New York: Quartz; 2018

[28] Hanford E. The Troubled History of Vocational Education. Saint Paul, MN: American Radio Works; 9 Sep 2014

[29] Hoffman AM, Hoffman DB. A History of Vocational Education. 1976. Retrieved from: https://files.eric.ed.gov/fulltext/ED132283.pdf

[30] Darling-Hammond L. The Flat World and Education: How America's Commitment to Equity Will Determine our Future. New York, NY: Teachers College Press; 17 Apr 2015

[31] Sharma G, Sharma P. Importance of soft skills development in 21st century curriculum. International Journal of Education & Allied Sciences. 2010;**2**(2):39-44

[32] Kaliappan A, Hamid H. Industrial 4.0 generic skills needed among vocational colleges students in Malaysia. Journal of Pharmaceutical Negative Results. 15 Dec 2022;**13**(Special Issue 9):5924-5934

[33] Kamaruzaman M, Hamid R, Mutalib A, Rasul M. Comparison of engineering skills with IR 4.0 skills. International Journal of Online Engineering. 2019;**15**(10)

[34] Kamaruzaman FM, Hamid R, Mutalib AA, Rasul MS. Determination of 4IR generic skills constructs for engineering graduates. Journal of Positive School Psychology. 2022;**6**(3):243-257

[35] Kamaruzaman FM, Hamid R, Mutalib AA, Rasul MS, Omar M, Zaid MF. Exploration and verification of fourth industrial revolution generic skills attributes for entry-level civil

engineers. International Journal of Evaluation and Research in Education. 2023;**12**(1):121-130

[36] Mohd Adnan AH, Abd Karim R, Mohd Tahir MH, Mustafa Kamal NN, Yusof AM. Education 4.0 technologies, industry 4.0 skills and the teaching of English in Malaysian tertiary education. Arab World English Journal (AWEJ). 2019;**10**(4):330-343

[37] Rakowska A, de Juana-Espinosa S. Ready for the future? Employability skills and competencies in the twenty-first century: The view of international experts. Human Systems Management. 2021;**40**(5):669-684

[38] Savery JR. Overview of problem-based learning: Definitions and distinctions. Essential readings in problem-based learning: Exploring and extending the legacy of Howard S. Barrows. The Interdisciplinary Journal of Problem-Based Learning. (Bloomington, IN). 15 Jan 2015;**9**(2):5-15

[39] Pedaste M, Mäeots M, Siiman LA, De Jong T, Van Riesen SA, Kamp ET, et al. Phases of inquiry-based learning: Definitions and the inquiry cycle. Educational Research Review. 2015;**14**:47-61

[40] Guo P, Saab N, Post LS, Admiraal W. A review of project-based learning in higher education: Student outcomes and measures. International Journal of Educational Research. 2020;**102**:101586

[41] Nichols M, Cator K. Challenge Based Learning White Paper. Cupertino, California: Apple Inc.; Dec 2008

[42] Hapgood S, Czerniak CM, Brenneman K, Clements DH, Duschl RA, Fleer M, et al. The importance of early childhood stem education. In: Johnson CC, Mohr-Schoeder MJ, Moore TJ, English LD, editors. Handbook of Research on STEM Education. 1st ed. New York: Routledge; 2020. pp. 87-100

[43] Ismail Z. Benefits of STEM education In: K4D Helpdesk Report. Birmingham, UK: International Development Department; 2018

[44] Soylu Ş. Stem education in early childhood in Turkey. Journal of Educational & Instructional Studies in the World. 2017;**14**(4)

[45] Timms M, Moyle K, Weldon PR, Mitchell P. Challenges in STEM learning in Australian schools. In: Policy Insights Issue 7. Camberwell, Victoria: Australian Council for Educational Research; 2018

Chapter 5

Personal Leadership and Communication Abilities: Impacts on Organizational Performance

Manuel Sousa Pereira, Sílvia Faria, António Cardoso and Álvaro Cairrão

Abstract

The aim of this study is to understand the importance of communication within the management of an organization as a way to promote creativity, innovation, employees' engagement and competitive advantages. Leadership success seems to be related to the level and style of communication, the innovation strategy, the level of efficiency, the ability to plan and be proactive and, ultimately, the performance of the business itself. Thus, the authors propose to carry out an exploratory study with six active managers in the Portuguese market. The research aims to understand if it is important for managers to be perceived as a mediator. It is also our objective to know if the leader needs to be perceived as someone who is capable of inspiring, by betting on creativity, a proactive attitude and, above all, a collective vision of the organization itself, assertively communicated. Data indicate a consensual opinion on the part of the surveyed managers regarding the impact of leaders' communication skills on the company's performance. They all agree that the success of any organization is directly related to the ability of its managers to communicate and manage daily procedures.

Keywords: communication, business efficiency, personal leadership, creativity, innovation

1. Introduction

The choice of this theme arose from the need to understand the communication management in small, medium-sized and big companies in terms of personal and business dynamics, learning process and the motivation to develop employees and managers' leadership competences.

The success of business leadership will be addressed. Creativity, innovation, communication, strategic thinking and business efficiency will also be included. These aspects will be studied in order to understand their impact on individual motivation, business general performance and continuous improvement.

The authors decided to use a qualitative study, based on a convenience sample composed of individuals currently working as managers in companies, seeking to

 IntechOpen

incorporate recent or new ideas and thoughts on business leadership. These individuals had specific and relevant responsibilities in communication and brand's management. Bearing this in mind, three small companies, one medium-sized company and two large companies were selected, so as to match the Portuguese business reality, essentially composed of a reduced group of large companies (with less weight but with good practices, nationally and internationally) and a considerable number of small and medium-sized enterprises (SMEs) (99.9% in 2021).

The purpose of the interviews carried out is to understand which factors make global communication efficient, which are the most relevant aspects that promote this efficiency and, consequently, the relationship between managers' communication skills and employee's engagement and personal satisfaction. We also want to understand how leadership performance can impact on the organization's performance as a whole.

2. Personal leadership and communication

It can be said that good leadership is directly related to the ability to communicate values, thoughts and skills to others; this communication must be done in a simple and clear way, allowing receivers to perceive senders as visionaries, entrepreneurs and builders of their own destiny (e.g., [1]).

Leadership is the art of creating action; it is also the ability to create a common vision or the art of developing abilities and skills, leading to an efficient management of change trying to do the right things at all times [2].

On the issue of construction of the leadership process, Sprea [3] defines leadership as "... the process of conducting the actions or influence the behaviour and mentality of other person." Leadership is therefore a driving process that influences the behavior and ability of people. So, one can say that leadership has to do with motivating, managing and bringing all elements of an organization together around common goals. The purpose is to achieve specific aims and objectives. In this sense, leadership presupposes communicating to all the involved people their full potential, all their skills and abilities so that, individually or together, energy and solutions are found to achieve predefined goals [2].

Leadership is the art of leading to action, training the employees involved and controlling procedures [4, 5], contributing to a positive appreciation of people and the organization itself. According to the author, leadership consists of the art of highlighting the individuals' capacity, of valuing them and recognizing their importance. In this way, capacities are maximized and common action is achieved. Each human being has his talent, his experience and his characteristics. This makes him unique. As each person is unique, they should be allowed and encouraged to listen to their inner voice, make choices and be able to act, influence and inspire others to do the same. There are certain moments in life when someone is asked to use his abilities; when this happens within the scope of work (organization), the individual may not feel prepared or qualified to develop a certain task. The weight of responsibility can negatively impact the action. That's when a leader must act. It requires people to be recognized as capable of creating knowledge, holding skills that allow them to focus on the collective. For this to happen, communication is a must. It is essential to guide, add meaning to the potential of each person and use sensitivity, intelligence and flexibility. This is the only way to pass on the needed responsibility and freedom for efficient people management (e.g., [6]).

Delegating authority, passing responsibility and granting the necessary freedom for decision-making are crucial aspects for the success of any company. It promotes lower absenteeism degree, higher job satisfaction, effective team work, reducing turnover and leading to better productivity and profitability (e.g., [7]).

However, this requires the development of individual skills [8]. Developing human capital means developing individual skills. But it is not enough to have more training; it is essential to change the overall attitude, ask for responsibility, guide and encourage people to meet the organization's objectives. It is also crucial to give more autonomy and freedom of action, so that each person develops his own skills and competencies. To do all this, leaders need to be able to speak and hear attentively [9].

To be able to be a leader, one needs to clearly understand (1) company's goals and objectives and (2) the organization as a whole. It is also important to be able to communicate in an assertive way, be preservative, enthusiastic and proactive. Motivated individuals stay optimistic even through difficult times; socially skilled people, capable of entering into dialog and interact, develop empathy. These are key issues for a good leader and to manage teams (**Figure 1**) [8, 9].

According to Rego [10], there are specific factors that can help organizations achieve success. Shared leadership, well-defined vision and goals, focus on excellence, clear rules, financial incentives, ability to build trust, capacity to overcome individual interests and learn from mistakes are essential aspects that a leader must be able to deal with. And for successful leadership, Lowney [11] considers important to review the ideas about leadership and how to help leaders to shape up themselves. The author highlights that any leader must be aware of his strengths and weaknesses and adapt his personal characteristics to changes and challenges, both in personal and business terms.

Strong leadership depends on determination, initiative, honesty, a positive and constructive approach toward market challenges and the ability to communicate.

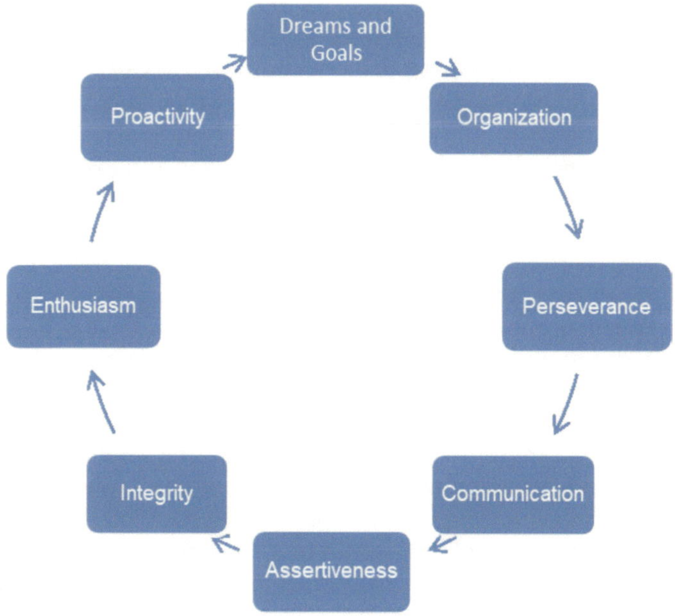

Figure 1.
Personal leadership. Source: Adapted from Santos [8].

Companies also depend on the same factors to achieve the desired success. Rego [10] stated that an organization managed with a feeling of positivity ends up positively influencing their workers' productivity and the overall performance. This, in turn, seems to improve interpersonal skills, team spirit and confidence levels. In other words, according to the author, proper communication can lead to the projection of positivity in organizations. This visibly influences the level of satisfaction, personal development, interpersonal relationships and overall performance. On the contrary, negative environment and lack of communication lead to apathy, depression, low interest in sharing information and experiences and high turnover intention. A leader's ability to communicate may or may not leverage the performance of the company as a whole. Leaders need to choose the most effective communication practices in order to achieve and positively influence organization's performance (e.g., [12, 13]).

3. Corporate strategic thinking

Strategic planning has become a growing need. It is the only way for a company to meet the new requirements of technological innovation, trends, customers' needs and to achieve productivity and sustainability, while meeting other organization's goals. Strategy leads to competitive advantages (e.g.: [14–16]). Corporate strategic thinking depends on managers' communication skills. Managers and entrepreneurs need to monitor the market carefully. They need to analyze the new market trends to then implement a business plan in line with the users or consumers' attitudes and needs as far as products or services.

Organizations need to define a set of strategic objectives, involving all employees, committing them in structural and sustainable change to achieve previously defined results. On the dynamics of strategic thinking, Gonzalez and Atencio stated [17] that managers need to previously know the different management tools, their basic features and interrelations so as to properly use them. They also need to be aware of market tendencies to adopt proper strategies. To implement the right strategies, leaders must be able to know internal strengths and weaknesses and, then, choose the ones who best suit the organization's vision, mission, values and daily activities [18]. So, to these authors, strategic success depends on the right choices, based on three dimensions: (1) customer focus, (2) activities undertaken and (3) market tendencies. These dimensions need to be analyzed in comparison to competitors' actions.

To implement strategic planning, companies need to involve all employees. Make them speak, trying to get new ideas, new solutions, developing skills and competencies. The business strategy also implies a dynamic transformational leadership [19]. This will be the result of the leader's ability to change the employees' basic values, beliefs and attitudes, stimulating their commitment to the company [20, 21]. Thus, the leader must be capable of providing a positive organizational environment, based on reciprocal communication. This will lead to a better understanding of desired behaviors and attitudes, impacting on the organization as a whole. According to Rego and Cunha [10], managing employees' motivation is a central concept in management and organizational behavior. It consists in using proper stimulus that provides action, movement and persistence, combined with a reward element.

The role of rewards in workers' motivation is complex. It involves different perspectives and needed actions, because every person is unique. Psychologists were the ones who most studied the issue of individual motivation. Dualistic theories split motivation into two types: intrinsic and extrinsic [22]. If we focus on managing people and companies, intrinsic motivations are the ones related to promote job satisfaction, compliance with standards and the achievement of personal goals (e.g., [23]). Extrinsic motivations have the purpose to satisfy indirect or instrumental needs. That is why money is usually the means to an end. Understanding how to motivate the workforce is essential to promote a dynamic and pleasant work environment. Leaders need to identify which intrinsic and extrinsic factors play an important role in employees' motivation, use and communicate them assertively (e.g., [23, 24]).

4. Innovation, creativity and business efficiency

Innovation is one of the most important aspects in terms of business management, therefore impacting on financial results, human resource management and the capacity to think strategically and adapt to market tendencies [25, 26]. However, true innovations occur, in general, slowly and over time. It can result in (1) creative combination of different forms of production; (2) marketing or communication strategies; and (3) new ways of doing things (processes). Ferreira [27] and Neely et al. [28] highlighted the need for management practices that encourage and support the innovation, through the integration of information, knowledge and expertise and the proper understanding of the external and competitive environment, competition, technology and consumer behavior.

Nowadays, companies act in mature and complex markets, with very demanding consumers [6, 25]. This requires individual and collective capacity to absorb and transform knowledge into truly differentiated products and services, good marketing practices and human resources management policies [29, 30].

Cota and Mark [31] related creativity to innovation, referring to the fact that creativity is a soft skill that must be shared by all managers of a company; more, it should be part of the organization's values.

One of the aspects inherent to creativity is to provide all employees increased motivation to make a contribution, with new or reused ideas [32]. To Frade ([33], p. 5) "... while creativity is the generation of new ideas, innovation is the translation of these ideas into new products or processes." This perspective considers individuals and groups' creativity as a starting point for innovation ([34, 35]; Anderson et al., 2004).

This creativity will always be objectively oriented in its application or implementation, because this is the only way to prove the innovative performance and their acceptance or relevance [36]. Sousa and Monteiro [37] consider creativity as an ongoing process that guides the individual and group initiative, leading to constant innovation and building profitable organizations.

In Porter's perspective [38], innovation is primarily responsible for the creation and maintenance of benefits, therefore ensuring organizations' continuity and sustainability. Kaufmann and Tödtling [39] add that a successful innovation contributes to improve the company's competitive position in the market segment. This is in line with Bateman and Snell [40]: innovation is a key source of competitive advantage, next to competitiveness in cost, quality and speed. The authors consider innovation as a factor that leads to the creation and maintenance of competitive advantage, therefore, the guarantee of continuity and profitability of any organization. Thus, innovation serves as the structural lever that ensures the company's future: (1) achievement of initial objectives; (2) stable economic and financial resources; and (3) company growth and capacity to reinvest.

According to Braga [36], the implementation of innovative projects should value aspects such as delegation, empowerment, trust and support of thinking and creative work. Consequently, innovation goes against routine and improves the perceived leadership quality. This happens when the top management values the individual and collective work, as well as the ideas presented by employees.

In this context, the more engaged employees are in tasks and activities, constantly helping to find solutions to the organization's problems, the more satisfied and motivated they will feel. Creative organizational environments are collective work structures, where all employees have access to the same information and share a common corporate culture. This leads to individual initiative, promotes innovation and adds value to the business dynamics, in a perspective of growth and sustainability [10]. It also promotes a favorable environment.

5. Methodology

This study aims to analyze the impact of personal leadership and communication abilities on organizational performance. A semi-structured interview was developed as a way to understand how does a manager's personal communication style affect the overall company communication. Other questions were included to relate the leader's quality of communication to the employees' satisfaction, their engagement and willingness to actively give ideas, look for alternative solutions and strive to achieve organizational goals.

According to Albarello et al. [41], an interview is the most appropriate instrument that allows the researcher to identify different cultural patterns present in the speech. More than mere words, gestures, facial expressions and tone of voice everything can be analyzed in detail when compared to a written questionnaire. It is, therefore, a more complete and detailed method of obtaining information.

Six people with communication and management responsibilities were selected by convenience [42] from among the authors' contacts: (1) Paula Arriscado, the Human Resources Director at Salvador Caetano; (2) Paulo Vilhena, CEO & Founder at Paulo Vilhena, Lda; (3) Jorge Sequeira, Human Resources and Communication Responsible at Team Building; (4) Salvato Trigo, Chairman of the Board of Directors of the Fundação Ensino e Cultura Fernando Pessoa (Fernando Pessoa University (UFP)); (5) Adelino Cunha, CEO & Founder at I have the Power; and (6) José Albuquerque, Communication Responsible at Nors, Auto Swedish. Salvador Caetano is a Portuguese company with more than 7000 employees, now present in 41 countries with more than 20 brands, car sales and distribution company. Paulo Vilhena Lda is a small company with 15 employees, providing consulting services. Team Building is a small company in the area of training and behavioral management. UFP and/or Fernando Pessoa Teaching and Culture Foundation (FFP) is an organization that aims to develop activities to promote education: culture, scientific research, professional and corporate training and public health. I have the Power is a small company with 18 employees, coaching specialist. Nors represents the Volvo brand at the Portuguese market and is also involved in some other economic activities, mainly in the industry; it completes 90 years in 2023.

The interviews were carried out in person, around five main topics: (1) Leader's personal communication skills and impact on the overall company communication; (2) the need to involve all employees in effective communication, creative thinking, innovation and company's performance; (3) the importance of having satisfied employees and the impact of their satisfaction in terms of communication; (4) managers' communication skills as an important soft skill to promote a company's success; and (5) what characteristics should a leader have so that he can develop fluid and capable communication. In each of these five topics, the main ideas given by each participant will be presented. Subsequently, answers were analyzed using the Content Analysis technique: inferences based on the text material obtained and its objective contextualization [43]. A phased content analysis was carried out, according to Bardin [44]: organization of the responses obtained; exploration of the gathered material (coding and categorization) followed by treatment of the results (inference and interpretation).

6. Findings and discussion

Trying to understand what is the impact of communication on the total performance of a company and what shapes trust, motivation, satisfaction and positive attitudes and understanding among employees, main trends in existing literature indicate that good leadership seems to be directly related to the ability to communicate, therefore, impacting on a company's success (e.g., [12]). This study is based on the approach of the communication capacity of a leader and managers in the results of the company as a whole. Thus, this relationship was assessed, through the exchange of ideas in the form of individual interviews with top managers of some Portuguese companies.

6.1 How do leaders' personal communication skills influence the overall company communication?

Participants revealed consensus views on this topic. Paula Arriscado, from Salvador Caetano (large company), stated that the success of a company is related to its managers' ability to communicate and manage the daily routines. This in turn requires managers to be aware of the ability of the company, as a whole, to perform the necessary functions, with the needed energy and within the stipulated timeframes to allow it to achieve its objectives as an organization. In this sense and according to this manager, the efficiency of personal communication is the ability to lead men and women in pursuit of a common goal. This is essential to keep the company's profitability. This is a prerequisite for the company to subsist in the market, therefore, a prerequisite to have reasons to communicate to the market. It confirms the importance that efficient internal communication has for the efficiency and effectiveness of the company and for its enlightening communication to the market and stakeholders. Paulo Vilhena, from Paulo Vilhena, Lda (small company), believes that companies reflect the leaders who run them. He thinks that a leader tends to attract people like him. "We tend to attract people similar to ourselves and tend to select people like us." By acting in this way, managers try to surround themselves with people who speak "the same language." That is, who will understand the logic of the speech they will have. For this reason, and from the outset, there is a relationship between a manager's communication style and his or her leadership style. This will be reflected in the day-to-day activities of the company and also in the way employees identify themselves in it. An enthusiastic leader exudes enthusiasm. Collaborators who absorb enthusiasm become enthusiasts. This ends up being reflected in the performance of the company. Also, in line with these two opinions, Jorge Sequeira, from Team Building (small company), thinks that leadership happens through example. An example is given by the way he works, the way he reacts to everyday situations and the way he deals with and informs other employees of what is being done and what needs to be done. This component of knowing how to communicate, of setting an example, is essential for employees to replicate. They understand the way forward, imitate good practices and end up working as a team in pursuit of a common goal. A manager is practically always communicating, whether in what he says, writes or through data analysis and decision-making. This has a direct impact on the company's performance that, in turn, also impacts the company's overall communication (internal and external).

Salvador Trigo, from UFP (Fernando Pessoa University, a medium-sized company), said that managers need to always take care to comply in their relationship with others: appropriate treatment, appropriate words and appropriate examples. In this perspective, respect and consideration are two essential variables to use in any form of communication, regardless of being internal (to employees) or external (to the market). He also believes that a leader has to be extremely inspiring and have to give utmost confidence. Like in the army, do the best for his/her team. The way a manager speaks must encourage initiative. The speech needs to be adapted to the receptors; however, in order to lead others to do what the company needs them to do, the way of speaking must be convincing. And one can only convince another person when words are directly related to actions. Therefore, a manager who knows how to use the right words and adopt the right actions will be contributing to a successful company, since he will have in his workers someone who understands him/her and identifies with him/her.

Adelino Cunha, from I Have the Power (a small company), started by saying that the relationship between leaders' capacity to communicate and the company's overall communication and performance is undeniable. To this manager, the internal communication reflects the leadership style. Any manager needs to be aware of how to communicate since this will be reflected in the company's general perception. Leaders should be inspiring. They need to reassure employees and make them feel comfortable at work. Managers also need to learn from other workers and adapt their speech. A company is made by the people who work for it. There is no need for managers or leaders if there is not a sufficient number of work teams to carry out all the activities required by the Organization. From top managers to employees at the bottom of the hierarchy, everyone matters. They are a whole. A company only exists if everyone makes an effort. A company only exists when all their elements manage to understand each other and it is the managers who must promote this general understanding. Then there is what it communicates to the market: a reflection of what happens internally. It is essential that a manager knows how to communicate and adapt his speech to the internal and external reality for the company to continue to exist. Read "in and out" information and prepare an adequate answer.

José Albuquerque, from Auto Swedish (large company), agrees that individuals' communication skills impact on organizations' communication quality. According to this participant, a leader is someone who is empathetic. Individuals tend to follow those who tell them what they expect to hear. They follow those who set an example, in actions and words. But mostly in actions. Thus, everything a manager does turn out to be communication.

The manager identifies situations and informs; he must listen, ask for suggestions. He makes decisions and informs. And in this continuous process, he is communicating. If he communicates assertively, he will have an aligned team. An aligned team adequately performs its functions. Faced with this, the company fulfills its promises and, therefore, is also automatically communicating. For everything to work and for the company to remain competitive and profitable, there is an unequivocal relationship between the leader's and/or managers' communication skills, the positive perception of the company's communication in general and its success. **Table 1** summarizes main ideas and compares with already existing literature:

Topic	Main parts of the interviewee's speech	Content vs literature
Personal Leadership and Communication vs. Overall performance: • "... good leadership is directly related to the ability to communicate values, thoughts and skills to others"; • "...Leadership is therefore a driving process that influences the behavior and ability of people"; • "...This, visibly influences the level of satisfaction, personal development, interpersonal relationships and overall performance	**P. Arriscado:** "the success of a company is related to its managers' ability to communicate and manage the daily routines"; "This is essential to keep the company's profitability. This is a pre-requisite for the company to subsist in the market, therefore, a pre-requisite to have reasons to communicate to the market."	Agrees
	Paulo Vilhena: "...companies reflect the leaders who run them. He thinks that a leader tends to attract people like him... By acting in this way, managers try to surround themselves with people who speak "the same language"; "... This ends up being reflected in the performance of the company."	
	Jorge Sequeira: "...This component of knowing how to communicate, of setting an example is essential for employees to replicate"; "...This has a direct impact on the company's performance."	Agrees
	Salvador Trigo: "...a manager who knows how to use the right words and adopt the right actions will be contributing to a successful company."	Agrees
	Adelino Cunha: "... the relationship between leaders' capacity to communicate and the company's overall communication and performance is undeniable."	Agrees
	José Albuquerque: "...individuals' communication skills impact on organizations' communication quality. According to this participant, a leader is someone empathetic. Individuals tend to follow those who tell them what they expect to hear"; "...For everything to work and for the company to remain competitive and profitable, there is an unequivocal relationship between the leader's and/or managers' communication skills, the positive perception of the company's communication in general and its success."	Agrees

Table 1.
Topic 1, answers and literature.

6.2 The involvement of employees for effective communication and consequent creativity thinking, innovation and business performance

All the participants agree that employees' involvement is essential. And employees are only involved if they are well informed. This topic was understood as a reinforcement of the previous one. Comments from all the participants stated that involving employees in the decision and communication process can positively increase the overall communication and performance strategies. Workers will proactively share ideas and concerns, actively listen to their managers and leaders and, therefore, feel more connected and engaged with the company's objectives. By encouraging them to listen and to speak, managers will for sure be able to develop effective internal and external communication. At the same time, involved employees give ideas, suggestions and this leads to creative approaches to the market (products and services) and company needs (procedures). This will have a positive impact on creativity and innovation that, in turn, leads to better business performance.

Topic	Main parts of the interviewee's speech	Content vs literature
• Employees' involvement for Effective communication and Business performance	**P. Arriscado:** "... only involved employees develop a serious commitment to the company, enjoying belonging to the staff and developing their activities with extra energy."	Agrees
	Paulo Vilhena: "...Engaged employees are the first to communicate positively. They act proactively and are not afraid to give ideas and show their point of view. This promotes dialog and raises productivity levels."	
	Jorge Sequeira: "... Involved employees are, usually, satisfied individuals; they will be part of an active communication, intern and externally."	Agrees
	Salvador Trigo: "... involved and encouraged employees tend to talk and end up revealing many aspects that need improvement, thus impacting the company's performance."	Agrees
	Adelino Cunha: "...Engaged contributors are individuals who identify themselves. They know that they are indispensable to the success of the company. Therefore, knowing how to listen, let people talk and analyze their suggestions can indicate the path that the company needs to follow to remain competitive in the market."	Agrees
	José Albuquerque: "...a successful company needs to control turnover. This can only be achieved by involving people. We have to let employees trust the company's management and listen to them carefully. Often, they are the ones who contact customers and competitors. Their point of view should be the starting point for countless daily decisions."	Agrees

Table 2.
Topic 2, answers and literature.

The opinion of two of the participants is highlighted: Paula Arriscado believes that only involved employees develop a serious commitment to the company, enjoying belonging to the staff and developing their activities with extra energy. They will proactively give suggestions on products' promotion and even procedures and "this will provide important insights to the organization" in the sentence "They will proactively give suggestions on products' promotion and even procedures and this will provide important insides to the organization". In line with this opinion, Jorge Sequeira believes that team spirit depends on two-way communication. And only united teams identify with the company's objectives and promote ways to achieve them. Involved employees are, usually, satisfied individuals; they will be part of an active communication, internally and externally. **Table 2** summarizes main ideas:

6.3 The influence of employees' satisfaction on communication

In general, all participants agreed that satisfied employees tend to communicate proactively.

Paulo Vilhena highlighted that individual's happiness also depends on the quality of the relationships he/she establishes with other individuals. If someone has a good working environment, feels recognized and involved in the decision-making process he/she will feel happy, motivated to do the best. For example, when working at a commercial department, feeling good and in line with the company's strategy and objectives, one will be capable of selling anything.

Topic	Main parts of the interviewee's speech	Content vs literature
• Employees' satisfaction impact in Communication	**P. Arriscado:** "...The daily concern of a human resources manager should be to promote a good working environment for its employees, regardless of the sector in which they work. Implementing employer branding strategies lead the company to be considered the best place to work. If an employee develops this perception, he will be an excellent asset with regard to communication (internal and external)."	Agrees
	Paulo Vilhena: "...Workers who do not feel professionally fulfilled develop a negative image of the company; and because a negative experience creates more buzz than a positive experience, the company risks facing negative (spontaneous) communication. So yes, employee satisfaction has a direct impact on a company's communication and image."	Agrees
	Jorge Sequeira: "... as I already said, satisfied individuals; will be part of an active communication, intern and externally."	Agrees
	Salvador Trigo: "...Anyone who feels integrated into a company, recognized and involved ends up developing satisfaction. Satisfied employees, like satisfied customers, are the first to talk about the company, the brand and recommend its products or services."	Agrees
	Adelino Cunha: "...Only satisfied employees develop positive communication. More: spread by word of mouth."	Agrees
	José Albuquerque: "...From my personal experience, satisfied employees speak convict and positively about the company: they believe in it and identify with it, recommending it to others, either as an employer or as a supplier of goods and/or services."	Agrees

Table 3.
Topic 3, answers and literature.

José Albuquerque believes that employees are very proud to belong to and work in Auto Swedish (Volvo). Paula Arriscado said the same about Salvador Caetano's workers. So, to all the participants, it is essential to promote job satisfaction in order to have engaged workers. Engaged workers will be proud to be working in that company and, through their initiative, will be drivers of positive internal and external communication. **Table 3** states main contributions:

6.4 How do managers' personal communication skills influence the overall company performance?

To all participants, personal communication skills are directly related to any company's success. Managers who are good at communicating enable good teamwork, rapid problem-solving, and the capacity to promptly answer to market demands and tendencies. They will also build empathy with the other workers, therefore promoting a positive work environment and culture. Good communicators are also those who absorb information from the outside and synthetize it to the other company's workers. Creativity and Innovation are perceived by them as the only way to stay competitive in mature markets. So, by investing in communication skills and in a

Topic	Main parts of the interviewee's speech	Content vs literature
• Managers' personal communication skills vs. overall company performance	**P. Arriscado:** "...90% of a manager's time is spent communicating: reading, analyzing data, writing reports and talking to different people. It is a soft skill that any manager must know how to use and improve."	Agrees
	Paulo Vilhena: "...If a manager is not a good communicator, he will not be able to convince others to act in accordance with the organizational objectives. It will negatively impact the company's results. The opposite is also true."	Agrees
	Jorge Sequeira: "...Managers, at the top, intermediate level or line managers, need to know how to argue, how to listen and understand. Only then will they be able to have ideas aligned with the internal and external needs of the company."	Agrees
	Salvador Trigo: "...an integral part of a manager's training is the development of communication skills. A manager is always communicating. And the success of the organization depends on his/her communication competences.".	Agrees
	Adelino Cunha: "...Those who know how to act and communicate assertively lead others to believe and replicate attitudes. A manager who acts in this way will be contributing to the success of the company."	Agrees
	José Albuquerque: "...Observe, listen, speak and listen again. It is from this continuous process of communication that a manager can assert himself and lead a team to achieve general objectives."	Agrees

Table 4.
Topic 4, answers and literature.

communication-friendly environment, managers will be working to improve the overall company performance and long-term success and profitability.

Paula Arriscado said that she started at the Marketing Department, responsible essentially for external communication. The company knew that she had a PhD in Communication. After some years, she was invited to embrace a new project: human resources management. The company bet on using her communication skills to develop a more friendly work environment, since they believe that satisfied and motivated workers are individuals with higher productivity and lower turnover intention. She is now having a huge challenge: develop proper communication to allow higher degrees of motivation and counteract a trend toward job abandonment. So, to her and to Salvador Caetano as a whole, personal communication skills do impact the overall company's performance. **Table 4** has the key answers:

6.5 Characteristics of a leader for communicating effectively

To reinforce the relationship between a leader's ability to communicate and a company's performance level, participants were asked which main characteristics a leader should have.

Salvador Trigo said that a leader has to have the ability to properly identify his target and then communicate in an understandable way. So, any leader needs to be a simplifier. By this it is meant that an ideal characteristic for a leader is to be able to not complicate things; deal with simplicity and clarity with everyday situations.

Paulo Vilhena combines this ability to simplify with another characteristic: being able to listen.

To Jorge Sequeira, empathy is the prerequisite, followed by the capacity to storytelling: awaken feelings and tell good stories that serve as good examples.

Paula Arriscado said that leaders need to enjoy to share: getting people involved in their projects. Not being afraid to share: knowledge, information and ideas. This will encourage others to act in the same way.

José Albuquerque added the capacity to stay rational, objective and transparent. Be an empathic person, someone that people like to hear but also trust to talk with.

To Adelino Cunha, a leader must be an example, in words and actions. Set a good example. Leaders also need to hear and understand others' point of view. **Table 5** summarizes the main ideas:

Topic	Main parts of the interviewee's speech	Content vs literature
• Leader's characteristics for Efficient communication	**P. Arriscado:** • "Enjoy to share; involve workers in daily decisions; • inform about good and not so good results; • Involve employees in setting goals; • Interact, tell stories and give examples."	Agrees
	Paulo Vilhena: • "Being able to listen; • Capable to simplify; • Pragmatic."	Agrees
	Jorge Sequeira: • "Empathy; • Storyteller; • Be exemplary."	Agrees
	Salvador Trigo: • "Good listener and speaker; • Knowledge and experience; • Adapt to change; • Learn through benchmarking."	Agrees
	Adelino Cunha: • Self-motivated; • Experience and strong formation; • Good speaker and listener; • Exemplar.	Agrees
	José Albuquerque: • "Empathy"; • Curiosity; • Capacity to listen; • Capacity to adapt speech to different public.	Agrees

Table 5.
Topic 5, answers and literature.

In general, the interviewees corroborate the existing literature, by consensually agreeing that the communication skills of leaders and managers in general have an impact on the performance of companies as a whole. Storytelling, directly or indirectly, was recognized as one of the most efficient ways to allow managers to explain ideas, share knowledge and deal with internal conflicts properly. This demands for good communication skills. Managers that invest in communication competences, being able to speak and listen, will for sure overcome possible barriers that individuals may build for their personal protection (e.g., [2]).

7. Conclusion

According to the state of the art, leadership is the capacity to create action, build skills and control things (e.g., [3, 4]). Leaders must be able to gather all the available information, internal and external, treat it and put it at the disposal of their coworkers in an understandable way [1, 9]. By having communication skills and leading others by example (actions), they promote job satisfaction [10]. Satisfied workers tend to develop positive feelings and, when properly motivated with extrinsic and intrinsic stimuli, act proactively [22]. So, proper communication can lead to positive organizational environment. In turn, positivity impacts workers' satisfaction, promotes personal desire for improvement and overall performance. Manager's communication skills have a huge impact on employee engagement, personal satisfaction and organizational success [10]. Communication builds trust, empowers employees, promotes responsibility and puts everybody performing at their best (e.g., [23, 24]).

Organizations need to implement strategic thinking. For that, all employees must be involved and committed. Strategy leads to competitive advantages (e.g.: [14–16]). In mature and competitive markets, creativity and innovation are two essential aspects to be included in any company strategy [25, 26]. They are key issues to competitive advantage, ensuring any company's future, profitability, growth and capacity to reinvest [25, 36, 40].

After analyzing the interviews carried out and the content of all the responses, there seems to be a consensus regarding the impact of leaders' communication skills on the overall performance of companies. In fact, all participants agree that the success of a company is related to its managers' ability to communicate and manage the daily routines. It seems that companies reflect the leaders who run them. So, in other words and according to data obtained, a global and efficient communication depends on the leaders' communication skills, on one side, and on employees' involvement on the other side. All the participants also agreed that involving employees in the decision and communication process can positively increase the overall communication and performance strategies, leading to creativity, innovation and better business performance.

Managers identify situations and inform others about it. They ask for suggestions, then make decisions and communicate them. In this continuous process, managers are always communicating. If this communication is assertive, an aligned and motivated teamwork is achieved. This, in turn, leads everybody to adequately perform their functions. Facing an increase in productivity and quality, companies are able to respond in line with market needs, therefore increasing competitiveness. Leaders that are good at communicating enable good teamwork, rapid problem-solving and the capacity to promptly answer to market demands and tendencies. They will also build empathy with the other workers, therefore promoting a positive work environment and culture. Employees will feel satisfied and engaged with the organization. The respondents' comments highlight the leaders' capacity to communicate as a drive for quality internal and external communication, capable of highlighting a company's strengths. If the leader communicates effectively, his team and the market are able to understand the brand's positioning and the bases of differentiation. Communicating implies strategic thinking. Define answers to internal and external questions; this presupposes a commitment to creativity and innovation. These are two crucial points for good internal and external performance.

To summarize, our study seems to prove that leaders with good communication skills promote understanding and team spirit. On the other hand, they perceive market issues and the need to create and innovate. Strategic thinking becomes part of the company's DNA and that of its employees. Everyone ends up being involved in this spirit of curiosity and proactivity. Thus, the good communication skills of a leader and his workers, the involvement of the company as a whole, strategic planning and commitment to creativity and innovative responses contribute to good levels of organizational performance. This is in line with previous literature and allowed answering the research questions. However, it presents a certain character of novelty by focusing on the Portuguese market, revealing a growing concern on the part of entrepreneurs with aspects related to (1) communication; (2) strategic thinking; and (3) the implementation of human resources policies aimed at employee satisfaction.

The authors recommend that this study should be replicated to a larger number of companies. To analyze, for example, two specific economic sectors—e.g.: textile and footwear industry, since they represent a large part of the Portuguese business fabric. This would allow, by comparison, a more comprehensive and enlightening understanding.

Acknowledgements

We would like to thank all participants for their kindness and availability for their active participation in this study.

Conflict of interest

No conflict of interest.

Notes/thanks/other declarations

Thanks to all the participants who agreed to participate in this research, sharing their own experience and enriching the acquired knowledge: Paula Arriscado, Human Resources Manager at Salvador Caetano; Paulo Vilhena (Paulo Vilhena Lda); Jorge Sequeira (Team Building); Salvador Trigo (UFP); Adelino Cunha (I have the Power) and José Albuquerque (Auto Swedish).

Author details

Manuel Sousa Pereira[1*], Sílvia Faria[2], António Cardoso[3] and Álvaro Cairrão[1]

1 ESCE, Polytechnic Institute of Viana do Castelo, Valença, Portugal

2 Universidade Portucalense, Porto, Portugal

3 FCHS, University Fernando Pessoa, Porto, Portugal

*Address all correspondence to: msousa.manuel@gmail.com

References

[1] Wikaningrum T, Yuniawan A. The relationships among leadership styles, communication skills, and employee satisfaction: A study on equal employment opportunity in leadership. Journal of Business and Retail Management Research. 2018;**13**(1):138-147

[2] Mládková L. Leardership and storytelling. Procedia – Social and Behavioral Sciences. 2013;**75**(3):83-90. DOI: 10.1016/j.sbspro.2013.04.010

[3] Sprea J. Emotional intelligence: The differential in competitive educational organizations. 2009. Available from: https://repositorio.iscte.pt/bitstream/10071/2050/1/Disserta%c3%a7%c3%a3o%20de%20mestrado%20Joseney%20Sprea%20oficial%20versao%206%2c0.pdf [Accessed October 10, 2013]

[4] Covey SR. The 8th Habit from Effectiveness to Greatness. Lisbon: Ed Dinalivro; 2005

[5] Rabiul MK, Shamsudin FM, Yean TF, Patwary AK. Linking leadership styles to communication competency and work engagement: Evidence from the hotel industry. Journal of Hospitality and Tourism Insights. 2023;**6**(2):425-446. DOI: 10.1108(JHTI-09-2021-0247

[6] Maçães M. Manual de Gestão Moderna Teoria e Prática. Coimbra: Actual Editora; 2018

[7] Elnaga A, Imran A. The impact of employee empowerment on job satisfaction theoretical study. American Journal of Research Communication. 2014;**2**(1):13-26. Available from: http://www.usa-journals.com/

[8] Santos MJ. Human Resource Management: Theory and Practice, Sociology Dossier. 2004. Available from: http://www.scielo.br/pdf/soc/n12/22259.pdf [Accessed November 23, 2013]

[9] Goleman D. What makes a leader. Creative Management. 2004;**2004**:82-91

[10] Rego A, Cunha MP. Positive Leadership. 2nd ed. Lisbon: Ed Syllabus; 2010

[11] Lowney C. Heroic Leadership. Lisbon: Ed Word; 2006

[12] Sabino LR, Neto MTR, Morais M, Santos VF. Leadershio, communication, and resistance influence Orgamizational performance. Latin American Business Review. 2021;**22**(3):265-286. DOI: 10.1080/10978526.2021.1897469

[13] Santoso NR, Sulistyaningtyas ID, Pratama BP. Transformational leadership during the Covid-19 pandemic: Strengthening employee engagement through internal communication. Journal of Communication Inquisy. April 2022:1-24. DOI: 10.1177/01968599221095182

[14] Adomaco S, Tran MD. Sustainable environmental strategy, firm competitiveness, and financial performance: Evidence from the mining industry. Resources Policy. 2022;**75**:102515. DOI: 10.1016/j.resourpol.2021.102515

[15] Amini M, Rahmani A. How strategic agility affects the competitive capabilities of private banks. International Journal of Basic and Applied Sciences, Vl. 2023;**10**(1):8397-8406. Available from: https://ssrn.com/abstract=4408544

[16] Farida I, Setiawan D. Business strategies and competitive advantage: The role of performance and innovation.

Journal of Open Innovation: Technology, Market, and Complexity. 2022;**8**(3):163. DOI: 10.3390/joitmc8030163

[17] González B, Atencio E. Strategies servicio: el elements for business success in multiciencias. Economic sciences sociales y Maracaibo. 2010;**26**:139-145

[18] Cusumano MA, Constantinos CM. Strategic Thinking. Rio de Janeiro: Ed Campus Publisher; 2002

[19] Pereira M. Personal Marketing. Lisbon: Ed Book Site; 2011

[20] Judge TA, Bono JE. Five-factor model of personality and transformational leadership. Journal of Applied Psychology. 2000;**85**(5):751-765

[21] Podsakoff MW, Mackenzie SB, Bommer WH. Transformational leadership behaviors and substitutes for leadership the determinants of employee satisfaction, commitment, trust, and organizational citizenship behaviors. Journal of Management. 1996;**22**:259-298

[22] Reiss S. Intrinsic and extrinsic motivation. Teaching of Psychology. 2012;*39*(2):152-156. DOI: 10.1177/0098628312437704

[23] Frey BS, Osterloh M, editors. Successful Management by Motivation: Balancing Intrinsic and Extrinsic Incentives. Germany: Springer Science & Business Media; 2001

[24] Singh R. The impact of intrinsic and extrinsic motivators on employee engagement in information organizations. Journal of Education for Library and Information Science. 2016;**57**(2):197-206

[25] Carvalho JMS. Inovação e Empreendedorismo ideia implementação informação impacto. Porto: Vida Económica; 2016

[26] Freire A. Innovation: New Products, Services and Business to Portugal. Lisbon: Ed Word; 2006

[27] Ferreira MP, Reis NR, Serra FR. Marketing for Entrepreneurs and Small Businesses. Port: Ed Lidel; 2009

[28] Neely AD, Adams C, Crowe P. The performance prism in practice. Measuring Business Excellence. 2001;**5**(2):6-12

[29] Catalão J. A Arte da Guerra na Criatividade e Inovação. Lisboa: TOPBOOKS; 2014

[30] Rodrigues J, Faria S, Rua OL. The impact of creativity as a foremost attraction for a business through social media: The power of Instagram. In: Borges AP, Vieira E, editors. Proceedings of the International Conference of Applied Business and Management (ICABM2022), 14-15 July 2022. Porto, Portugal: ISAG - European Business School. Repositório Institucional UPT; 2022. pp. 221-224. Available from: http://hdl.handle.net/11328/4659

[31] Cota BV, Mark PG. Innovative Marketing. Lisbon: Ed Catholic University Publisher; 2007

[32] Siegel SM, Kaemmerer WF. Measuring the perceived support for innovation in organizations. Journal of Applied Psychology. 1978;**63**:553-562

[33] Frade JR. Innovate with Initiative, Autonomy, Demand for Innovation, Climate for the Production and Innovation. Portugal: University of Lisbon; 2008

[34] Amabile TM, Conti R, Coon H, Lazenby J, Herron M. Assessing the work environment for creativity. Academy of Management Journal. 1996;**39**(5):1154-1185

[35] Hunter Bedell KE, Mumford MD. Climate for creativity: A quantitative review. Creativity Research Journal. 2007;**19**(1):69-90

[36] Braga AM. Factors Influencing the Decision-Making Innovate in Portuguese Companies. Portugal: University of Tras-os-Montes and Alto Douro; 2010

[37] Sousa FC, Monteiro LP. Organizational innovation: The effectiveness of the method of creative problem solving. Portuguese and Brazilian. Journal of Management. 2010;**2010**:38-49

[38] Porter ME. The Competitive Advantage of Nations. Rio de Janeiro: Ed Campus; 1998

[39] Kaufmann A, Tödtling F. Science-industry interaction in the process of innovation: The importance of boundary-crossing between systems. Policy Research. 2001;**30**:791-804

[40] Bateman TS, Snell SA. Administration - Building Competitive Advantage. São Paulo: Ed Atlas; 1998

[41] Albarello L, Digneffe F, Hiernaux J-P, Maroy C, Ruquoy D, Saint-Georges P. Practice and Research Methods in Social Sciences. Lisbon: Gradiva; 1997

[42] Pestana M, Gageiro J. Data Analysis for Social Sciences. The Complementarity of SPSS. Lisbon: Syllabus Issues; 2005

[43] Bauer MW, Gaskell G. Pesquisa qualitativa com texto, imagem e som: um manual prático. Porto: Editora Vozes; 2015

[44] Bardin L. Análise de Conteúdo. 13th ed. Lisboa: Edição Vozes; 2011

Chapter 6

Unlocking Growth: Exploring Senior Management Programme's Learner Experiences in India's Blended Learning Landscape

Durgesh Tripathi and Surbhi Tandon

Abstract

COVID-19 pandemic has significantly transformed the landscape of education, leading to a widespread acceptance of digital education. Senior executives are recognizing the potential of digital education to improve their skills, networks and leverage the brand value of top business schools. This study aims to investigate the perceptions, motivations and experiences of senior managers enrolled in a Senior Management programme offered by Indian Institute of Management, Calcutta (India), delivered in a blended mode. Through interviews of 29 learners, the research tries to investigate the perceptions and motivations for joining the course, advantages, and limitations of the course and mapping their overall experiences. The key findings of the study reveal that most learners joined the programme for the upskilling opportunities along with a strong inclination towards gaining the alumni status of the premier institution and leveraging the brand value of 'IIM' tag. The learners believed that such courses were the best option for the working professionals as it provides them with the flexibility and opportunity to upgrade their skills. It is essential to map and analyse the experiences of the learners for developing more nuanced blended learning courses aligned with the needs of twenty-first century and Industrial Revolution 4.0.

Keywords: blended learning, learner experiences, corporate India, lifelong learning, business schools, upskilling, Indian workforce

1. Introduction

> *"The illiterate of the 21st century will not be those who cannot read and write, but those who cannot learn, unlearn, and relearn."—Alvin Toffler*

Raghav Gupta, Managing Director of India, and APAC at Coursera, stated in 2021 during a Times Higher Education Webinar titled 'Upskilling and reskilling India's present and future workforce with digital education' [1] that the country has been facing 'double disruption' due to the ongoing COVID-19 pandemic and the automation taking place in the industry, both of which have implications for the future of businesses and the workforce. He pointed out the four interconnected phenomena that are taking place in the country, which revolved around job losses in the pandemic, corporates prioritising the reskilling of their employees as automation and digitalization are changing the way businesses are being conducted and transacted, remote work, and predictions for the creation of newer jobs in the future that require digital and data-oriented skills. All these phenomena are taking place in the country. Whilst another panellist on the webinar brought up an important aspect of how individuals are taking the responsibility of reskilling and upskilling themselves in an ever-changing modern work environment, particularly with the rise of gig and digital economies, Dwarika Prasad Uniyal, pro vice chancellor of RV University, said that individuals, especially mid-tier management, are feeling that they are ill-equipped to deal with the challenges of the modern workplace and keep pace with the changes that are taking place in the business world. He is of the opinion that they are utilising digital education, particularly in the form of blended courses, as a means of avoiding becoming "redundant" in the workforce and enterprises.

1.1 Upskilling trends in India

According to the Upskilling Trends Report, 2023 [2], which was published by the edtech platform Great Learning, 83% of Indians aim to take up courses and certificates that would enable them to upskill themselves. This percentage is significantly higher than the global average of 74% for that specific year. On the other hand, the survey suggests that over 71% of professionals in India feel positive about maintaining their existing employment and roles. This percentage is significantly higher than the average of 59% that is seen across the world. According to the findings of the survey, the most in-demand and widely acquired talent in India in 2022 was data science. This was followed by software engineering and management. Learners with more than 8 years of experience were most interested in artificial intelligence and cloud computing (**Figure 1**).

The city of Bengaluru, also known as the Silicon Valley of India, had the biggest demand for professional development courses. This was followed by the cities of Chennai, Hyderabad, Mumbai, Pune, and Delhi in that order. According to the report [3], some of the most common motivations for enrolling in upskilling courses were the desire to advance in one's career, to receive a higher salary package, to gain new skills and expertise, particularly technical skills, and to satisfy the need to remain relevant in the face of the challenging macroeconomic conditions that exist in a world that has been affected by a pandemic. Among the many probable motivations for obtaining new skills and competence, one of the most common is the ability to easily migrate to different fields. It was revealed that there were gender differences among those who were participating in the upskilling courses; however, the inequalities were found to be significantly more pronounced among those who had more than 8 years of experience. The gender inequalities were seen probably as a result of the time, effort, and financial resources required to participate in such courses and certifications, as well as the necessity of balancing work duties and the requirements of caregiving (**Figure 2**).

1.2 Need for twenty-first century skills in India

Both S&P Global and Morgan Stanley [4] believe that India is on track to become the third largest economy in the world; however, their estimates for the year differ. S&P Global and Morgan Stanley both believe that India will become the third largest

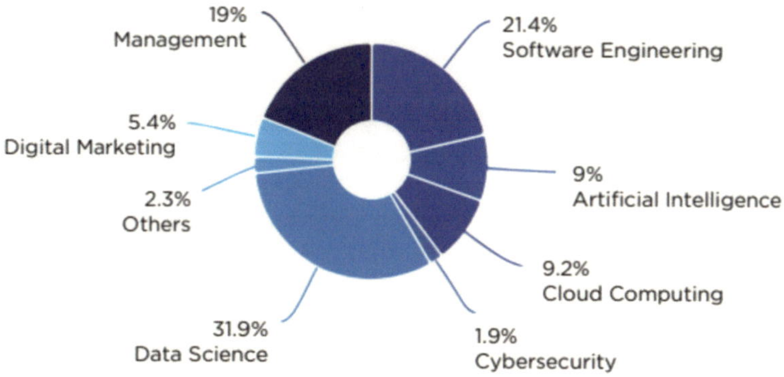

Figure 1.
The image showcases the top skills acquired by learners in India through upskilling courses in 2022 as per the upskilling trends report released in 2023. Source: https://www.mygreatlearning.com/blog/upskilling-trends-in-india/

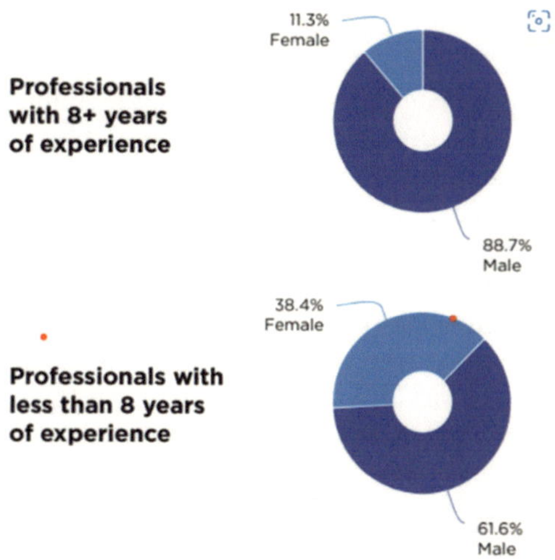

Figure 2.
The image showcases the vast gender differences in those taking up upskilling courses in the workforce as per the upskilling trends report released in 2023. Source: https://www.mygreatlearning.com/blog/upskilling-trends-in-india/

economy in the world. According to a prediction by S&P Global, India will pass both Japan and Germany by the year 2032; however, Morgan Stanley predicts that this milestone would be reached by India by the year 2031. The following are some of the factors that have been identified as contributing to such growth in the foreseeable future: an average nominal growth of gross domestic product of 6.3% in the post-pandemic period; the continuation of the financial liberalisation; labour market reforms; investments in infrastructure and manufacturing; low-cost labour; energy transition; and the availability of digital infrastructure, to name a few. Nevertheless, India is confronted with the unusual problem of a shortage of the workforce that will support the economy, particularly in terms of twenty-first-century skills in emerging industries such as artificial intelligence, 5G equipment manufacturing, semiconductors, electric vehicle technology, carbon capture, medical equipment manufacturing, defence manufacturing, climate technology, and the banking sector, amongst others. This presents a challenge that is unique to India. According to an article that was published in May 2023 in Fortune India and titled "The New-Age Skill Gap," [5] it was pointed out that Indian corporates are encountering difficulty in acquiring the suitable talent with the appropriate abilities that are required in the twenty-first century. Businesses in India such as the Tata Group, the Adani Group, Mahindra & Mahindra, Reliance Industries, the Vedanta Group, and L&T (Larsen and Tubro) are struggling to find qualified workers in the Indian labour force market. Companies such as L&T, which already employs a workforce of 200,000 people, needed to hire 1500 additional engineers in order to expand their operations into new markets. These new markets include hydrocarbons, defence, electric vehicles (EV), heavy engineering projects, and green hydrogen, amongst others. Even the freshly hired engineers were obligated to participate in a training programme that lasted for a full year before they were allowed to start working. The corporation has also made the decision to spend Rs. 100 crores annually in order to provide the new staff it hires with the necessary abilities for the twenty-first century. Tata Consultancy Services (TCS), which also provides business consulting services, is having trouble recruiting qualified candidates. Even though FMCG businesses like Hindustan Unilever (HUL) have undertaken a "skill analysis" of their 3000-strong frontline sales team and feel that many of them may have excellent personal selling and influencing skills, they lack the skills necessary to work with data. The company has made a commitment to enhancing the capabilities of its 21,000 staff members by the year 2025. This will be accomplished through a combination of in-class and on-the-job training courses developed in cooperation with the edtech platform Khan Academy and ITI (Industrial Training Institutions).

According to Future of Jobs Report (2023) [6], there will be creation of 69 million new jobs whereas there will also be a decline in the 83 million job worldwide creating a deficit of about 14 million jobs i.e., 2% of the total employment. According to the report, many clerical and secretarial jobs would be eliminated in future due to Artificial Intelligence. The report also states that there would be increased demand for specialists in fields like artificial intelligence, machine learning, data specialists and scientists as they are the most prominent emerging sectors of the economy. The Future of Jobs Report, 2023 also points out that there is a talent deficit as the 60% of the companies surveyed for the report are facing challenges in bridging the skills gaps whereas 53% of the companies are unable to find employees and attract talent with the adequate skills to transform their businesses and prepare it for the future. Thus, there seems to be need to invest in the existing workforce and employees and reskill or upskill them to make them relevant for the changing times and business situations. Organisations are fast realising that there is an urgent need to invest in their employees and provide them with the opportunities as well as the financial resources so that they can adapt to the changing workplace and its norms (**Figure 3**).

1.3 Government initiatives for upskilling and digital education

With multiple entry and exit points, a focus on digital education, the establishment of an academic bank of credit, and the ability to pursue multiple degrees concurrently, India's new National Education Policy (2020) [7] has provisions to make it easier to develop skills for the twenty-first century and pursue lifelong opportunities. It aligns with Sustainable Development Goal 4, which promotes high-quality education for all, by emphasizing a multidisciplinary approach with a learner-centric focus [8]. The establishment of the National Educational Technology Forum, the creation of

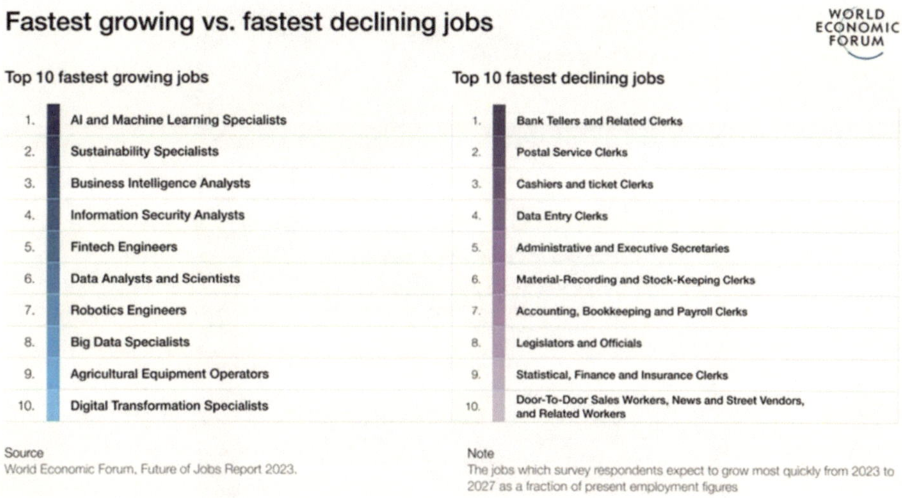

Figure 3.
The image showcases the top 10 fastest growing sectors and top 10 fastest declining jobs in the job markets across the globe as per the World Economic Forum's Future of Jobs Report, 2023. Source: https://www3.weforum.org/docs/WEF_Future_of_Jobs_2023.pdf

MOOCs (Massive Online Open Courses) to be specifically created in regional languages, the training of faculty members in the planning, carrying out, and assessment in digital learning environments, and investments in digital infrastructure can all be used to analyse the policy's greater emphasis on digital education [9]. The National Education Policy, which was created in 1986 and attempts to address the needs of the next generation, is replaced by the new policy. In the budget for 2023, the Union Finance Minister announced the creation of 30 International Skill India Centres [10] as part of the Pradhan Mantri Kaushal Vikas Yojana 4.0, recognising the need for upskilling, particularly in 21st-generation skills. The curriculum plans to teach the latest technologies like coding, artificial intelligence, robotics, mechatronics, IOT, 3D printing, drones, and soft skills. To maintain India's reputation as the "pharmacy of the world," the budget also promised the creation of multidisciplinary courses to teach skills linked to producing cutting-edge medical equipment (**Figure 4**) [11].

Employees who use advanced digital skills, such as cloud architecture and software development, report higher job satisfaction and contribute $507.9 billion to India's annual gross domestic product (GDP), according to a study titled "Asia Pacific Digital Skills Study: The Economic Benefits of a Tech-Savvy Workforce" [12] that was commissioned by Amazon Web Services. Since 2017, Amazon Web Services has taught approximately 4 million people in advanced digital skills, particularly those linked to cloud computing, for the Indian workforce. According to the survey, at least 21% of firms that run most of their business on the cloud have quadrupled their annual revenues, compared to 9% that rely on it either partially or not at all. According to the survey, 92% of employers anticipate incorporating expertise in blockchain, AI, cryptocurrency, and quantum computing into their standard operating procedures and business practises.

1.4 Blended learning and leveraging its potential for the upskilling and reskilling

Blended learning is an educational approach which is a combination of the online and offline learning experiences. It is also often called as the hybrid mode or mixed

Figure 4.
The infographic is released by press information bureau with the highlights of the union budget, 2023 showcasing the present government's commitment toward youth for the upskilling courses and preparing them for the twenty-first century skills. Source: pib.gov.in/PressReleaseIframePage.aspx?PRID=1895304

mode of learning. It combines the features of the traditional face-to-face classroom experiences as well as digital education. Some of the important features of blended learning are mix of delivery methods, flexibility in time schedules and learning styles, integration of technology in the pedagogy through different aids such as learning management systems, multimedia content, discussion forums, digital tools, availability of personalised learning along with group activities assignments, peer learning, online quizzes, collaborative learning opportunities, availability of learning analytics to track learner's progress and development to name a few.

According to the Guide to Blended Learning by Commonwealth of Learning released in 2018 [13], multiple studies have showcased that blended learning gives the opportunity to the learn collaboratively, develop creative thinking and tailor their experiences to serve their individual needs and personal goals. The book also offers insights into three basic models of the blended learning which may be tweaked and differentiated to varying degrees to design, develop and deliver multiple courses and programmes catering to the needs of the learners, curriculum framework and institutional factors. The three models of blended learning are:

a. *Flipped classroom or flipped curriculum*: In this model, the classroom teaching or face-to-face teaching is the primary mode of instruction however, the students also have access to online resources to support their learning experiences. The students may be provided with open educational resources (OERs), podcasts, online exercises related to the topic/subject to be discussed in the classroom. The students have access to the online resources independently. It may include group learning through online medium such as webinars or seminars.

b. *Blended block model*: This model incorporates both online sessions and face-to-face learning with carefully planned sequence of activities to facilitate the process of learning. Such a model considers the pedagogical goals and pragmatic considerations whilst designing the courses and is a useful model for designing and implementing courses for the working professionals and geographically distributed learners. It is usually designed in a manner where the online sessions are followed by a block of face-to-face learning such as group presentations, case studies.

c. *Fully online model*: As the model's name suggests, it has provisions for digital or online sessions and opportunities for learning, however, it is also a blend of online synchronous learning such as online classes, webinars, tutorials and asynchronous activities like discussion forums, pre-recorded videos, individual assignments, quizzes integrated through learning management systems (LMS) or otherwise.

According to Online Education in India: 2021 report by KPMG [14], India's online reskilling and online certification market is mature with the growth rates of about 38% (Compound Annual Growth Rate-CAGR) and the factors attributed for the high growth are high adoption rate amongst the target audience, convenience factor and the need to continuously evolve oneself with the changing technology and the needs of the contemporary times. The report estimated that India's market size for reskilling and online certification is about 463 million USD in 2021 which has risen from the 93 million USD in 2016. The report states that India's market is oligopolistic in nature with subscription model being the most preferred model adopted by the users. The average course duration for reskilling programme ranger between three to 6 months with a cost of around Rs. 8000 (INR) to Rs. 16,000 per course. The courses provide access live classes, instructor led projects and case studies, however, some courses also offer value added services such as recruitment assistance and paid freelance projects undertaken during the courses. The report states that an average user enrols themselves in two courses in a year for reskilling themselves in the evolving contemporary times whereas they may enrol in such courses five times in their entire lifetime. Working Professionals are generally looking for courses that immediately adds value to their profiles after the completion of the course especially in Tier 1 cities in India whereas Tier 2 users are looking for niche courses. However, the courses may have a low shelf life as the course content easily becomes obsolete due to the fast-paced changes in technology and their usage in various industries but the course updation on a regular basis remain a challenge as it is an expensive and time-consuming process. The report also points out that technology related courses are evenly distributed amongst various across different regions and tiers whereas business management courses are highly demanded in Tier 1 and Metro cities. The report also states that high demand for certification courses is due to the rise in disposable incomes of the employees and an aspiration to distinguish themselves or their curriculum vitae from their peers in the work environment. However, some of the key challenges faced by the learners are connectivity issues, pricing of the course and the choice of brand for the course selection. Some of the key motivational factors pointed out by the report for adopting online certification and reskilling programmes are convenience, no requirement of travelling to a physical classroom and self-paced learning especially in the urban centres. Reduced travel time and flexibility offered is a key factor for adoption of the courses.

Thus, upgrading the skills of the Indian workforce and preparing them for upcoming opportunities and challenges appear to be achievable through digital education especially blended learning programmes considering that working professionals have work as well as familial responsibilities. India has a thriving digital education sector for a variety of uses, such as competitive examination preparation, skill development, and upskilling initiatives. As they can include both online learning and practical experiences like apprenticeships, campus visits, immersive activities, group projects, live classes, and offline meetups, among other pedagogical aspects, blended learning programmes are thought to be the most suitable mode of learning for upskilling programmes.

2. Review of literature

Hrastinski [15] refers to blended learning as an umbrella phrase. He asserts that blended learning is more than just integrating online and offline instruction; it also includes a variety of methodologies and elements. According to him, blended learning encompasses a range of pedagogical strategies, information technology tools, and instructional methods. Although there is no universally accepted definition of blended learning or what it entails, the phrase was first used in the 1990s. Graham (2006) [16] feels that the online teaching and learning process is an amalgamation of the conventional offline teaching and learning processes in a computer-mediated environment, in contrast to [17] who view the integration of the online teaching and learning process in the curriculum framework to be "thoughtful." On two features of blended learning, which is a thoughtful combination of in-person instruction and learning and online interactions, there does appear to be agreement: it should be "planned" and "pedagogically valuable." However, there seems to be a consensus on two aspects of blended learning, which is a judicious mix of face-to-face teaching and learning along with online interactions: that it should be 'planned' and 'pedagogically valuable.'

Bordoloi et al. [18] contend that education in the twenty-first century should be a combination of customized, "productive," and "collaborative" in character, with a focus on holistically developing the potential and creativity of the students. They suggest that blended learning—a combination of face-to-face (F2F) and technology-enhanced instruction—could be the most effective model for the holistic development of students, who would then be both critical and creative thinkers and problem solvers. They also think that blended learning technology, together with carefully thought-out methodology, content, and course materials that are in line with modern needs, can act as catalysts to assist the nation advance faster than other nations. Their study, "Perception towards online/blended learning at the time of the COVID-19 pandemic: an academic analysis in the Indian context," demonstrates that blended learning is viable in the Indian context for the twenty-first century, particularly in emergency or extraordinary circumstances like war or pandemic. They demonstrated a favourable perspective and connection between online learning and the delivery of instruction, training, and skills through mediated environments. They believe that soon, new instructional technologies will become crucial. Whilst Hass and Joseph [19] investigated how business school students at a liberal arts university in the Southwest of the United States felt about online versus traditional face-to-face courses. The study found that students in both groups—those exposed to online learning and those taking traditional courses—demonstrated a willingness to participate in online programmes. However, the researchers recommended a blended or hybrid form of instruction for these kinds of programmes.

Another study, "Can MOOCs Reskill and Upskill the Indian Workforce for the Industrial Revolution 4.0?" which is a thorough literature review highlights the inherent weaknesses of MOOC courses in skill upgradation due to the high attrition rate offered through government-sponsored MOOC platforms like SWAYAM (Study Webs of Active-Learning for Young Aspiring Minds). Many students in the Indian context do not complete their courses. The fact that the course materials were unable to meet the needs of the variety of learners—some of whom would have prior knowledge or even experience, whilst others would be beginners—is a significant factor in the high attrition rates. Other frequent causes for course abandonment include the digital divide, lack of national framework for the MOOC ecosystem, and issues with credit transfer. The findings also showed that the Canadian government understands the critical necessity for workforce upskilling and reskilling every few years due to the changing nature of the world and the introduction of newer technology that affect how we behave. The government has acknowledged the necessity for boot camps and the creation of MOOC courses to provide its workers with twenty-first century skills.

Kumar and Pande [20] in their research paper titled "Technology-mediated learning paradigm and the blended learning ecosystem: what works for working professionals?" assert that blended learning courses offer ease of access, interactive pedagogy and have a high contextual significance. They proposed a learning paradigm for the working professionals especially related to blended learning programmes which is based on the earlier formulated learning paradigm of 'learning as participation'. The researchers believe that such blended learning programmes are context-centric, focussed on acquisition of specific skills and enables collaborative and peer learning. They also identify the key success factors for the blended learning ecosystem for the working professionals. User-centricity is identified amongst the key factor. They have recognised varied factors which play a key role in the satisfaction of the learners and effective learning in the blended learning courses which are—Institutional factors, Faculty-related factors, Student-related and Pedagogy related factors.

3. Research objectives

The paper attempts to understand the perceptions and motivations of a blended learning programme through investigating the learner experiences. Following are the research objectives of the research article:

1. To understand the perceptions and motivations of the learners to join a blended learning programme especially for those in senior or middle management levels.

2. To assess the advantages and limitations of blended learning programmes run by business schools

3. To analyse the overall experience of the learners enrolled in a blended learning programme.

4. Research methodology

It is a qualitative research study that employed a descriptive methodology with an emphasis on conducting structured interviews with students enrolled in the Indian Institute of Management Calcutta's (IIM Calcutta) Senior Management Programme (SMP). We intend to explore the learner's experiences, viewpoints, and insights surrounding their enrolment in the SMP. The primary purpose of this study is to determine how learners perceive and benefit from the SMP at IIM Calcutta, which is delivered in a blended mode. The Alfred P. Sloan School of Management (MIT), the Government of West Bengal, the Ford Foundation, and Indian business collaborated to create the Indian Institute of Management, Calcutta, as the country's first national institution for post-graduate courses and management research, in 1961. It is regarded as one of Asia's finest business schools. The course began in June 2023 and was still in progress at the time of the study. It is a 12-month programme designed to teach strategic leadership abilities and ease the transition into senior management roles, particularly in an evolving business environment. According to the website (https://www.iimcal.ac.in/ldp/SMP), the programme's stated objectives [21] are:

a. equip them with analytical skills,

b. enhance their existing functional competencies,

c. transform them into strategic leaders.

The course is delivered in a blended format, with online instruction on weekends, particularly Sunday, to accommodate the demands of working professionals, and two campus visits (5 days) at the programme's midpoint and finish. The students had already been on one of the programme's planned campus visits when the study was done. A total of 150 students were enrolled in the programme, and 29 SMP students—21 men and 8 women—were interviewed for this study. The participants ranged in age from 34 to 50 and held senior management positions such as project managers, directors, associate directors, vice presidents, and chief financial officers (CFOs), among others. The course includes both on-campus and online instruction, as well as pedagogical tools and exercises like case studies, role-plays, games, quizzes, and simulations. Except for one person who just left their position, these participants all hold middle- to senior-level management positions in global firms and government agencies. We have mostly depended on conducting in-depth structured interviews with an approach that permits open ended questions and in-depth investigation of each participant's experience with the SMP in order to gather data. The questions revolved around the themes of the perceptions and motivation for joining the course considering their well-established position and job profiles in the industry/domains, advantages and limitations of the blended learning programme, strategies, and challenges to align their work, family responsibility and learning goals, organisational support for the senior management programme and their overall experience. The interviews were transcribed and then the recurrent patterns, themes and insights were identified from them to gain valuable insights into the learner's experiences.

5. Findings and results

5.1 Perceptions and motivations of the learners to join a blended learning programme especially for those in senior or middle management levels

Some of the main reasons for joining the Senior Management Programme are: leveraging the brand value of the Indian Institute of Management, which is a premier management institution in India with a strong reputation in Asia; a medium for networking opportunities with industry professionals, particularly those in key decision-making positions; opportunities for skill enhancement and upskilling; and preparation for important leadership positions that may become apparent. As a result, several of the unique responses were (**Figure 5**).

> *"To equip myself with skill sets that would help me transition from being a functional manager to a suitable role in general management."*

> *"Discovering what is beyond present leadership role and understanding present industry standards, that can help build better workplace and sustain growth with meeting future needs."*

DOI: http://dx.doi.org/10.5772/intechopen.1003640

Figure 5.
The image showcases the main motivations for joining the senior management programme at IIM, Calcutta. Source: Formulated by the researchers.

5.1.1 Long-term and short benefits of the senior management programme

Some of the short-term benefits of participating in the course included: transitioning from the government to the corporate sector; promotion purposes, including elevation to the post of COO/CEO level job; upskilling; adding value to the current role and organization in the corporate sector; technical learning; learning new management trends and patterns; and gaining an edge on the resume due to the host institution's high reputation and leveraging the brand value. Long-term benefits of taking the course include developing strategic decision-making skills, improving decision-making abilities, understanding the challenges and opportunities in various leadership roles, alumni networking, accelerated advancement from current roles, and attracting recruiters. Some of the learners' distinctive responses were as follows:

> *"It would help upskill and expand my knowledge base further; and also my appreciation & understanding of how various functions operate in leadership roles. It would definitely equip me with skill sets to becoming a better leader with a more wholesome, enriching experience & outlook."*

> *"It gives good insights into Strategic Decision Making by exposing participants to all important Corporate Functions".*

> *"It will help me understand the dynamics of business apart from technology roles and help me to grow in management role."*

> *"It will help to get a holistic view of all functions of the business and might be useful if am trying for more senior management roles".*

5.1.2 Advantages and limitations of blended learning programmes run by business schools

According to the learners, the benefits of the senior management programme included the opportunity to grow and acquire new skills, networking opportunities, updated course content, sharing knowledge and discussions with peers, particularly on critical issues of the day, and alumni status. The remote learning opportunity and the flexibility that comes with it to balance work, family responsibilities, and learning needs; accessibility to course materials, including text materials and videos, at all times through the learning management system; time management; and the ability to learn from home represent a few of the standard benefits indicated by respondents. Many respondents stated that blended learning programmes are the only way for working professionals to improve their knowledge and abilities (**Figure 6**).

Some of the common challenges and concerns raised by the learners enrolled in Senior Management Programme are large batches in an online set-up, rushing of the syllabus in the classes, prolonged and unnecessary time spent on Questions and Answers Sessions or Discussions leading to time constraints to comprehensively cover the syllabus, lack of access to course instructors except for the Sunday and offline campus visits, technical glitches including access to learning modules and videos, lack of individual attention, less opportunities for networking in online interactions, personal interactions and touch with the educators, problems with Learning Management Systems, balancing work, family responsibility and learning goals, instructional designs as some crucial topics could be taken up during the offline classes in campus visits, depth missing in some subjects, coping with the speed of the course or consideration of the needs of the diverse learners, examinations during the travel time among others (**Figure 7**).

5.1.3 Organisational support for the upskilling course

As the majority of course participants are working professionals with high-profile professions in senior and middle management, organisational support is essential for participation in and effective completion of a blended learning programme. As a result, it is important to have organisational support in order to speed up learning and develop the necessary abilities. Out of 29 students, two had their courses paid for by their organisations; however, six students received no funding from the latter. Whilst two students received some support from the organisation for the course. Others have received varying degrees of assistance from their company, ranging from leaving work during institution visits to helpful managers who helped them manage their time and workload. Since it is a weekend course, many respondents chose not to ask the organisation for assistance and instead paid the tuition with their own funds or resources. Following are a few of the learners' novel answers to organisational help from the organisation:

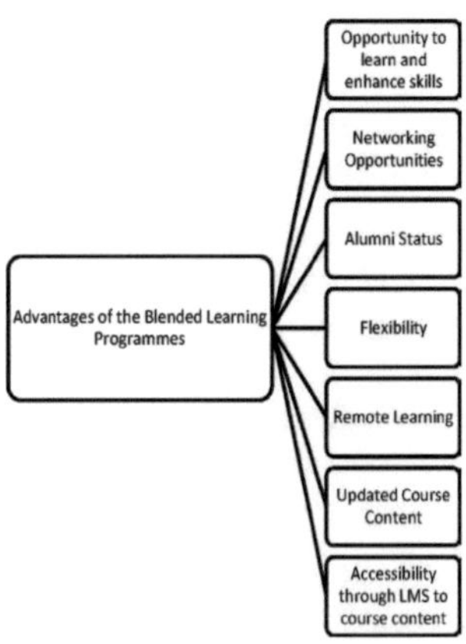

Figure 6.
The infographic showcases the advantages of the blended learning programmes as experienced by the learners. Source: Formulated by the researchers.

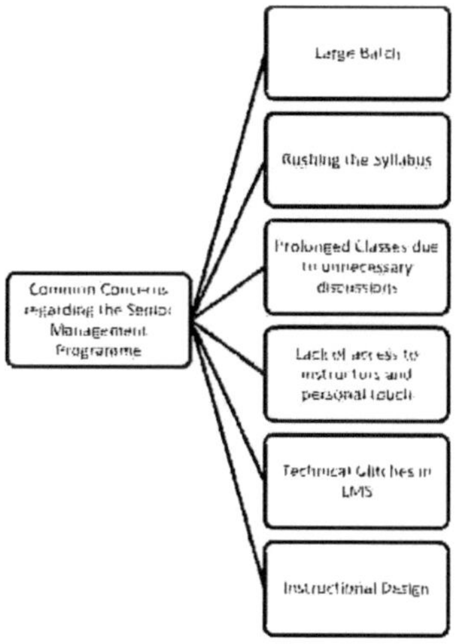

Figure 7.
The infographic shows the common concerns and challenges faced by the learners in the Senior Management Blended Learning programme. Source: Formulated by the researchers.

> *"Only support that I asked was to allow attending lectures in office as we have office on Sunday as well".*

> *"My organization has been very supportive in providing necessary leaves and time offs for campus visits. Rest my work is not hampered due to this so company has no problem".*

> *"They have supported and encouraged me a lot for this course. They have partially paid fees for this course."*

5.2 Overall experience of the learners enrolled in a blended learning programme

The overall experience of the senior management programme received a range of views, but the majority of respondents evaluated it as "good" to "excellent," with only two respondents out of the 29 giving the programme a "average" rating. Many respondents agree that it is a useful alternative for working professionals who may have few other opportunities to improve abilities and acquire new management topics. The course ended up being the best choice available because one of them said that the employer would not permit sabbaticals for learning opportunities. However, another responder thought they should have chosen an offline or live course that would have lasted for three or 6 months and had more focused modules. Most responders think it's a fantastic chance to network with people from all backgrounds and occupations. Some respondents brought up the restriction that they could not participate in online role-playing games or presentations. The vast size of the batch, which included 150 students, upset many of those who responded. Some people valued the peer learning chances, whilst others think the college ought to host gatherings and networking events for students who reside in nearby cities. Some respondents praised the programme's high standards of instruction and faculty members, whilst others noted that the programme's case studies were outdated and not appropriate for India's conditions. Still other respondents wished for fewer areas to be covered in greater depth. According to one of the responses, the training has inspired him to embark on new endeavors and search for startup possibilities. Important comments on the overall experience include:

> *"It has been a good experience. Senior or middle-aged professionals get an opportunity to remotely acquire management degree or certification, which otherwise would have meant taking a sabbatical etc. Not all companies support break for education."*
>
> *"Overall experience has been good in terms of learning through case studies and peer learning. Networking has been an important facet of this program which I liked. Only thing I disliked is the batch size of 150 people which is too big to interact with and sometimes makes online classes difficult to moderate."*
>
> *"Ok experience. Difficult to focus in offline model, but since it is was working individuals do not have much of a choice. Also, in online we cannot do role plays, presentations etc. Syllabus needs to be improved and case studies need to be more relevant to Indian ecosystem and current scenarios (most of the case studies are 20–30-year-old). However, we are trying to make the best of it by learning from fellow mates and the books given."*

6. Conclusion

India boasts a substantial workforce poised for potential reskilling and upskilling soon. Blended learning programmes emerge as a compelling medium to cater to the diverse needs of working professionals across various industries and domains. This approach offers inherent advantages owing to its adaptability and flexibility in the context of remote learning. Some of the important findings of the study reflect that the blended learning programmes especially for the management fields should monitor and calibrate the size of the batch, faster response, and redressal of the complaints regarding the learning management systems and other technical glitches, updated course content which is relevant to the Indian business environment and transforming business needs. The course should include case studies and relevant examples catering the needs of the modern workplace where automation, data analytics, artificial intelligence, generative language models, internet of things are already making inroads in the organisations. Overall, the courses and programmes for the working professionals should be meticulously designed and strategically planned, considering the demands of future job markets and the cultivation of leadership skills to confront contemporary challenges. Embracing blended learning programmes should become increasingly prevalent to address the evolving learning requirements and opportunities for knowledge sharing, thereby equipping individuals with the essential skills demanded by the twenty-first century. Future research is recommended for designing more effective blended learning programmes that caters to the needs of the learners as well as fulfils the intended learning outcomes of the such programmes.

7. Limitations of the study

Extensive literature regarding the effectiveness of the blended learning programmes particularly for the management programmes and overall, for the generalised learnings and understanding was not available. The study was conducted whilst the course was still underway and the overall experience, satisfaction level and perceptions regarding the course and blended mode of learning may differ at the end of the course. Since, the study considers the experiences and the insights of the limited number of learners, future studies may be required for more nuanced understanding for designing more user-centric and effective blended learning programmes especially for the management studies. Also, the study could be replicated with different age-cohorts may yield different results especially Millennials and Gen -Z.

Acknowledgement

We would like to extend our sincere gratitude to Mr. Mohit Pandey, Regional Head (Sales), DBS Bank, India for his kind assistance and cooperation in facilitating the interviews with the other learners at the Senior Management Programme, 2023, offered by IIM, Calcutta. We would like to express our heartfelt gratitude and appreciation for the participants of the study for to taking out the time to provide us with their valuable insights, experiences, and feedback on the Senior Management Programme.

Author details

Durgesh Tripathi* and Surbhi Tandon
University School of Mass Communication, Guru Gobind Singh Indraprastha University, New Delhi, India

*Address all correspondence to: drdurgeshtripathi@ipu.ac.in

References

[1] Upskilling and reskilling will be key for India's future workforce [Internet]. Times Higher Education (THE); 2021. Available from: https://www.timeshighereducation.com/hub/coursera/p/upskilling-and-reskilling-will-be-key-indias-future-workforce

[2] Basu S. More Indians intend to upskill in 2023 compared to global counterparts: Great learning report. The Economic Times. 2023. Available from: https://economictimes.indiatimes.com/jobs/mid-career/more-indians-intend-to-upskill-in-2023-compared-to-global-counterparts-great-learning-report/articleshow/99765075.cms 3

[3] Learning G. Report: Upskilling trends in India for 2023. Great Learning Blog: Free Resources what Matters to shape your Career! 2023. Available from: https://www.mygreatlearning.com/blog/upskilling-trends-in-india/

[4] Shan LY. India may become the third largest economy by 2030, overtaking Japan and Germany. CNBC. 2022. Available from: https://www.cnbc.com/2022/12/01/india-to-leapfrog-to-third-largest-economy-by-2030.html

[5] The New-age Skill Gap [Internet]. 2023. Available from: https://www.fortuneindia.com/long-reads/the-new-age-skill-gap/1125806

[6] World Economic Forum. Future of jobs report 2023 [Internet]. 2023. Available from: https://www3.weforum.org/docs/WEF_Future_of_Jobs_2023.pdf

[7] National Education Policy. Ministry of Human Resource Development Government of India. 2020. Available from: https://www.education.gov.in/sites/upload_files/mhrd/files/NEP_Final_English.pdf

[8] Tripathi D, Tandon S. Can MOOCs reskill and upskill the Indian Workforce for the Industrial Revolution 4.0? European Conference on e-Learning. 2022;**21**(1):417-424

[9] Will NEP. Give a much needed boost to online education in India? [Internet]. India Today. Available from: https://www.indiatoday.in/education-today/featurephilia/story/will-nep-give-a-much-needed-boost-to-online-education-in-india-1713926-2020-08-22

[10] Budget 2023-24: For Jobs of the Future, FM Announces PMKVY 4.0 to Boost Skilling. The Economic Times; 2023. Available from: https://economictimes.indiatimes.com/small-biz/sme-sector/budget-2023-24-for-jobs-of-the-future-fm-announces-pmkvy-4-0-to-boost-skilling/articleshow/97516875.cms

[11] National Education Policy formulated to empower Youth and help "Amrit Peedhi" realize their dreams. Available from: https://www.pib.gov.in/PressReleasePage.aspx?PRID=1895304

[12] Bureau BB. Employees with advanced digital skills contribute $508 bn to India's GDP: Report. BusinessLine. 2023. Available from: https://www.thehindubusinessline.com/economy/employees-with-advanced-digital-skills-contribute-508-b-to-indias-gdp-report/article66541100.ece 7

[13] Guide to Blended Learning [Internet]. Available from: https://oasis.col.org/server/api/core/bitstreams/888d37d6-2e2d-4859-940d-36df969621e5/content [Cited November 9, 2023]

[14] A study by KPMG in India and Google [Internet]. 2017. Available from:

https://assets.kpmg.com/content/dam/kpmg/in/pdf/2017/05/Online-Education-in-India-2021.pdf

[15] Hrastinski S. What do we mean by blended learning? TechTrends. 2019;**63**(5):564-569. Available from: https://link.springer.com/article/10.1007/s11528-019-00375-58

[16] Güzer B, Caner H. The past, present and future of blended learning: An in depth analysis of literature. Procedia—Social and Behavioral Sciences. 2014;**116**:4596-4603. Available from: https://www.sciencedirect.com/science/article/pii/S187704281401009X

[17] DRandy G, Kanuka H. Blended learning: Uncovering its transformative potential in higher education. The Internet and Higher Education. 2004;**7**(2):95-105

[18] Bordoloi R, Das P, Das K. Perception towards online/blended learning at the time of Covid-19 pandemic: An academic analytics in the Indian context. Asian Association Open University Journal [Internet]. 2021;**16**(1):41-60. DOI: 10.1108/aaouj-09-2020-0079

[19] Hass A, Joseph M. Investigating different options in course delivery – traditional vs online: Is there another option? International Journal of Information and Learning Technology. 6 Aug 2018;**35**(4):230-239

[20] Kumar R, Pande N. Technology-mediated learning paradigm and the blended learning ecosystem: What works for working professionals? Procedia Computer Science. 2017;**122**:1114-1123

[21] Senior Management Programme (SMP) | IIM Calcutta. Available from: https://www.iimcal.ac.in/ldp/SMP

Section 2

COVID-19 Impact on the Workplace and Work Arrangements

Chapter 7

Does Working from Home Work?

Jacques Bughin and Michele Cincera

Abstract

Remote work ("WFH") was often the default mode of working during the recent pandemic, because of lockdown. But beyond this one-off effect, the question remains whether remote working will endure and become part of the "new normal". We formalize a simple company-employee work-at-home decision model, which takes into account both worker preferences and the company's strategic incentive to invest in supporting work-at-home practices. The model predictions are then tested on a large sample of global firms across the world, regarding their evolution in WFH intensity and how WFH changes correlate with labor productivity changes. We find that technologies facilitating WFH, and to a lesser extent, active human resources, are needed to make work from home more productive. Said otherwise, the future of WFH depends on how technology will be able to "augment" labor effectiveness.

Keywords: work from home (WFH), labor productivity, technology augmentation, human resources, work automation

1. Introduction

By 2022, Shopify, a well-known global next-generation e-commerce platform had secured a perennial flexible work arrangement scheme across its entire workforce, centered around the possibility of working from home (WFH). By that time, Accenture has already implemented an effective flexible work policy, with nearly 100% of employees working remotely. The significance of WFH was also clearly demonstrated during the peak of the COVID-19 pandemic, as social lockdowns pushed many firms and workers to resort to it. Looking at the period pre-COVID, WFH was limited, used by barely 15% of the European population [1].[1] In less than 6 months, during the lockdown of the pandemic, WFH quickly doubled to reach 40% of workers in both the United States and Western Europe [2].

But despite all claims, WFH is failing to automatically scale as a "new normal". Not everyone is a Shopify's, and even companies championing WFH are backtracking, such as Disney or Starbucks. Scholars themselves disagree, from the optimistic view of Barrero et al. [3] to the cautious views recently expressed by Harvard Professors Edward Glaeser and David Cluter on the need to go back to the office (2021).[2]

One reason for some limited WFH effects is simply that not all jobs are suited for WFH [4]. Another reason is that remote work practices have an ambiguous impact on

[1] jrc120945_policy_brief_-_covid_and_telework_final.pdf (europa.eu)

[2] Remote work is bad for productivity—and for your career—The Washington Post.

labor productivity, as flexibility benefits are quickly bypassed by the sense of exclusion and by a lack of team performance spillovers [5, 6]. A final issue is organizational, whereby remote workers may *hinder* the performance of their team colleagues, given a lack of coordination [7]; especially a too high-level of WFH [8].

This research analyzes the trajectories made by large (mostly multinational) firms regarding WFH, pre- and post-COVID, with a goal to better understand the corporate drivers, especially productivity gains-linked to the adoption and expansion of WFH. The originality of the research is threefold. First, most recent studies on WFH productivity resort to workers' surveys (e.g., [9, 10]). When studies take the pulse from the employer side, they have mostly relied on self-assessed productivity gains, e.g., Erdiesk [11], or have concentrated on very specific firm case studies [12, 13]. Here, we perform a statistical analysis of corporate revenue productivity changes and WFH density changes at the firm-level to derive estimates of the productivity benefit of WFH. Second, we lay out an analytic model of remote work as background to our empirical specifications—many studies rely on conceptual, rather than analytical models to define their empirical strategy, but they lack the insight that, for instance, complementary resources to remote work are critical to boost competitive advantage and boost WFH diffusion. Finally, our study covers a relatively large survey of 4000 firms, in ten countries—this is to be compared to the average sample of about 400 datapoints in the analysis of the 26 studies on productivity impact of remote work by Anapko et al. [14].

We confirm that WFH trajectories are different among firms, with the pandemic playing a catch-up, and most heavy WFH-centric firms exhibiting better revenue growth, *but* mostly to the extent that they have invested in complementary human resources and technology capabilities. Thus, WFH is not automatically part of "new normal", but will clearly depend on the firm complementary capabilities in both HR and work technologies.

2. Remote work: evidence to date

WFH dates a long way back and was pushed by workers to limit time loss in commuting, and work–family conflict [15, 16]. Studies also highlight that WFH is an effective way to boost workers' happiness, and their engagement [17]. According to Anapko et al. [14], the US Congress and the European Union had long approved legislation supporting remote work, but WFH remains rampant as technically challenging for years. For instance, large US firms resorted to remote work as a way to limit commuting during the two main oil energy crises in the 1970s.

The rise of connectivity and new digital technologies, including the internet, mobile, and the first applications of videoconferencing since this new century, have solved most of technical problems linked to WFH and boosted the rollout of more remote work practices. In this context, seminal studies such as Bloom et al. [12] or Anderson and al. [17] had confirmed that WFH could be a powerful tactic for firms, as it reconciles workers' delight with productivity uplift.

More recently, the COVID-19 pandemic has become a major catalyst to resort to remote work as a main work practices. Results of new studies on the productivity of remote work, however, still raised skepticism as to whether WFH could generate labor productivity gains. For example, a study on UK workers by Mandall et al. [18] concluded that only a minority of UK workers could complete as much work during the first wave of the pandemic as during pre-COVID. In Japan, Morikawa [19] suggested that WFH productivity was only 2/3 of the level achieved at the workplace. Using a sample of 10,000 skilled professionals at a large Asian IT services company, which all shifted to WFH during the pandemic, Gibbs et al. [20] found that total hours worked increased by roughly 30%, but the average output did not significantly change, leading to a productivity drop in total of about 20%. Ipsen et al. [21] have concluded that a majority of Danish WFH workers could complete the same amount of work or more than when working at a workplace, but still 40–45% of them were less productive. Equivalently indecisive results were found for advancing countries such as Indonesia and the Philippines [22, 23].

The merits of those COVID-19 studies have been to highlight that productivity gains are not warranted but depend on a possible few key mediating factors. The first factor is organizational agility: in fact, most firms were possibly ill-prepared to deploy WFH as an urgent action out of lockdown. The second factor is that WFH productivity depends critically on the ability of workers to leverage technologies for effective WFH. In particular, a recent research by Bai et al. [24] demonstrates that digital technologies could boost WFH as well as enhance corporate performance. Tønnessen et al. [25] note that digital ability is not enough—rather digital knowledge *sharing* is the key driver of remote work on productivity.

Our research contributes to the debate by assessing the WFH trajectories of large firms across a worldwide survey performed by late 2021, at the time of COVID-19 pandemic got controlled by the rollout of effective RNA-based vaccines. The advantage of the study is that it measures WFH intensity at the level of the firm *before and after* the pandemic. This gives us insights into the dynamic pattern of WFH, which is largely missing in the literature. Second, we capture parallel data on both human resource practices and work technology investment spent that may act as clear mediators on how WFH deployment ultimately correlates with firm performance. In the next section, we lay out a simple analytic model of WFH intensity, that highlights the channels by which firm performance can be affected by remote work. We then continue with the empirical analysis.

3. A simple model of WFH optimal decision

3.1 Framework

We consider a representative worker working only for the focal firm, who values work and leisure equally. The worker receives a salary, w per unit of time worked, L, but her utility out of work is also shaped by the fact that she works remotely, or not. We note $L_i = LP_i + LH_i$, where.

LH_i (LP_i) is remote (on premises) labor. The worker utility is given by:

$$U_i = (1 - L_i) + (1 + \gamma).wi\ L_i \tag{1}$$

Where $0 \leq LH/_{LP} \leq 1$ is the share of work under remote, $0 < \gamma < 1$ is the preference toward remote work. Regarding the firm, the firm sells a product, Y, with a product demand:

$$P^{\kappa} = Y_i \tag{2}$$

Where $1/\kappa$ is the absolute price elasticity.

As in task based models [26, 27], the product, Y, is made of the aggregation of m tasks in the range (0, 1) that could be done either by on premises or remote labor. Suppose further that tasks are ranked such that remote labor increase its competitive advantage for the high-end of tasks. Firm optimization implies that aggregating over all tasks, there is a portion, $0 \leq 1/\tau \leq 1$, where $w.LH_i/Y_i = w.LP_i/Y_i$, above which all tasks are done remotely.

As tasks are fully substitutive between remote and on premises, then the aggregation of tasks production function is equivalent to a Cobb-Douglas of the form:

$$Y = (1 + t).(\tau.LP)^{1/\tau}.(\tau/_{\tau-1}\ LH)^{1-1/\tau} \tag{3}$$

And $(1 + t)^{(\tau-1)/\tau} = (Y/_{LH})$ as we normalize $Y_i/_{LP\ i} = 1$ [27].

The firm maximizes its profit, but strategically, has been investing complementary assets, I, upfront, before production with a rental cost, r, to secure the best benefit of remote work. Among others, I includes the collaboration software tools and video conferencing hardware to support connectivity and r is the rental price of I. We note:

$$Y/LH = 1 + 1/_{\lambda}.I^{\lambda} \tag{4}$$

and $0 \leq \lambda \leq 1$, so that the *lower* λ, the higher the effectiveness of I to boost WFH productivity

Firm thus decides on I, then selects labor mix based on equilibrium with workers labor supply.

3.2 Equilibrium

As a subgame perfect equilibrium, the solution is found backward.

3.2.1 Final stage: labor demand stage

Thus, using (2) and (3) in the latest stage, the profit maximizing firm choses Y, such that:

$$Y = ((1 + \kappa).w)^{1/\kappa} \tag{5}$$

Further, following the production side, and the Cobb-Douglas, the labor demand is implictly given by

$$w = 1/_{\tau}.Y/_{LP} = 1/_{\tau} \tag{6}$$

$$w = (\tau - 1/_{\tau})\ Y/_{LH} \tag{7}$$

or

$$LP/_{LH} = 1/_{\tau-1} \tag{8}$$

The optimal labor supply implies:

$$w = 1/_{1+\gamma} \tag{9}$$

which means that at labor market equilibrium:

$$\tau = 1 + \gamma \tag{10}$$

$$L = \left(\gamma^2 + 1\right)/_{\gamma(1+\gamma).}\ LH \tag{11}$$

And thus, the optimal split of labor is given by:

$$LP/L = (1 - \gamma)/(\gamma 2 + 1); LH/_L = \gamma(\gamma + 1)/\left(\gamma^2 + 1\right) \tag{12}$$

3.2.2 WFH investment stage

In the first stage, the profit including investment, I, in remote labor is given by

$$\Pi = \kappa.((1 + \kappa)/(1 + \gamma))^{1/\kappa} - rI \tag{13}$$

As firm wants to maximize profit, first-order condition set to zero thus implies that:

$$\delta\Pi/\delta(Y/LH).\delta(Y/LH)/\delta I = r \tag{14}$$

And from (4) and (14), one can compute that :.

$$\delta(Y/_{LH})/_{\delta I} = \lambda.(Y/_{LH} - 1)/_I \tag{15}$$

$$\delta\Pi/\delta\left(_{Y/LH)=}\ \kappa.(1 + t)\right. \tag{16}$$

Inserting (15)–(16) into (14), one finds:

$$rI = \lambda.t.(1 + t).\kappa \tag{17}$$

where from (3) and definition of t, we also have:

$$(1 + t) = (1 - \kappa).(1 + \gamma)/\gamma \tag{18}$$

Integrating (18) into (13), final equilibrium profit is

$$\Pi = \kappa.((t + \kappa)(1 + \kappa)/(t + 1))^{1/\kappa} - \lambda.t.(1 + t) \tag{19}$$

Using Eq. (18), we have thus demonstrated that:

Proposition 1: Firms have an interest to invest in complements to the extent that are able to boost remote above on premise remote work productivity.

Proposition 2: The incentive grows with product market power and workers appetite for WFH.

The proof of the above is done by assessing marginal profit and investment increase in function of the market attractiveness, κ, average productivity of (and preference toward) WFH, t (γ), as well as the degree of effectiveness of investment spent, 1/λ. Also, final profit reduces to κ. (1+ κ) $^{1/\kappa}$ if no gain prevails in selecting WFH over on-premises productivity, as in this case, the firm does not waste resources to invest in no WFH uplift.

4. Empirical research design

4.1 Empirical model

The previous section implies that firm revenue productivity, P.Y/L should be tied to the remote work intensity, especially in the function of remote work complements investments that signal that firms anticipate productivity uplift by shifting toward WFH. We can test this prediction with the following generic empirical equation, at the ith firm level:

$$\Delta(PY/L)_i = b_0 + b_1.\Delta(LH/L)_i + b_2.TECH_i{}^*\Delta(LH/L)_i + u_i \quad (20)$$

Where u is an error term, $\Delta x/_x$ is the difference in x measured before and post-COVID; the dependent variable is revenue per employee (PY/L), LH/L is share of remote labor., and $TECH_i{}^*\Delta(LH/L)_i$ measures the technology complement to WFH, while the core hypothesis we want to test is that the coefficients: b1,b2 > 0.

The equation above is rather generic and is amended the following way. First, we adjust the equation to account for adjustment costs. The first is that productivity path out of investing in WFH has been recently shaped by the pandemic. The pandemic has indeed led to a urgent shift to WFH due to lockdown, which is not correlated to productivity, but rather to the simple ability to function [18, 19, 21]. If this overshooting takes time to absorb, it may weight on the positive dynamics of productivity gain post-COVID. We thus would include a variable, ADJUST, measuring how well the workforce has adjusted to the new digitally remote work induced by the pandemic.

Second, our model is especially concentrated on technology complements, but other elements may support new flexible works, e.g., such as much more inclusive human resources. As our survey discussion will allude to hereafter, we have measured the degree of HR involvement of firms around three key dimensions beyond purely financial, that is emotional balance, employability, purpose and relationship management. Those three dimensions are important as new working arrangements such as remote work require tools training ("employability", [28]), induce new forms of interactions and bonding ("relationship management", [7]), and move the emotional state like fear of exclusion ("emotional balance", [17]). Following the literature for construct validity [29], we have built an index on those three dimensions based on a ranking from how firms made themselves accountable for those dimensions, on a Likert scale 1–7 (1 not at all, 4 neutral, 7 definite). Recentering on 4 = zero and scaled down by 9, we have built a variable, HR varying between (−1, 1), with −1 (1) meaning that the firm has been not at all (fully) accountable for those practices. Third, regarding technology investment, we separate between degree of deployment (TECHD = 0, no deployment, 1, pilot, 2 = scaling, 3 fully scaled) of remote collaborative technologies to support WFH and degree of investment on those tools (TECHI =0, no investment, 1 = Moderate, 2, Average, 3 = significant). This separation allows to separate input (investment) from output (deployment) as indicator of technology support to remote work.

Based on the above, the amended equation becomes:

$$\begin{aligned}\Delta(PY/L)_i = a_0 &+ b_1.\Delta(LH/L)_i + b_2.TECHD_i{}^*\Delta(LH/L)_i \\ &+ b_3.TECHI_i{}^*\Delta(LH/L)_I + b_4.HR_i{}^*\Delta(LH/L)_i + b_5.(ADJUST)_i \\ &+ b_6.Z_i + u_i\end{aligned} \quad (21)$$

We also add a large set of control (vector Z) that are typically known to affect labor productivity outside WFH. We include both a measure of digital technology maturity (DK), and R&D intensity (RD), as both types of capital is also associated with higher labor productivity [30–34]. The information collected concerns the use of 10 digital technologies: cloud, mobile, broadband access, edge computing, IoT, robotics, machine learning, computer vision, advanced RPA, NLP/NLG. The last four are AI-related. Our measure of maturity is the index from 0 to 10, where each technology used for commercial use is coded 1, 0, 5 if adopted but only used at stage of experimentation, and 0 otherwise. This kind of construct has been used and validated e.g. by Lee et al. [32].

We also include company size, scope (B2C versus B2B versus B2B2C), as well as the fact that companies are, or not, global multinationals. Industry and geographies fixed effects are included, capturing elements like product market features affecting revenue potential, workers skills, and occupation types that affect the technical feasibility of WFH [4].

Our main hypothesis extends to b_1, b_2, b_3, $b_4 > 0$, and Eq. (21) is estimated both by OLS and mostly by Instrumental variables, given the endogeneity of $LH/_L$, and the WFH cross-effects. We use the pre-COVID WFH intensity variable as first instrument. The second instrument is the industry weight at the leave-one-out mean. The method works similarly as a generalized moments method [35].

4.2 Sample

Eq. (24) relies on a top executives' survey designed by a major global consultancy, and administered online by an independent agency, by the fall of 2021. The survey covers a large set of firm practices during three periods (pre-, during-, and post) COVID-19 lockdown pandemic. The survey focuses on large firms, across 10 key countries (Europe: France, Germany, UK, Italy, and Spain); North America (US and Canada) as well as in APAC, China, or Japan. It also covers 17 NACE-2 aggregate sectors. Appendix provides more background on the sample, as well as its representativeness. The full sample comprises 4015 firms, with 2/3 of firms generating 1–10 US billion by end of 2020. Large firms have the advantage to diffuse new practices faster than others [3, 36]. The average company grew revenue by 9% cumulative over 2018 to 2021, thus including the acute phase of the covid-19 pandemic, and 3 years change in labor productivity has been 4.7%, for companies generating EBITDA margin in the range of 15% and return on capital employed of 6% during the 3 years.

WFH intensity in the sample is reported to have been 16.5% by 2018, growing to 24.6% post-COVID. **Table 1** provides the distribution of the dynamics of WFH

WFH intensity	Before COVID	After COVID
Less than 10%	34.8	13.2
Between 11 and 25%	43.4	44.2
Between 26 and 40%	15.3	29.5
Between 41 and 75%	5.1	10.3
Over 75%	0.6	2.0

Source: survey, authors computation, based on total sample, N = 4015 firms

Table 1.
WFH density (%) distribution in sample, pre- and post-COVID.

Stage	Automation (%)	WFH tools (%)
Not started	9	6
Pilot	42	22
Scaling in the organization	32	42
Scaled up in whole enterprise	17	30

Source: survey, authors' computation, based on total sample, N = 3930 firms (balance stands for firms for which the technology has no application for their business.

Table 2.
State of work technology diffusion large global firms, pre-COVID.

densification among the sampled companies. If there has been a net *increa*se in the portion of WFH practices, the most visible shift has happened at the bottom of the distribution, with low WFH intensive firms catching up, possibly, as per the necessity out of the lockdown during the COVID pandemic. More importantly, we notice that about one-third of companies have *also reduced* their WFH intensity post-COVID to a level (lower than) before pre-COVID.

Regarding remote work technologies, **Table 2** shows that about 70% of large companies in the sample had rolled out digital collaborative tools for enterprise use, but only 30% of firms were exploiting those technologies at scale across the whole enterprise. This state of use is in line with other surveys (e.g., [3]). We observe quite some variance by sectors, with sectors such as retail and healthcare being more limited in the rollout at scale, as lots of activities still are made in face-to-face in those sectors.

As already mentioned, the absorption by employees of those new technologies may take time. **Table 3** reports how employees have been able to settle, even enjoy, the new digital environment (variable, "ADJUST"). Half of the respondents claim that the digital remote shift has been fully absorbed, for about 15% of companies that are still struggling with remote tech absorption.

Finally, **Table 4** provides a view of HR practices beyond administrative pay, and linked to employability, emotional balance, and relationship/team management. On average, firms are starting to deploy those HR practices, but it remains largely unsettled.

Regarding control variables, the survey does not have quantitative measures of investment in digital technologies but provides a split between stage of use, between experimentation and the level of commercial exploitation. The ratio of exploration to

Employees feeling about digital remote routine:		
	Settled (%)	**Enthusiastic (%)**
Strongly disagree	0.40	0.70
Disagree	1.20	2.00
Neither	13.20	10.40
Agree	35.50	40.80
Fully agree	49.80	46.20

Table 3.
Workflow integration of WFH technologies, 2020, large global companies.

	Not at all (%)	Not really (%)	A bit (%)	Partially (%)	Growing (%)	Almost (%)	Completely (%)	Index (%)
Emotional	0.8	1.4	11.6	26.7	28.8	21.7	9.0	9.0
Relational	0.4	0.8	9.3	25.0	32.3	23.5	8.8	10.0
Employable	0.2	0.8	5.8	18.9	29.5	31.9	12.9	14.0
Index computed with data presented on partially (4), completely = 1; not at all = −1.								

Table 4.
HR practices, 2020, large global companies.

exploitation of AI technologies is roughly 65/35 (see also Zolas et al. [36]). Concerning R&D, the average firm spends close to 4.5% of revenue on R&D, or above the typical range of firm [37].

4.3 Results

Table 5 reports the results with fixed country and industry effects included (but not reproduced for clarity). The first two columns report the OLS, and then the last two concern IV estimations. For each type of estimation, we present first the simplest equation without the cross-effects, then including the cross-effects. Regarding the IV, we have performed the first stage regression linked change in WFH with WFH pre-COVID, and "leave the focal firm out" means WFH change at the dyad industry/geography level. We have confirmed the IV relevance for the WFH variable, either through the Hansen J test (P = 0.02), or Stock and Yogo's F-test (F > 18.2). We then

Variables	**.(1) OLS**		**.(2) OLS**	
	Coefficient in %	**Stdev**	**Coefficient in %**	**Stdev**
Constant	3.01***	1.22	3.55*	1.87
WFH (points %)	0.21	0.14	0.19*	0.09
ADJUST (in %)	n.a.	na	2.92***	0.43
TECHD*WFH (points %)	n.a.	n.a.	0.71	0.39
TECHI*WFH (points %)	n.a.	n.a.	0.79*	0.41
HR*WFH (points %)	n.a.	n.a.	1.09**	0.41
RD (points %)	0.42*	0.18	0.37*	0.16
DK (percentage points)	1.02	0.86	1.22*	0.66
SIZE (in billions)	−0.4	0.78	. −0.39***	0.11
B2C+	.−3.12*	1.66	.−3.02*	1.63
B2B2C+	-0.35	0.67	.−0.69**	0.34
Firm is global+	2.54**	1.22	2.21***	0.67
industry dummy	Y		Y	
country dummy	Y		Y	

Variables	.(3) IV		.(4) IV	
	Coefficient in %	**Stdev**	**Coefficient in %**	**Stdev**
Constant	3.09**	1.56	3.28***	1.08
WFH (points %)	0.25	0.16	0.18	0.11
ADJUST (in %)	na	na	3.51***	0.78
TECHD*WFH (points %)	n.a.	n.a.	0.99***	0.28
TECHI*WFH (points %)	na	na	0.83**	0.32
HR*WFH (points %)	n.a.	n.a.	0.74*	0.41
RD (points %)	0.21*	0.12	0.24**	0.1
DK (percentage points)	0.98*	0.46	1.08**	0.49
SIZE (in billions)	. −0.49***	0.15	. −0.52	0.37
B2C+	.−3.02*	1.63	.−2.01*	1.08
B2B2C+	.−0.69	0.45	.−0.32*	0.18
Firm is global+	1.03***	0.37	1.33***	0.68
industry dummy	Y		Y	
country dummy	Y		Y	

*Note: Adjusted R-square are respectively 0.225; 0.412; 0.264; 0.452; variables are measured as difference post- and pre-COVID, or a window of 3 years; ***p < 0.01, ** p < 0.05, *;. +: default is B2B; country: US and industry: hightech.*

Table 5.
Productivity and work from home change, global firms.

used the fitted value from this first stage to build the new variables WFH and cross-effects as second stage regression shown in **Table 5**.

Regarding controls, a F-test on the joint significance of industry effects, as well as country effects, show that both effects are relevant at 1%. Regarding other firm control productivity variables, global firms exhibit better labor productivity growth than other firms (about 2 point of nominal labor productivity for 3 years), but this effect cancels out when accounting for firm size, as global firms exhibit larger revenue than average, and higher revenue firms tend to have lower labor productivity growth (minus 5 points over 3 years) in this sample. We find that digital technology penetration as well as R&D are associated with higher labor productivity growth (for a joint marginal effect of about 1 to 1.5 points over 3 years). Those effects tend to be lower than the early literature on the effects of digital technology on labor productivity growth, e.g., [30].

Those effects tend to be lower than the early literature on the effects of digital technology on labor productivity growth, e.g., [30].

Coming to our various hypotheses, on the effect of WFH, a right tail F-test, is strongly significant at 1%, confirming that labor productivity change is positively linked to the rollout of WFH practices, as well as technologies/human resources complements supporting those practices, in line with our model predictions. Looking variable by variable, we, however, find that the effect of WFH intensity on labor productivity growth is not significant per se; what matters are really the cross-effects, as well as the ability of employees to absorb those digital technologies for remote working practices.

The above clearly settles the case that WFH is a relevant positive trend as claimed by Barrero et al. [3], but this is a profitable trend for corporations to the extent that employees can get used to this new type of environment, and that firms invest in enough technology and human practice complements to support the shift, to get returns in the form of higher labor productivity.

From the sample, we do not have access to level of the investment made to technology that favors remote work, but the fact is that technology spent and absorption to support effective WFH are a large contributor, at the sample mean, bringing from 6 to 7 points in labor productivity growth over 3 years. This uplift is relatively large to secure a strong return to technology investment made. Finally, besides technology, organization matters. Workers must adapt to those new digital remote technologies to deliver performance. The fact they do not fully adjust to those new digital remote work practices costs about 1 points of productivity growth. Likewise, firms that have a strong proactive human resource approach that alleviates the transition costs to remote work will support a better productivity gain said otherwise, technology augments labor effectiveness.

Regarding the estimates, a firm that manages HR to account for all positive elements of emotional balance and employability, and invests at scale in remote collaborative tools to support the best context for remote work, might generate 3 points of extra labor productivity, versus a firm not willing to invest and support WFH, after controlling for company size, profitability and industry/location. This type of estimate is relatively in line with some of the most favorable remote work case studies reported in the literature such as Bloom et al. [12] for an online Chinese travel portal, or Choudhury et al. [13] during their investigation of a shift from work from home to work from anywhere at the US patent office. Finally, in our sample, about 2/3 of companies has boosted WFH practices since pre-COVID, thus, the net effect should be clearly positive on the economy [38].

5. Conclusion

Working from home is part of the known trend toward more flexible work arrangements. While the pandemic has accelerated the shift out of premises work, the fact is that the trend is not necessarily natural, and will only materialize if there is common incentives by employers and workers to commit to WFH. Despite some high profiles of companies pushing for full flexibility, there are as many brand names reverting back from extensive work-from-home, questioning who will actually buck the trend. The originality of this research is to consider the firm's viewpoint, as being the ultimate investment maker regarding the adoption and rollout of those technologies. We also test the impact of technology adoption among a large sample of more than 4000 global firms and across 15 countries.

We formalize a task-based model of the firm that only invests in technology and human resources to the extent they can complement WFH productivity uplift. The prediction tested on the full sample, suggests that WFH must interwork with technology and HR support to augment labor productivity gains. We find that the effect of WFH boosts labor productivity on average for our sample of large global firms. The effect is positively linked to the rollout of technology tools, suggesting that the question of the future of WFH is closely linked to the future of technology deployment to complement work tasks [3, 39].

The above study has some notable restrictions. First, regarding sample, the data are survey-based and variables such as WFH are reported as range. Second, company respondents are not fully identified and thus we cannot match the survey with other external sources. Third, data does not give any insights of workers skills and capabilities. This is a critical missing piece of information as the skill distribution will shift both the potential for the technical opportunity of WFH and the ability of workers to quickly absorb and master new technologies. The way we control for skill distribution is through industry control, but this may not be enough, and significant difference may exist at firm-level. Fourth, the sample concerns large global companies, and results may not necessarily be generalizable to smaller firms. Finally, productivity performance is measured by the end of 2021, or post-pandemic lockdown. As shown by the significance of the ADJUST variable, companies may still be partly influenced by the effect of the pandemic, and productivity effect may only arise longer-term.

Acknowledgements

The authors thank Accenture Research for access and some support work on the data. All errors are our own.

Appendix

See **Tables A1** and **A2**.

Revenues change	2 years before COVID-19 (%)	6 months COVID-19 (%)	End of 2021 (%)
More than 10% decline	0	2	1
Between 5% and 10% decline	1	10	4
Between 0% and 5% decline	4	20	27
No change	5	21	13
Between 0% and 5% growth	46	25	24
Between 5% and 10% growth	37	19	22
More than 10% growth	6	3	9

Table A1.
Evolution revenue (pre-COVID = 2018, post-COVID, end of 2021).

Measures	Metrics	Sample	Benchmarks
Financials:	Profit change Q3-Q1,2020	Minus 28% worldwide	Minus 35% for the S&P 500
	Profit growth precovid, 2019/18	7.1% worldwide	7.3% worldwide publicly quoted companies

Measures	Metrics	Sample	Benchmarks
	profit growth post covid, 2022/21	6.1% worldwide	6.4% worldwide publicly quoted companies
Capabilities			
Innovation	innovation spent decline 2020	Minus 8%	Minus 5–10% [5]
Agility	companies versed in agile method	65%	70%, KPMG, 2019
Digitization	Share of tech used	55% for European sample companies	> 50%, EIB, 2020
Sustainability	% ESG engagement US	83% for US sampled companies	70%, Harvard Law School
Work from home	% employees working from home	17% in top 5 European countries,2018	13% same scope, WEF, 2017
		27% in top 5 European countries, 2022	25% same scope, Eurostat, 2022
		19% in US, 2018	14%, firms more than 1000 people; PEW, 2017

Sources: Author based on KMPG, World Economic Forum, Damodoran web site; EIB, McKinsey, Eurostat, Harvard, Pew project.

Table A2.
Sample representativeness.

Author details

Jacques Bughin[1,2]* and Michele Cincera[1,3]

1 Université Libre de Bruxelles, SBSEM, Times[2], Belgium

2 Machaon Advisory, Value Verse and Fortino Capital, Antwerpen, Brussels, Belgium

3 ECARES, Belgium

*Address all correspondence to: jacquesbughin@machaonadvisory.com

References

[1] Boeri T, Giupponi G, Krueger AB, Machin S. Solo self-employment and alternative work arrangements: A cross-country perspective on the changing composition of jobs. Journal of Economic Perspectives. 2020;**34**(1):170-195

[2] Chernoff AW, Warman C. COVID-19 and implications for automation. National Bureau of Economic Research. 2020;**2020**:w27249

[3] Barrero JM, Bloom N, Davis SJ. Why working from home will stick. National Bureau of Economic Research. 2021; **2021**:w28731

[4] Alipour JV, Falck O, Schüller S. Germany's capacity to work from home. European Economic Review. 2023;**151**: 104354

[5] OECD. Productivity Gains from Teleworking in the Post COVID-19 Era: How Can Public Policies Make it Happen? Washington, DC, USA: OECD Publishing; 2020

[6] Tremblay DG, Paquet R, Najem E. Telework: A way to balance work and family or an increase in work-family conflict? Canadian Journal of Communication. 2022

[7] Van der Lippe T, Lippényi Z. Co-workers working from home and individual and team performance. New Technology, Work and Employment. 2020;**35**(1):60-79

[8] Kazekami S. Mechanisms to improve labor productivity by performing telework. Telecommunications Policy. 2020;**44**(2):101868

[9] Barrero JM, Bloom N, Davis SJ. COVID-19 is also a reallocation shock. Brookings Papers on Economic Activity. 2020;**2020**(Summer):329-371

[10] Etheridge B, Tang L, Wang Y. Worker productivity during lockdown and working from home: Evidence from self-reports. Covid Economics. 2020;**52**: 118-151

[11] Erdsiek D. Working from home during COVID-19 and beyond: Survey evidence from employers. ZEW – Centre for European Economic Research Discussion Paper. 2021;**2021**:21051

[12] Bloom N, Liang J, Roberts J, Ying ZJ. Does working from home work? Evidence from a Chinese experiment. The Quarterly Journal of Economics. 2015;**130**(1):165-218

[13] Choudhury P, Foroughi C, Larson B. Work-from-anywhere: The productivity effects of geographic flexibility. Strategic Management Journal. 2021;**42**(4):655-683

[14] Anakpo G, Nqwayibana Z, Mishi S. The impact of work-from-home on employee performance and productivity: A systematic review. Sustainability. 2023;**15**(5):4529

[15] Pratt JH. Home teleworking: A study of its pioneers. Technological Forecasting and Social Change. 1984;**25** (1):1-14

[16] Tremblay DG, Paquet R, Najem E. Telework: A way to balance work and family or an increase in work-family conflict? Canadian Journal of Communication. 2006;**31**(3):715-732

[17] Anderson AJ, Kaplan SA, Vega RP. The impact of telework on emotional experience: When, and for whom, does telework improve daily affective well-being? European Journal of Work and Organizational Psychology. 2015;**24**(6): 882-889

[18] Mandal SC, Boidya P, Haque MIM, Hossain A, Shams Z, Mamun AA. The impact of the COVID-19 pandemic on fish consumption and household food security in Dhaka city, Bangladesh. Global Food Security. 2021;**29**:100526

[19] Morikawa M. Work-from-home productivity during the COVID-19 pandemic: Evidence from Japan. Economic Inquiry. 2022;**60**(2):508-527

[20] Gibbs M, Mengel F, Siemroth C. Work from home & productivity: Evidence from personnel & analytics data on IT professionals. In: University of Chicago, Becker Friedman Institute for Economics Working Paper, (2021-56). 2021

[21] Ipsen C, Kirchner K, Hansen JP. Experiences of Working from Home in Times of COVID-19: International Survey Conducted the First Months of the National Lockdowns March-May, 2020. Kgs.Lyngby, Denmark: DTU; 2020. pp. 1-33

[22] Susilo D. Revealing the effect of work-from-home on job performance during the COVID-19 crisis: Empirical evidence from Indonesia. Journal of Contemporary Issues in Business and Government. 2020;**26**(1):23-40

[23] Brandão S, Ramos M. Teleworking in the context of the Covid-19 pandemic: Advantages, disadvantages and influencing factors–The workers' perspective. Revista Brasileira de Gestão de Negócios. 2023;**25**:253-268

[24] Bai JJ, Brynjolfsson E, Jin W, Steffen S, Wan C. Digital resilience: How work-from-home feasibility affects firm performance. National Bureau of Economic Research. 2021;**2021**:w28588

[25] Tønnessen Ø, Dhir A, Flåten BT. Digital knowledge sharing and creative performance: Work from home during the COVID-19 pandemic. Technological Forecasting and Social Change. 2021;**170**: 120866

[26] Zeira J. Workers, machines, and economic growth. The Quarterly Journal of Economics. 1998;**113**(4):1091-1117

[27] Acemoglu D, Restrepo P. The race between man and machine: Implications of technology for growth, factor shares, and employment. American Economic Review. 2018;**108**(6):1488-1542

[28] Veld M, van der Heijden BIJM, Semeijn J. Home-to-work spillover and employability among university employees. Journal of Managerial Psychology. 2016;**31**(8):1280-1296

[29] Peccei R, Van De Voorde K. Human resource management–well-being–performance research revisited: Past, present, and future. Human Resource Management Journal. 2019;**29**(4):539-563

[30] Damioli G, Van Roy V, Vertesy D, Vivarelli M. AI technologies and employment: Micro evidence from the supply side. Applied Economics Letters. 2022;**2022**:1-6

[31] Hall BH, Lotti F, Mairesse J. Evidence on the impact of R&D and ICT investments on innovation and productivity in Italian firms. Economics of Innovation and New Technology. 2013;**22**(3):300-328

[32] Lee YS et al. When does AI pay off? AI-adoption intensity, complementary investments, and R&D strategy. Technovation. 2022;**118**:102590

[33] Nicoletti G, von Rueden C, Andrews D. A matter of capabilities, incentives or both? European Economic Review. 2020; **2020**:128

[34] Baumann J, Kritikos AS. The link between R&D, innovation and productivity: Are micro firms different? Research Policy. 2016;**45**(6):1263-1274

[35] Goldsmith Pinkham P, Sorkin I, Swift H. Bartik instruments: What, when, why, and how. American Economic Review. 2020;**110**(8):2586-2624

[36] Zolas N, Kroff Z, Brynjolfsson E, McElheran K, Beede DN, Buffington C, et al. Advanced technologies adoption and use by US firms: Evidence from the annual business survey. National Bureau of Economic Research. 2021;**2021**: w28290

[37] Conte A, Vivarelli M. Succeeding in innovation: Key insights on the role of R&D and technological acquisition drawn from company data. Empirical Economics. 2014;**47**:1317-1340

[38] Bughin JS, Berjoan S, Yong Y. "Net better off?" why companies should scale new, tech-based flexible work practices. The European Business Review. 2022;**11**: 106-111

[39] Perez M, Sanchez M, de Luis CP, Jimenez R. The differences of firm resources and the adoption of teleworking. Technovation. 2005;**25**: 1476-1483

Chapter 8

Flexible Work Options in the COVID-19 Period

Jacob Ongaki

Abstract

The use of flexible work options, including telecommuting, was key to business success during COVID-19. Whether employees working remotely from their home setting or employer-provided location provided both the business and employees to perform their work roles and attend to personal scheduling challenges. This chapter will examine the success and setbacks of using flexible work arrangements during the COVID-19 pandemic. However, it is important to point out that technology plays a big role in business success because it provides tools for workers to fulfill their roles and earn a living. We would wrap up the chapter by providing mechanisms on how employees can learn from COVID-19 to be more prepared to mitigate business risks and how businesses can embrace flexible work arrangements to incentivize employees to be more productive, whether working from home or at the office.

Keywords: flexible work schedule, COVID-19, technology, work schedule conflict, remote

1. Introduction

The worldwide COVID-19 pandemic caught organizations, governments, and individuals by surprise. Businesses and governments reacted quickly to limit social interaction to prevent the spread of Coronavirus, famously known as COVID-19. It was evident that the government lockdown prevented the widespread use of COVID-19. Businesses moved swiftly and transitioned from traditional corporate structures to remote workforce arrangements or working from home. Working remotely entails employees working outside their regular office locations, including distant corporate sites, hotels, or at-home offices. The state of uncertainty of the COVID-19 pandemic exerted pressure on the organizational system of people management and ways to ensure supply and distribution centers satisfy and meet customers' needs. This ensures a mode of longevity and business survival [1]. The COVID-19 pandemic disrupted manufacturing and affected global economies, resulting in a global recession. The recession wiped out most of the capital market value including the 401K retirement assets. This was a far-reaching consequence compared to the previous recessionary period including the global financial crisis of 2008.

The change in technological advancement [2] has enabled multitasking roles in many workplaces and employees working from home. The improvement in technology has also contributed to an increased need for flexible work arrangement programs, especially virtual work or telecommuting. These practices provided employees with options on when, where, and how to fulfill their work roles. Work and family are two competing spheres for similar resources. These competing roles (work and home) are often problematic and challenging for employees to balance work and family responsibilities. Conversely, leaders have to confront and address it. Work and personal life are the most important domains in a worker's life. Because people are involved in multiple roles (employee, spouse, parent, child, and elderly caregiver) in their lives, this variety of roles has contributed to increased work–family conflicts. The role pressure of participation in one domain (such as the family role) makes it difficult to participate in another domain (such as the work role) and vice versa. However, the advancement in information technology and the ability for employees to work remotely has changed the way the workplace operates. It is no longer an incentive for employees to work from home but a natural fit-in during the COVID-19 lockdown.

Working from home was perceived negatively until the pandemic outbreak in early 2020. The COVID-19 pandemic opened doors for many employees to utilize flexible work options and work remotely. It was documented that the use of flexible work options was not standardized across all employees and deemed a privilege even when in the company's policy [3]. Businesses warmed to embrace the use of flexible work arrangements as an alternative for employees' productivity regardless of where they worked, whether working from home or at the office. The COVID-19 pandemic necessitated remote work. It became a reality for many employers, providing employees with work flexibility, autonomy, and choices on how they accomplish their work. In health emergencies, many kinds of flexible work have been implemented without regulation and adopted as substitute working modes [4]. Remote working is not new; however, it has become prevalent over the last few years to avoid the spread of COVID-19 in workplaces and public gatherings.

Modern technology enabled smart working and resolved work issues that never received attention until the pandemic outbreak [4]. For example, in Italy, remote work or employees working from home saw a jump from 28% to 82% during the pandemic [5]. In 2020 the United States, 96% of colleges and universities provided their education services online; however, the number of online educations decreased by the year's end [6]. Despite the working-from-home stereotype and stigma, many benefits have surfaced (work efficiency at work, concentration on tasks, and a less stressful environment) to enrich work-life balance [7]. Many employers have embraced working from home because of the cost and healthcare benefits and the availability of workers around the world [8]. It is worth pointing out that social isolation due to a lack of employee interaction, skill sharing, and a 24-hour reduction of personal time may contribute to negative effects and affect employee performance and health [9]. The younger generation of workers, the older generation, is more likely to work from home, be adaptable to technology, have an advanced education level, are single and without children, or even live far away from home [2].

Many have suggested that working from home has failed employees to differentiate work-life balance. Modern workers will be faced with the challenges of managing multiple responsibilities including work and personal roles. This was true during COVID-19, when parents struggled to balance work roles and their kid's schooling online because of the lockdown. Changes to family structures and demographics since the mid-1980s have increased employees' responsibilities toward work and family in many industries in the United States and worldwide. This is a concern to work interference with personal life, hence impacting employees' work performance (lack of work ethic and structure) due to work-life imbalance that may lead to an overwhelmed employee's role and deterioration of one's welfare [2]. Conversely, role theory assumes that participation in one role makes engaging and fulfilling other roles difficult because of fixed resources such as time and energy. Excessive role interference could lead to psychological and physical exhaustion and result in negative outcomes such as burnout, reduced job satisfaction and performance, or increased employee turnover.

In higher education, the negative effect was real during the COVID-19 pandemic. A study that surveyed teachers expressed high-stress levels, burnout, poor office ergonomics, and an unpleasant workplace [10]. The increased workload, lack of peer interaction, organization climate, and role ambiguity were factors to blame for the poor quality of education. It is clear that technology will continue to advance and transform the workplace. Many public and private workplaces use computer systems to store and retrieve information on time easily. COVID-19 may have been seen as an introduction to a remote working environment; however, the workplace transformation is well documented in history. COVID-19 brought the issue to the forefront and further discussion. This could involve the merits and demerits of remote work (including in higher education), mainly working from home. Organizations need to draft and implement policies that enable workers to be well-positioned and deliver products and services should similar crises of COVID-19 strike [11]. The unprecedented times and diverse outcomes have led researchers and practitioners to grow interest in flexible working arrangements designed to optimize when, how, and where work can be accomplished. Widespread advances in information technology and the Internet have enabled many workers to fulfill and manage multiple roles from any location.

2. Employers and employees' challenges

Remote work or working-from-home arrangements emanated in the 1980s, but emphasis and research picked up in the 2000s, and employers began to consider flexible work policies to attract and retain talents [12]. Studies produced mixed results on the purpose and benefits of this program [2]. An employer would like increased productivity as an incentive for an employee to have a work-life balance that allows multitasking, a quieter environment, a flexible schedule (start and end workday), fewer hours of commute, reducing sick days, and taking care of family members [13]. The lack of limited working from home for better communication, collaboration, and idea generation in the workplace which could have otherwise been limited when working from home. Leaders such as Marissa Mayer limited remote working at Yahoo for the same reasons.

The COVID-19 pandemic outbreak may have changed business preparedness during a crisis or unplanned business disruptions and continuity. Technology and flexible work schedules were vital to business success during the pandemic. Remote work and flexible work arrangements altered the norms of the workplace. However, the COVID-19 pandemic and government actions balanced the equation and made it easier for employers and employees to use flexible work options [12]. COVID-19 has shifted the traditional working to another of working of a modern worker. Flexible work arrangements were largely argued in the context of helping employees balance work demands and that of a family. However, the COVID-19 pandemic added another layer to the use of flexible work as a necessity for organizations to operate and employees to fulfill their roles and responsibilities. Hall [14] argued that "Stay-at-home orders, day-care closures, distance learning, and bandwidth requirements were just some of the things that may not have been fully considered before COVID-19." This could be true in support of traditional work in which employers leveraged working from home as a benefit to employees. This is no longer the case because employers need to operate and achieve shareholders' goals. This could not have been the case without employees' willingness to work during the pandemic. Many workplaces were never prepared for this type of outbreak and lockdown mandated by governments. This is normally thought of by first responders and medical professionals or essential workers reporting to work. The pandemic brought the world to a standstill, allowing opportunities for remote access requirements and affected businesses including the healthcare industry, education systems (teachers and students), and retail (affected customers).

The organizational challenges were associated with employees failing to fit in and adapt, leading to increased boredom, anxiety, anger, frustration, isolation, feelings of unworthiness, and lack of support [15]. It has been documented that employees' stressors and social impact during the COVID-19 pandemic [1].

- Duration of quarantine—the longer the isolation, the worse the psychological stress.
- Fear from infection of self or family members.
- Frustration and boredom are linked to a change in routine, reduced contact, lack of work if unable to work virtually, and reduced ability to do daily activities.
- Inadequate supplies of food, water, and health supplies.
- Inadequate information because of either poor government communication, institutional communication, or workplace communication.

After isolation, the following stressors were reported:

- Financial loss because of changes in work circumstances, potential change in working hours and wages.
- Stigma, especially, if one was exposed to a virus.

Employers reacted to quickly determine better ways to provide resources securely (Zoom and Teams) in the COVID-19 environment. Also, the pandemic period brought about many challenges to employees required to work from employer-provided working locations. The daycare or Zoom learning for young kids, the elderly, and sick family members taxed employees. However, those working remotely from home found it manageable despite the multitasking of the family and attending to work requirements. Organizations have tasted the benefit of thinking outside the box about working in a better environment. This is a discussion that employers must confront to be prepared to turn challenges into opportunities leveraging the advancement in technology and information communication. Although the pandemic surfaced the issue of work–family conflict and vice versa, the benefits outweigh the cost of working from home or remotely. Research supports remote work that shows remote working has a positive effect on work–family conflict but decreases workplace well-being. Also, family interference with work has a nonsignificant negative effect on employee well-being largely because of self-efficacy and job autonomy [16].

Research findings suggest the importance of managerial support and organizational commitment for the success of flexible work arrangements, job satisfaction, and the use of technology [17]. Employers were not willing to offer and implement remote work until the pandemic struck. If any, the benefits were given to a few including the higher up. The COVID-19 pandemic was the last straw that broke the camel's back. After the mandated business lockdown, there was a drastic shift from working in an office environment to working from home. Held [18] stated that 13% of their workforce worked remotely before the pandemic compared with 50% after the pandemic. Also, the flexible work option was primarily used to alleviate work–family conflict and vice versa, and the program used sparing. It turned out that family configurations and care obligations were not factored in situations of school and daycare closures that increased parental role conflict [19].

The lack of IT infrastructure and the availability of the Internet complicated the work-from-home program. Also, the availability of working tools such as approved laptops or communication devices to connect to the company's virtual working space network systems (company folders, emails, working data, or shared drives). The lack of resources and support affected employees' effective transition to working from home, which affected employees' attitudes [12]. Therefore, technological setbacks and the lack of proper communication hindered employees from expanding their expertise during the uncertain COVID-19 period.

3. Employers preparedness

The use of technology can enhance the challenges during workplace crises. Working from home could mean access to a large pool of talent worldwide. The openness for employers to create workplace-friendly policies would mitigate a crisis. With the implementation of virtual meeting tools, organizations are no longer confined to a particular geography when defining business goals and strategic initiatives. This inherently enhances business continuity strategies as flexible hours and geographical diversity increase the ability to continue operations during an event that significantly impacts a particular region. Technology has its challenges as cyber-attacks continue to increase. This is an area in which companies must invest resources in their network and best security practices to safeguard business assets and customer information. For example, security with backup systems and data recovery practices protocols. This would translate into growth opportunities for internal and external stakeholders to feel safe online. The best practices must be enhanced to vendors and suppliers for a better workplace. The company goals must be communicated downstream and invested in employees' training of purpose. Accurate and timely messages could mitigate rumors on the Internet, safeguarding the company's image to the public. Technology will continue to dictate the success of businesses in the future. This means employees use technologically advanced working tools provided with adequate training to succeed at their work. Job security is a major concern among employees because of outsourcing of tasks. Job security is also a factor in lower productivity among many employees. Employees working from home or remote locations should be supported with adequate benefits and continued performance evaluation. Supported employees often always suggest possible solutions to many workplace problems and challenges.

Employees generally tend to cope and adapt well under stressful situations and rise to the task. Like 9/11, COVID-19 unified the international community, and this is true for employees. Even with resilient employees, employers must develop programs available to safeguard one's well-being including psychological or developing mental illness from a difficult work environment, either from home or an employer-provided workstation. The COVID-19 pandemic warned businesses to enhance and prepare for severe unanticipated threats, testing organizational preparedness in a modern era. Performing risk assessments even though COVID-19 may be termed as an outlier in historical context, and it is more likely an infectious disease outbreak will occur. Businesses will not be immune from it. Companies must be ready to activate measures (remote working) to ensure fewer business interruptions.

4. Leaning forward

The loss of some traditional workers because of the pandemic may have changed the workforce operations. Technology will accelerate into the future, and so will cyber security challenges. Businesses including governments ought to have learned from peers and COVID-19 lessons. Less employee and customer interruptions could mean a well-prepared business environment. But we live in a world where we are interdependent in the supply chain and distribution. Leave alone global connections. There were supply delays and shortages during the pandemic, which resulted in business closures. What if technology fails or a cyber-attack puts business operations on hold [14]? Even with traditional work, technology is utilized. This seems scary, but it could happen, and businesses and the government should invest in R&D to avoid it happening soon. Working remotely will only be possible with the availability of the Internet connected to devices or central business stations. The connections and virtual collaboration and webinars, social media blogs, and email will be derailed to share and communicate information for businesses to operate. Do not wait for the crisis to happen; be proactive and anticipate challenges and how to overcome them. Technology, preparedness employees, and working remotely should be part of the business model. The pandemic may have paved the way for the remote work model; however, recovery plans must be initiated and implemented considering unforeseen events that can halt business operations. It is necessary to assess the type of business and industry to incorporate potential risks that could include financial, operational, legal, regulatory, reputational, and others to be better prepared and how businesses can recover quickly with less impact [14]. Preparedness includes assessment of resource dependencies, employee deployment, hardware infrastructure, applications, equipment, and supplies. Employees make a company thrive and achieve its goals. Despite the emphasis on remote work, it is important to maintain certain aspects of employee presence to boost morale by sharing professional and personal experiences. Cultural interaction can occur even when working remotely. The leadership must create ways to ensure that human interaction is not lost. This could mean virtual check-ins, recreational events, happy hours, workouts, team-building exercises, awards, and employee recognition to feel part and parcel of an organization. Social interactions boost morale and creativity free of business obligations. The COVID-19 period challenges workplaces and opens opportunities for how employees work. Working from home has become the norm, and some organizations have yet to return employees to their traditional workplaces. Employees often turn challenges into opportunities and contribute to the growth of an organization. However, there are still many gaps to fill.

The use of flexible work schedules and remote work must be incorporated as part of the strategy. A greater focus should be on anticipation of similar challenges beyond the COVID-19 pandemic, such as when the possibility of working from home will not be possible. This will not only enhance organizational readiness but also operational capabilities [14].

Organizational leaders could leverage resources and empower employees, provide leadership support, gather feedback, and communicate employee growth opportunities that reinforce their work engagement in uncertain and challenging times [20]. This means that employees must learn to adapt through employer-offered training and mentorship to perform to their potential of self-efficacy, self-awareness, and self-accountability [21]. Regardless of how we move forward as businesses and workers, remote work and employees working from home should be part of the company's strategic positioning in a global economy. Organizations use COVID-19 as a case study to innovate and enhance the way employees work, adapt, and respond to the impact of macro events and pandemics to create sustainable business growth and longevity that values important assets, workers. The strategies could not work in isolation without incorporating technology and safeguarding information from increased cyber-attacks that could halt business operations.

Lastly, organizational preparedness and leaning forward means a smart workplace like a smart classroom in higher education. Global smart workplace companies are on the rise, exceeding USD 47 billion in 2023. The ever-increasing demand for smart offices provides solutions for companies to combat working from home or remote access and, most importantly, prevent cyber-attacks [22]. The focus shifts from organizational survival during COVID-19 to long-term strategies that center on implementing measures to transform businesses and adapt to modern ways of a smart and sustainable working environment, assuring revenue and productivity in uncertain times or preparedness for unforeseen macro events [23]. Successful businesses should have strong technological infrastructures to support work system interfaces and connections. Studies have found that technology moderates the work implications, particularly the COVID-19 outbreak, and affects employees' performance [24]. Organizations are not fully developed technologically to support many working avenues including working from home or remotely; thus, a greater emphasis is required to support a smooth, smart place working environment or a new normal post-COVID-19 period. The reinforcement of home office and adapting and investing in technology to limit loss in the event of occurrences of COVID-19. This infrastructure will improve employees' performance and the quality of work. Opportunity to enhance work platforms and digitalization efforts to cope with and benefit employees and organizational outcomes in the event of the inevitable or severe disruptive events of the COVID-19 pandemic. Others have argued that technology is not a problem for employees' work, but the physical isolation among workers contributes to the deterioration of group relations in a business during periods of lockdown situation [25].

5. Conclusions

The use of flexible work options, popular during the COVID-19 pandemic, has decreased, and employers require workers to return to office space. A recent telework survey in the South Bay region of Los Angeles shows a substantial increase in usage during the pandemic. The post-pandemic or after the government relaxed social gathering restrictions, telework, and flexible scheduling have seen some organizations return workers to the physical workplaces. The study suggests that it is unlikely that flexible work practices will return to the COVID-19 levels [26]. It might as well be a good case for workers returning to their workplaces, but it pegs the lesson learned. Studies have recommended that businesses modify policies and practices to motivate and maintain the level of their workforce for a healthier work environment, better work-life interface, and job security to increase productivity during the COVID-19 pandemic [27]. Companies that react quickly to macro crises increase employees' productivity, and job satisfaction, and reduce turnover rates. Organizational leadership and management must be sensitive to employee job security, health, work-life balance, pay, and favorable work practices responses [27]. As discussed earlier, the macro COVID-19 pandemic focused on work-from-home programs and changed the discussion on how employers' employees adapt and learn. Research has shown that the COVID-19 challenges and working from home created an avenue for employers to develop a program policy on managing the duality of work-life balance, understanding that it is a win-win situation [28]. The work-life policies must enhance the company goals and vision that work collaboratively and provide employees with tools to minimize work-life conflict [12, 28]. Capitalizing on digital platforms and advancing information communication can enhance work engagement during uncertain times such as COVID-19, and work-from-home programs could play a pivotal role. Employees learn to adapt to existing technological protocols and develop new techniques to coordinate work more efficiently [29].

Conflict of interest

No conflict of interest.

Author details

Jacob Ongaki
Colorado Mesa University, Colorado, USA

*Address all correspondence to: jongaki@coloradomesa.edu

References

[1] Bussin MHR, Swart-Opperman C. COVID-19: Considering impacts to employees and the workplace. South African Journal of Human Resource Management. 2021;**19**(1):1-5. DOI: 10.4102/sajhrm.v19i0.1384

[2] La Torre G, Chiappetta M, Mazzalai E, Gresele R, Bazzo G, Pederzolli G, et al. Smart working perception in banking companies' employees during the COVID-19 pandemic: A cross-sectional pilot study. Work. 2022;**73**(2):363-376. DOI: 10.3233/WOR-211152

[3] Smyth C, Cortis N, Powell A. University staff and flexible work: Inequalities, tensions and challenges. Journal of Higher Education Policy & Management. 2021;**43**(5):489-504. DOI: 10.1080/1360080X.2020.1857504

[4] Mascagna F, Izzo AL, Cozzoli LF, Torre GL. Smart working: Validation of a questionnaire in the Italian reality. Senses and Sciences [Internet]. 2019;**6**(3):805-827. Available from: https://sensesandsciences.com/index.php/Senses/article/view/169

[5] Basso G, Formai S. Il lavoro da remoto in Italia durante la pandemia [Internet]. Banca d'Italia; 2021 Jan [cited 2021 Jun 17] p. 13. Available from: https://www.bancaditalia.it/media/notizia/il-lavoro-da-remoto-in-italia-durante-la-pandemia

[6] College Crisis Initiative [homepage on the Internet]. Davidson College; 2021. Available from: https://college crisis.shinyapps.io/dashboard/

[7] Vittersø J, Akselsen S, Evjemo B, Julsrud T, Yttri B, Bergvik S. Impacts of home-based telework on quality of life for employees and their partners. Quantitative and qualitative results from a European survey. Journal of Happiness Studies. 2003;**4**:201-233

[8] Di Tecco C, Ronchetti M, Russo S, Ghelli M, Rondinone BM, Persechino B, et al. Implementing smart working in public administration: A follow up study. La Medicina del Lavoro. 2021;**112**(2):141-152

[9] Nakrošienė A, Bučiūnienė I, Goštautaitė B. Working from home: Characteristics and outcomes of telework. International Journal of Management Reviews. 2019;**40**(1):87-101

[10] Kotowski SE, Davis KG, Gerding T. Almost a year in: Virtual offices remain an ergonomic trouble spot. Work. 2021. Available from: https://www.researchgate.net/publication/358317005_Almost_a_year_in_Virtual_offices_remained_an_ergonomic_trouble_spot

[11] Horton N, Jacobs K, Davis K, Kotowski S. How does the working environment transition impact perceived work-related quality of life for postsecondary teachers within the United States? Work. 2022;**71**(2):417-421. DOI: 10.3233/WOR-210819

[12] Yeo RK, Li J. Breaking the silence of psychological impact while working from home during COVID: Implications for workplace learning. Human Resource Development International. 2022;**25**(2):114-144. DOI: 10.1080/13678868.2022.2047149

[13] Xiao Y, Becerik-Gerber B, Lucas C, Roll SC. Impacts of working from home during COVID-19 pandemic on physical and mental wellbeing of office workstation users. Journal of Occupational and Environmental Medicine. 2021;**63**(3):181-190. DOI: 10.1097/JOM.0000000000002097

[14] Hall T. Business continuity beyond COVID-19: Lessons learned and the

"illusion of preparedness". Journal of Business Continuity & Emergency Planning. 2022;**16**(1):45-52

[15] Brooks SK, Webster RK, Smith LE, Woodlands L, Wessely S, Greenberg N, et al. The psychological impact of quarantine and how to reduce it: Rapid review of the evidence. The Lancet. 2020;**395**(10227):912-920. DOI: 10.1016/S0140-6736(20)30460-8

[16] Xu G, Wang X, Han X, Huang S (Sam), Huang D. The dark side of remote working during pandemics: Examining its effects on work-family conflict and workplace wellbeing. International Journal of Disaster Risk Reduction. 2022;**79**. DOI: 10.1016/j.ijdrr.2022.103174

[17] Seal CR, Rawls KM, Flaherty PT, Fan D, Sanchez S, Garcia Guzman M. Flexible work arrangements and employee work attitudes: A case-based inquiry of a small non-profit response to crisis. Journal of Organizational Psychology. 2021;**27**(4):93-101

[18] Held JM, C.E.B.S. Measuring the impact of COVID-19 on employee benefits. Benefits Quarterly. 2021;**37**(1):57

[19] Minkus L, Groepler N, Drobnič S. The significance of occupations, family responsibilities, and gender for working from home: Lessons from COVID-19. PLoS One. 2022;**17**(6):1-17

[20] Van Steenbergen EF, van der Ven C, Peeters MCW, Taris TW. Transitioning towards new ways of working: Do job demands, job resources, burnout, and engagement change? Psychological Reports. 2018;**121**(4):736-766. DOI: 10.1177/0033294117740134

[21] Xanthopoulou D, Bakker AB, Demerouti E, Schaufeli WB. Reciprocal relationships between job resources, personal resources, and work engagement. Journal of Vocational Behavior. 2009;**74**(3):235-244. DOI: 10.1016/j.jvb.2008.11.003

[22] Abhishek S. Smart Workplace Market Size, Share, Industry Analysis, Key Players, Business Opportunities, Development Status, Challenges and Impact of COVID-19. M2PressWIRE. 2020. Available from: https://www.abnewswire.com/pressreleases/smart-workplace-market-size-share-industry-analysis-key-players-business-opportunities-development-status-challenges-and-impact-of-covid19_496497.html?utm_source=dlvr.it&utm_medium=facebook

[23] Smit M. Workplace inclusion: The COVID-19 impact. Human Resources Magazine. 2020;**25**(4):12-15

[24] Narayanamurthy G, Tortorella G. Impact of COVID-19 outbreak on employee performance – Moderating role of industry 4.0 base technologies. International Journal of Production Economics. 2021;**234**:108075. DOI: 10.1016/j.ijpe.2021.108075

[25] Jackowska M, Lauring J. What are the effects of working away from the workplace compared to using technology while being at the workplace? Assessing work context and personal context in a global virtual setting. Journal of International Management. 2021;**27**(1):1075-4253. DOI: 10.1016/j.intman.2021.100826

[26] Prager F, Rhoads M, Martínez JN. The COVID-19 economic shutdown and the future of flexible workplace practices in the South Bay region of Los Angeles County. Transport Policy. 2022;**125**:241-255. DOI: 10.1016/j.tranpol.2022.06.004

[27] Cao J, Hamori M. Adapting careers to the COVID crisis: The impact of the pandemic on employees' career

orientations. Journal of Vocational Behavior. 2022;**139**. DOI: 10.1016/j.jvb.2022.103789

[28] Dumas TL, Sanchez-Burks J. The professional, the personal, and the ideal worker: Pressures and objectives shaping the boundary between life domains. Academy of Management Annals. 2015;**9**(1):803-843. DOI: 10.1080/19416520.2015.1028810

[29] Malik P, Garg P. Learning organization and work engagement: The mediating role of employee resilience. International Journal of Human Resource Management. 2017;**31**(5):1-24. DOI: 10.1080/09585192.2017.1396549

Chapter 9

Transforming the Skies: Managing Remote Workforce at a Maintenance, Repair, and Overhaul (MRO) Aviation Company

Benito Gonzalez Jr. and Sohel M. Imroz

Abstract

Remote work, also known as telecommuting, is a flexible working arrangement that allows employees to work from remote locations outside of corporate offices. Remote workforce management is the practice of effectively leading and managing remote employees and teams. While remote work has been steadily increasing, its demand, popularity, and usefulness have skyrocketed since the COVID-19 pandemic. To be successful or even survive in this post-pandemic era, organizations cannot overemphasize the importance of effectively managing remote workforce. This chapter presents a case study explaining various issues of managing remote workforce based on a Maintenance, Repair, and Overhaul (MRO) company (Company A, pseudonym) in the aviation industry. The purpose of this chapter is twofold. First, it presents the challenges experienced by Company A when managing remote workforce and how the company supports its remote workers. Second, it explains how Company A is adjusting to this new mode of employment, which impacts fully remote, fully onsite, and hybrid employees. The chapter concludes by recommending companies managing remote workforce to adopt HR Hybrid Guidelines tailored to their needs. The chapter should be beneficial for readers interested in understanding the impact of remote employment and managing remote workforce in MRO aviation companies.

Keywords: remote work, telecommuting, maintenance, repair, and overhaul (MRO), aviation industry, hybrid guidelines

1. Introduction

As we are all aware, the COVID-19 pandemic has prompted numerous companies to roll out remote work policies. Nevertheless, the notion of remote work is not novel; it has gained increased traction in recent years. This chapter presents a case study explaining the advantages and disadvantages of a remote workforce and how it affects operational efficiency, workforce management, and collaboration in a Maintenance, Repair, and Overhaul (MRO) aviation company. The chapter also shares effective approaches to overseeing remote employees by describing various forms of remote

IntechOpen

work setups, including fully remote, entirely onsite, and hybrid personnel, while offering a hybrid on-call model as a recommendation. Lessons from this case study suggest that a remote workforce can have an influence on an organization's productivity and on the employees' collaborative efforts. In addition, the impact on the organization may happen in several ways depending on how the workforce chooses to accept remote work authorizations. By the conclusion of this chapter, readers should gain insightful perspectives on how remote work, if used correctly, could potentially enhance business results in the aviation sector.

According to Devara [1], "Maintenance, Repair, and Overhaul (MRO) services are essential for any industry that uses machinery to run operations. In the aviation sector, the term MRO aviation refers to all the activities that are aimed at ensuring that the aircrafts remain ready to fly at all times" (para. 1). The subject of this case study is an MRO facility in Texas, USA that has about 3,000 employees. To maintain anonymity, this company will be referred to as "Company A" in this chapter. It operates in the aviation industry and consists of departments with classes of employees such as aircraft technicians, mechanics, sheet metal technicians, electricians, and non-destructive inspectors (NDI) technicians [2, 3]. Each department of Company A has about 500–700 employees, with the manufacturing department having the most employees onsite (around 1,300). These departments are known as Hands-On-Labor (HOL) because their workers physically work on the products and parts that Company A produces or manufactures.

According to the Department of Labor (DOL) [4, 5], the number of jobs for aircraft technicians is around 151,400, with a potential to increase by 6% over the next 10 years. The typical work Company A employees do depends on the type and model of the aircraft they are working on, and they may also be manufacturing parts for these aircraft. Sometimes Company A performs Programmed Depot Maintenance (PDM) in which an aircraft goes through several phases of induction, inspections, repair, reassembly, testing, painting, and delivery back to the customers [6]. These customers may be the United States government or its foreign allies, although there are a few commercial private-sector aircraft programs as well.

The Federal Aviation Administration (FAA) dictates the maintenance schedule for different operations of MRO aviation companies like Company A per Section 14 CFR Part 43: Maintenance, Preventive Maintenance, Rebuilding, and Alteration, and Part 145: Repair Stations. In the legal framework established by the FAA through the Code of Federal Regulations (CFR), the guidelines that relate to the domain of Company A predominantly reside within Title 14 CFR, specifically in Part 43 and Part 145. These segments lay out the criteria and benchmarks governing aircraft maintenance and repair, along with the accreditation process for repair facilities engaged in MRO operations. Smaller repair stations may work on aircraft assemblies such as landing gear, flight control overhauls, or interior upholstery refurbishment per FAA Section Part 145 [7, 8].

Title 14 of CFR Part 43 commonly oversees the spectrum of aircraft maintenance, repairs, and overhauls. This section of the CFR lays out the parameters and standards governing the maintenance, repair, and overhaul procedures for aircraft. It encompasses a wide range of topics related to aircraft maintenance, such as inspections, repairs, modifications, and comprehensive overhauls, all designed to uphold the aircraft's safety and airworthiness. Part 43 precisely delineates the necessary qualifications of individuals performing these functions and sets out the protocols for executing maintenance tasks while documenting procedures and their results [7]. Part 145 of the CFR focuses on the certification and supervision of aircraft repair stations. This rule outlines the conditions and yardsticks that repair facilities need to follow to gain certification from the FAA for conducting aircraft maintenance, repairs, and modifications. This section encompasses various aspects of repair station operations, encompassing staff qualifications, facility prerequisites, equipment, protocols, documentation, and quality assurance protocols. Adhering to the directives laid out in Part 145 guarantees that repair stations sustain the required norms to safeguard the security and flightworthiness of aircraft undergoing maintenance and repairs [8]. The following section presents the most critical challenges experienced by Company A when managing remote workers and how to best support them.

2. Research, method and analysis

The study used qualitative research method approach employing phenomenological research design and incorporated heuristic inquiry with a purposeful sampling technique. Using the qualitative research method and phenomenological research design was appropriate in this study due to its objective of exploring an understudied central phenomenon, namely the experience of the MRO aircraft technician workers. The utilization of a heuristic inquiry strategy was necessary because it emphasizes the significance of a researcher's intimate first-hand experience, insight, and understanding of the phenomenon being studied [9]. A total of 50 employees participated in this study, and only seven of them were female. There were 15 participants with less than 5 years of experience, eight with 6–10 years, five with 11–15 years, 11 with 16–20 years, six with 21–25 years, and five with 26–40 years of experience. **Table 1** summarizes the number of participants in this study and their work experience. Data were also gathered from physical artifacts such as employees' weekly work schedules, FAA policy guidelines, and Office of Personnel Management (OPM) requirements

Type of employees	Years of experience	Number of employees
Male technicians	0–5	12
	6–10	4
	11–15	5
	16–20	11
	21–25	6
	26–40	5
Female technicians	0–5	3
	6–10	4
	11–15	0
	16–20	0
	21–25	0
	26–40	0
Total		50

Table 1.
Summary of participants and work experience.

documents. Data analysis was carried out using thematic analysis and by identifying themes and patterns in the collected data. Data analysis in this study involved breaking down the data into its component parts and then looking for patterns and themes that emerged from the data.

3. Challenges of managing a remote workforce and how to support remote workers

Managing a remote workforce within MRO aviation companies can pose certain challenges. With employees dispersed across various locations, ensuring everyone aligns and works toward shared goals can be quite demanding. However, with effective strategies in place, managing a remote workforce can be as, if not more, effective than managing an onsite one [10].

3.1 Lack of communication and collaboration

When most of the employees in Company A started working remotely, the PM noticed some frustration from the older team members who did not understand the new technologies imposed upon them for remote work and needed some training. This was something new to them since the older employees were used to using emails and desk phones to communicate and were communicating face-to-face with other team members by going to each other's cubicles or offices. The older Program Management Office (PMO) workers adjusted quickly to using cell phones to make phone calls, instant messages (IMs), and text messages since they have been using smartphones for a while now. The younger PMO workers, who were already used to doing everything from their smartphones or tablets, quickly adjusted to the new remote work technology. A program manager from Company A decided to have the older and younger employees work as a unit because of the technological understanding gap and suggested pairing an older employee with a younger one so they could learn from each other. Creating a remote worker buddy system paired one team member who is tech-savvy to help another team member who is less experienced using technologies. Those employees were learning the ropes of being remote employees and needed guidance on how to correctly use the new technologies that they were not familiar with. This buddy system helped strengthen the camaraderie between the PMO remote workers at Company A because they worked together as a team and helped each other to overcome these technological obstacles [11].

While collaboration may present challenges within a remote workforce, it also offers distinctive opportunities. With suitable tools and communication strategies, remote teams can effectively collaborate to achieve their objectives [10, 12]. For instance, at Company A, the Program Manager (PM) made sure that the PMO maintained effective communication with each of its team members and customers using technology while making sure that each member of the team was able to use the technology easily by adjusting to IMs on cell phones, using video calls, using chat instead of emails while using the computer, and using video conference software such as Microsoft Teams, Zoom, and or WebEx. It did cause some frustration within the group when someone did not know how to connect to a meeting or how to use virtual conference etiquette because they were not used to working remotely [13, 14].

3.2 Lack of timely access to information

When remote work was authorized by the executive leaders of Company A for the PMO team members, there were some challenges at the beginning. One of the major challenges was receiving the information on time to meet several deadlines, which caused minor delays when the PMO team members were adjusting to their newly founded remote work status. The onsite workers have now started to rely on sending the information by email, uploading it to a secure server, using screen share, and/or video conference meetings to pass along the information [15–17]. They had to quickly adjust on how and where to send the information because, in comparison to the pre-COVID-19 era, the PMO support workers would usually go to the operational site, manufacturing, or production floor to retrieve the information by a handoff paper copy from the MRO worker. If a signature was required on a document, then now the MRO worker would have to sign and scan it to send it to the PMO worker. This involved extra steps that the MRO onsite worker had to complete. The DocuSign software was implemented later to speed up the process of signing documents [16, 17].

Another example of software that was implemented involved the utilization of project management software such as Microsoft Project, Jira, Power BI, Tableau, and Minitab, which allows team members to track progress and communicate updates in real-time. This not only fosters better teamwork but also guarantees alignment and a unified focus on common objectives. However, it is crucial to emphasize that successful collaboration within a remote workforce hinges on well-defined anticipations, a program manager that adapts to the remote work environment, transparent communication, and a robust foundation of trust among the team members. The PM at Company A incorporated a trust-based management style in which PMO team members were able to manage their time and tasks effectively while still meeting all their goals, which helped keep their productivity at a high level because they were not being micromanaged [14, 16, 17].

3.3 Lack of face-to-face supervision

One of the fundamental practices for handling a remote workforce involves establishing transparent communication channels since face-to-face interaction is limited to video conferences and not in-person. In this effort, the program manager needed to set forth a communication management plan for the remote workers. According to this plan, the PM needed to do regular check-ins with remote employees utilizing collaboration tools like video conferencing and instant messaging and set explicit expectations for deadlines and deliverables. Moreover, it is crucial to trust the employees and empower them to independently manage their workloads. By fostering a culture of trust and communication, a robust and productive remote workforce can be nurtured [18].

The PM at Company A encouraged every PMO remote team member to maintain a detailed record of their work through proper documentation using memos, record their video conferences, enable read receipts option on their emails, and properly archive documents. This is valuable information during any lessons learned phase of the program. The PM conveyed to the PMO support remote workforce the importance of security and data privacy. A lot of information is going to be transmitted electronically since face-to-face interaction is very limited, and some of the information may be company-sensitive information. The Information Technology (IT) department established the use of email and document tags that can be assigned to sensitive information before the COVID-19 era, and the PM made the PMO remote workforce aware of this function and to use it. These email and document tags had a banner that stated: Sensitive, Internal Use Only, and/or Proprietary Information [14, 17].

3.4 Employee expectation of work productivity

While the operational, production, and manufacturing workforce took care of the HOL at Company A, they were supported by the Program Management Office (PMO), which usually consists of a program manager, contract manager, scheduler, planner, finance manager, and procurement specialist. The engineering workforce was also involved as a mix of HOL and PMO support depending on what needed to be done on the aircraft or on one of its components. The PMO efforts do not require the personnel to be near an aircraft, equipment, products, or parts. It is an advanced administrative duty that requires input from software, flow charts, process monitoring, and schedules. They establish timelines, assign resources to the schedule, set up Zoom call meetings with the HOL sector or customers, and procure and order parts just like they would do if they were at the organization sitting in a cubicle [19].

The Program Manager (PM) at Company A set forth certain requirements for each of the PMO team members if they decided to work remotely because the managing dynamic changed from an onsite workforce to a remote workforce. In this instance, everyone in the PMO department decided to work remotely, which helped the program manager easily adjust the management style. The PM needed to make sure that everyone on the team understood that they were going to be evaluated on the quality of their work, the timeliness of their deliverables, and their availability to other team members. Key Performance Indicators (KPI) were enhanced so the PM could successfully monitor the team's progress and provide up-to-date feedback to keep the PMO aligned with their set goals [20].

3.5 Technological issues

There are certain MRO workers at Company A who could work remotely because they did not need to be at the facility or near the aircraft. These types of workers were branded as non-essential during the COVID-19 era and could work out of the Program Management Office (PMO). Though very important to the organization, they can perform their work at any location if they have a work-issued cell phone and a work-issued laptop. Technology and the ability to connect to the worksite or its onsite servers or cloud servers is a very important aspect of working remotely [21]. Let us take, for example, those employees from Company A who must travel to work at different work sites but still need access to Company A's servers. None of this is new to Company A because the business development department has personnel who travel and connect remotely from any part of the country. Company A's technology during the pre-COVID-19 era was prepared to handle only around 30 personnel who may be on travel at the same time. The issue is that after the pandemic, a larger majority of the workforce is connecting remotely, and the organization's Information Technology (IT) department had to upgrade its servers and technology to be capable of handling all these remote workers' requests for connection to the servers [22].

Company A also had to issue everyone in the PMO department a company cell phone and laptop for remote work. In some cases, several PMO employees requested monitors and docking stations to take to their homes. However, the IT department had to acquire these monitors, cell phone plans, and laptops, which was an expense to Company A. This extra cost was provided by their budgeted capital funds for that financial quarter. A SharePoint site was also incorporated into the program so file transfers can happen easily among PMO support team members. The SharePoint site was used as a secure In/Out drop box in which files or documents were uploaded to respective folders and downloaded by team members who needed that information. The PMO team members communicated with each other by a quick IM or text message that the documents were uploaded so the other team members could download them. The SharePoint site was very useful because documents that could not be uploaded to emails due to their file size were easily uploaded and downloaded at the SharePoint site securely [23]. It is important to understand that the pandemic affected not only those employees who became fully remote but also those who had no choice but to remain fully onsite and who opted to be hybrid—two or three days working onsite and the rest of the week working from home. The following section elaborates on the impact of remote work on different types of employees at Company A—a fully remote, fully onsite, hybrid, and our proposed hybrid on-call schedule.

4. Impact of remote work on fully remote, fully onsite, and hybrid employees

4.1 Fully remote employees

Upon careful examination of various divisions within Company A, a noticeable trend emerges regarding the suitability of remote work arrangements. Specifically, the Information Technology (IT) department emerges as a prime candidate for a fully remote workforce structure. This conclusion is grounded in IT tasks, such as software development and troubleshooting, which are inherently conducive to remote execution. Moreover, remote IT personnel enjoy equitable access to tools and resources, fostering seamless collaboration [14, 17]. Conversely, a different perspective emerges for the maintenance department, indicating a more favorable alignment with an onsite workforce model. This determination is underpinned by the inherent physical nature of maintenance responsibilities, which encompass activities like aircraft inspections and repairs. This type of work cannot be done remotely because it requires HOL tasks to be performed. The localized presence of maintenance employees also facilitates effective coordination with other vital departments, including logistics and engineering [24].

Individuals working at Company A and enjoying the privilege of full-time remote work often shared their experiences of enhanced autonomy and flexibility. They expressed contentment in tailoring their work schedules according to their personal preferences, a practice that fosters a more harmonious equilibrium between their professional and personal spheres. This adaptability is of particular significance to those employees juggling personal commitments or those who thrive during unconventional working hours [25]. Remote employees of Company A also articulated the benefits of eliminating commuting stress and its financial implications. According to a group of remote workers, the absence of their daily commutes translated into more time available for work tasks or personal pursuits, contributing to their overall well-being.

The absence of interruptions and distractions that come with working in an office environment was mentioned by a few other employees. Working remotely makes them feel more focused and productive. They added, however, that working from home can make it challenging to keep business and personal lives distinct [20, 22].

These workers typically exhibit a high degree of focus and diligence in their work. As they have ready access to one another and can fix problems as they emerge, they frequently work efficiently with their coworkers and pass along on-the-spot experiences to one another. This is the same type of work environment that is happening within remote workers. Many of them are more readily available when called upon, even though they are working remotely. With the use of video conference calls and screen sharing, they can also pass along the experience from one employee to another with the use of technology [26].

Some managers at Company A, in the past, expressed confusion when they could not find a worker who was at the worksite but away from the cubicle or office because they were in another section of the building or in a meeting. The same goes for the onsite workers trying to find a manager or a director who is always busy in a meeting or with the door closed. Company A remote workers overcame such confusion because they can send a quick IM chat or look to see their online status if it is in the Available (Green), Busy (Red), or Away (Yellow) status. This is one of the adjustments that Company A had to make while working remotely. The issue may be the availability of the worker or manager, no matter if they are working remotely or onsite, which seems to be frustrating to the workforce [20].

4.2 Fully onsite employees

The case study revealed that the maintenance, repair, and overhaul departments of Company A achieve optimal performance with a fully onsite workforce. The rationale behind this lies in the intricate technical skills and hands-on responsibilities intrinsic to these departments, which are not amenable to effective remote execution. Conversely, departments such as human resources and marketing of Company A reaped benefits from a remote workforce, capitalizing on diminished requirements for physical presence and the potential of virtual communication tools to enhance management efficiency [23].

Several employees working onsite at Company A expressed a deep connection to their workplace, highlighting that the physical environment significantly contributes to their sense of belonging and self-identity. For these individuals, the workplace holds a central role in fostering social interactions and acting as a wellspring of motivation. Direct interactions with coworkers and managers enable instant communication, aiding in swift issue resolution and teamwork. The advantage of being physically present lies in the ability to engage in spontaneous conversations, exchange expertise, and receive guidance—factors particularly vital in the intricate field of aviation [21, 23]. It is worth considering that viewpoints can differ, and the appropriateness of exclusively onsite work hinges on variables like job responsibilities, individual situations, and inclinations. These observations underscore the intricate connection between being physically present, collaborative efforts, and the individual welfare of Company A employees.

The majority of Company A onsite employees found comfort in the regularity of commuting to a physical office, as it aided in setting clear distinctions between their professional and personal lives. A particularly notable challenge raised by those employees was the potential strain caused by lengthy commutes, both physically and mentally. Additionally, the fixed nature of the workplace restricts the flexibility to work from different locations, which can be a matter of concern for those who value varied environments to enhance their creativity and concentration [1, 2, 21]. The dedicated, fully onsite individuals of Company A exhibited a remarkable degree of concentration and conscientiousness in their tasks. Their adeptness at collaborating seamlessly within the team is facilitated by their ready proximity, enabling swift resolution of any challenges that may arise. However, fully onsite employees of Company A sometimes found it difficult to maintain a healthy work-life balance. Being physically close to their place of employment made it challenging for them to entirely disengage from work. Over time, this could result in burnout and decreased productivity [21].

Company A employees' perspective illuminated the merits of a fully onsite work environment in the MRO aviation domain, emphasizing the cultivation of camaraderie and collaborative dynamics since a lot of the employees are military veterans. They continue to hold certain core values from their military days, which they integrate into their work when they are onsite. Company A military veteran employees hold in high regard face-to-face interactions with peers and the sense of belonging to a closely-knit community. Nevertheless, certain employees voiced concerns regarding work-life equilibrium within the fully onsite paradigm. One individual brought attention to the challenge of mentally disconnecting from work due to its omnipresence, while another flagged the toll of extended commutes on personal time [3, 5, 27].

4.3 Hybrid employees

Hybrid workers at Company A facilities often expressed enthusiasm for the flexibility this setup offers. They emphasized the equilibrium between onsite and remote work as a notable advantage, affording them improved control over the interplay of their professional and personal lives. This adaptability also empowered them to navigate fluctuating project requirements while preserving a degree of independence over their schedules. These employees held in high regard the chance to harness the advantages from both realms. They found value in the face-to-face interactions and collaborative dynamics inherent to onsite presence, as well as the conducive environment remote work creates for tasks demanding deep focus. This fusion enabled them to effectively leverage their skill sets, fostering heightened job contentment and a genuine sense of accomplishment [26].

After examining several departments at Company A, the case study suggested that the hybrid workforce model functions best in departments that need a high level of collaboration and communication. This includes the engineering, maintenance, and quality control divisions. The idea of hybrid personnel has drawn a lot of interest and attention in today's dynamic workforce. Companies A has embraced the hybrid workforce model because of the rise of remote work requests and the demand for flexibility.

It is clear from past research that departments that largely rely on collaboration and communication are the ones where the hybrid workforce model works best. One staff member shared her appreciation for the flexibility afforded by the hybrid work arrangement, underscoring the improved work-life balance it creates. Company A hybrid employees also highlighted the economic savings from reduced transportation costs and a rejuvenating absence of commutes. Furthermore, the hybrid model contributed to a reduced carbon footprint, avoiding coworkers who go to the workplace while having the seasonal cold or flu and mitigating disruptions from impromptu cubicle or office interactions that could otherwise hinder or slow down productivity [26].

Yet other hybrid employees in Company A acknowledged the advantages of remote work but voiced a sense of disconnection from their team due to the absence of in-person interactions. Hybrid is a mix of both and may help those employees who need to be around people and then need to retreat for work-life balance. Personality may also play a role if someone is an extrovert. Extroverts would usually lean toward going to work and being among coworkers, while introverts would rather work from home [28]. Few Company A program managers and hybrid employees did note, however, that virtual meetings and team-building activities have effectively bridged this gap, facilitated by robust communication tools and technology literacy. Notably, those encountering difficulties with remote work were predominantly individuals less familiar with current technology that would help them stay connected no matter where they work [14, 17, 18].

The case study suggested that hybrid employees in Company A manifested remarkable adaptability and versatility compared to their counterparts who are exclusively onsite or exclusively remote. These individuals seamlessly oscillate between onsite and remote work modes seamlessly accommodating the organization's requisites and their individual preferences. As such, hybrid employees often attained a more gratifying equilibrium between work and personal life than those solely onsite or remote. This stems from their ability to embrace remote work when suitable. To optimize their efficacy and contributions toward the team's objectives, it is imperative for organizations to establish well-defined expectations and guidelines for hybrid work arrangements. According to [27], hybrid workers claim to be more productive when working hybrid than when working fully onsite or fully remote. Moreover, hybrid workers are even willing to take a small amount of a pay cut since they are not commuting to and from the office.

5. Lessons learned: adopting HR hybrid guidelines tailored to company needs

A key lesson from this case study suggests that within these departments, a blend of onsite and remote team members ushers in enhanced flexibility and quicker decision-making. Consider, for instance, an engineer working remotely collaborating seamlessly with an onsite technician, enabling real-time troubleshooting and expeditious issue resolution, thereby minimizing downtime. Moreover, adopting a hybrid workforce model in these domains can yield cost efficiencies by diminishing the demand for physical office space, curtailing operational expenditures, and optimizing equipment utilization. By adopting a hybrid schedule, Company A can benefit by having PMO remote employees in the workplace for several days during the week. According to the Office of Personnel Management (OPM) [29], hybrid schedules vary between organizations and are typically 2 days of remote work and 3 days at the workplace. By following the OPM guidelines, Company A must be aware that creating a hybrid work schedule program that combines the flexible work schedule and compressed work schedule establishments with the intention of providing unauthorized advantages to employees or agencies is not allowed [5, 12, 30].

This chapter recommends that Company A adopt a hybrid workforce on-call schedule, which can be beneficial to the company. This model proposes that the HOL workforce of Company A will have to be present at the MRO facility. The support team, which Company A has already deemed a non-essential workforce during the COVID-19 era, can take care of the administrative duties from home and come to the facility as needed. While a regular hybrid schedule consists of having to be at the facility at least 3 days a week, the hybrid on-call schedule would consist of going to the facility when necessary. The PMO support employee can be at the facility one day a week when there is not too much to do or up to four days a week if there is an uptick in work to be performed onsite. The increase in workload may be due to in-person meetings with a customer or end-user, Program Management Reviews (PMR), and Gemba walks—"a workplace walkthrough which aims to observe employees, ask about their tasks, and identify productivity gains" [31 para what is Gemba walk, 32]. Even Gemba walks are now transitioning to virtual observation using technology [32].

When Company A gives the option to PMO support workforce who can work at a facility, on the road while traveling, or at home, those PMO support employees may be more satisfied working for that organization. They would feel a sense that they are not obligated to come back to the facility forcefully just because a director or manager wants to "keep eyes on them." They understand that their productivity is being monitored and tracked but not micromanaged or accusatory. A trust compromise must be in effect between the Company A program manager and the Company A PMO support employees in which the program manager trusts them to do the work and that the PMO support employees trust that their work productivity will be monitored accordingly [33, 34].

Additionally, Company A PMO support workers fully understand that their type of work can be done remotely without the need to be tethered to a desk. Questioning the motive of why the organization wants them back onsite when they are just as productive working remotely. Company A is faced with having an empty infrastructure and having to pay minor costs to keep it as opposed to having it filled with workers and paying for the operational costs for electricity, air conditioners, or heat flow. Some of those costs are passed to the PMO remote and hybrid workers who had to upgrade their internet connection to comply with the Virtual Private Network (VPN) of the organization and pay more for electricity since they are working from home with more electronics such as laptop and monitors consuming more energy [12, 30]. Company A PMO support hybrid workers will have a mix of the decreased energy consumption benefits when they are onsite working and an increase of energy consumption when they are at home working. When considering the prospect of initiating trials with hybrid employees, it becomes crucial to factor in the potential cybersecurity vulnerabilities [14, 17]. The majority of risks mirror those impacting typical software or client-server architectures, encompassing concerns like buffer overflow, denial of service, spoofing, and similar issues. Protective measures entail the use of current operating systems, contemporary cryptographic solutions, permission frameworks, and cutting-edge authentication technologies [14, 16–18].

6. Conclusion

With the tug-of-war play that an organization is doing to bring back all the remote workers and the remote workers calling for working from home, the hybrid schedule seems to be a compromise between the two. A hybrid on-call schedule will better fit the needs of those employees who can go into the workplace because they are needed and not because they are forced to by the organization. Organizations will need to adjust to the hybrid workforce because it may start increasing job postings because it is what the employee is looking for. Hybrid on-call provides the proper work-life balance that the workforce has been looking for, and because of COVID-19, the organizations were forced to use it or would lose profit/revenue in their line of business. The MRO organization has already divided and selected who should be onsite employees and who should be remote/hybrid employees by classifying them as essential and non-essential. Essential personnel are basically their HOL workers who were required to be onsite employees during the COVID-19 era. The non-essential would be the remote/hybrid workers who had to stay and work from home. Hybrid On-Call is the best choice, which gives the freedom of selection to the employee to be onsite unless it is necessary.

Acknowledgements

The authors would like to acknowledge all the participants from Company A in this case study, especially the HOL aircraft maintenance workers and their PMO support group. This study could not have been completed without their time, attention, and willingness to talk to us.

Conflict of interests

The authors declare no conflict of interest.

Author details

Benito Gonzalez Jr.* and Sohel M. Imroz
Embry-Riddle Aeronautical University, Daytona Beach, FL, USA

*Address all correspondence to: gonzalb4@my.erau.edu

References

[1] Devara PB. All you need to know About Aviation MROs. Ramco. 2021. Available from: https://www.ramco.com/blog/aviation/all-that-you-need-to-know-about-aviation-mros

[2] Vieira DR, Loures PL. Maintenance, repair and overhaul (MRO) fundamentals and strategies: An aeronautical industry overview. International Journal of Computer Applications. 2016;**135**(12):21-29

[3] Efthymiou M, McCarthy K, Markou C, O'Connell JF. An exploratory research on blockchain in aviation: The case of maintenance, repair and overhaul (MRO) organizations. Sustainability. 2022;**14**(5):2643. DOI: 10.3390/su14052643

[4] Bureau of Labor Statistics, U.S. Department of Labor. Occupational Outlook Handbook, Aircraft and Avionics Equipment Mechanics and Technicians. 2023. Available from: https://www.bls.gov/ooh/installation-maintenance-and-repair/aircraft-and-avionics-equipment-mechanics-and-technicians.htm

[5] Hampson I, Junor A, Gregson S. Missing in action: aircraft maintenance and the recent "HRM in the airlines" literature. International Journal of Human Resources Management. 2012;**23**(12):2561-2575

[6] Dias NG, Santos LFFM, Melicio R. Aircraft maintenance professionals: Stress, pressure and fatigue. MATEC Web of Conferences. 2019;**304**:6001

[7] Electronic Code of Federal Regulations (e-CFR). Title 14 – Aeronautics and Space, Part 43 – Maintenance, Preventive Maintenance, Rebuilding, and Alteration. e-CFR. [Online]. Available from: https://www.ecfr.gov/current/title-14/part-43

[8] Electronic Code of Federal Regulations (e-CFR). Title 14 – Aeronautics and Space, Part 145 – Repair Stations. e-CFR. [Online]. Available from: https://www.ecfr.gov/current/title-14/part-145

[9] Patton MQ. Qualitative Evaluation and Research Methods. 3rd ed. Newbury Park: Sage Publications; 2002

[10] Ware J, Grantham C. Managing a remote workforce: Proven practices from successful leaders. The Work Design Collaborative. 2010;**151**:7-20

[11] Capgemini. The Future of work: From Remote to Hybrid. 2020. [Online]. Available from: https://www.capgemini.com/it-it/wp-content/uploads/sites/13/2021/03/The-Future-of-Work_Final.pdf

[12] Johnson A. The benefits and challenges of remote workforce in aviation industry. Journal of Aviation Management and Education. 2020;**2**(1):45-56

[13] Roy R, Stark R, Tracht K, Takata S, Mori M. Continuous maintenance and the future–Foundations and technological challenges. Cirp Annals. 2016;**65**(2):667-688

[14] Whitney L. How Remote Working Still Poses Security Risks for Organizations. TechRepublic. 2021. [Online]. Available from: https://www.techrepublic.com/article/how-remote-working-still-poses-security-risks-for-organizations

[15] Kamat SR, Hassan FM, Mahmood WH, Ani MF. Critical factors influencing project on effective maintenance, repair and overhaul (MRO) in aircraft aviation industry. Malaysian Journal on Composites Science & Manufacturing. 2021;**4**(1):1-10

[16] Ambrogio G, Filice L, Longo F, Padovano A. Workforce and supply chain disruption as a digital and technological innovation opportunity for resilient manufacturing systems in the COVID-19 pandemic. Computers & Industrial Engineering. 2022;**169**:108158

[17] Khan S. Towards MRO 4.0: Challenges for digitalization and mapping emerging technologies. 2023. DOI: 10.4271/EPR2023007

[18] Popovici V, Popovici AL. Remote work revolution: Current opportunities and challenges for organizations. Ovidius University Annals, Economic Science Series. 2020;**20**:468-472

[19] Tokgöz A, Bulkan S, Zaim S, Delen D, Torlak NG. Modeling airline MRO operations using a systems dynamics approach. Journal of Quality in Maintenance Engineering. 2018;**24**(3):280-310. DOI: 10.1108/JQME-05-2017-0037

[20] Cewinska J, Striker M. Managers' interference with employees' lifestyles while working remotely during COVID-19 pandemic. Sustainability. 2023;**15**:11870. DOI: 10.3390/su151511870

[21] Chandola DC, Jaiswal K, Verma S, Singh B. Aviation MRO: A comprehensive review of factors affecting productivity of Aircraft Maintenance Organization. In: 2022 Advances in Science and Engineering Technology International Conferences (ASET), 2022 Feb 21. Piscataway, New Jersey, USA: IEEE; 2022. pp. 1-7

[22] Kelly J. Digital Nomad: The New and Cool Trend of Working from Paradise—Or Anywhere in the World. Forbes. 2020. [Online]. Available from: https://www.forbes.com/sites/jackkelly/2020/09/08/digital-nomad-the-new-and-cool-trend-of-working-from-paradise-or-anywhere-in-the-world/?sh=516243704246

[23] Moin I, Harun K, Rahman N, Mohammad F. Personnel competency development for a successful digital transformation in aircraft maintenance, repair & overhaul (MRO) industry: A conceptual framework. Advances in Transportation and Logistics Research. 2019;**2**:426-432

[24] Hill J, Thomas AJ, Mason-Jones RK, El-Kateb S. The implementation of a lean six sigma framework to enhance operational performance in an MRO facility. Production & Manufacturing Research. 2018;**6**(1):26-48. DOI: 10.1080/21693277.2017.1417179

[25] Microsoft. The Next Great Disruption is Hybrid Work – Are we ready?. 2021. [Online]. Available from: https://ms-worklab.azureedge.net/files/reports/hybridWork/pdf/2021_Microsoft_WTI_Report_March.pdf

[26] Ziomek A. Motivation to work remotely in the face of organizational and cost conditions. Ekonomia i Prawo. 2023;**22**(2):399-418. DOI: 10.12775/EiP.2023.023

[27] FlexJobs. Productivity, Work-Life Balance Improves during Pandemic. 2020. Available from: https://www.flexjobs.com/blog/post/survey-productivity-balance-improve-during-pandemic-remote-work/

[28] Baer SM, Jenkins JS, Barber LK. Home is Private...Do Not Enter! Introversion and Sensitivity to Work–Home Conflict. Stress Health.

2016;**32**(4):441-445. DOI: 10.1002/smi.2628

[29] Office of Personnel Management. Comptroller General report B-179810, December 4, 1979, and 50 FLRA No. 28. 1995. Alternative Work Schedules (opm.gov)

[30] Burton A. Remote Work has Increased Steadily Since the 1960s—and it Will Likely Climb Upward for Decades, Stanford Research Finds. Fortune. 2023. Available from: https://fortune.com/2023/07/06/remote-work-increased-1960s-decades-office-technology/

[31] Safety Culture. Gemba Walk: Meaning, Process, and Examples. 2023. [Online]. Available from: https://safetyculture.com/topics/gemba-walk/

[32] Francis S. The Virtual Gemba. Products Finishing. 2020;**84**(12):24-27

[33] Permatasari CI, Yuniaristanto SW, Hisjam M. Aircraft maintenance manpower shift planning with multiple aircraft maintenance licenced. IOP Conference Series Materials Science and Engineering. 2019;**495**(1):12023. DOI: 10.1088/1757-899X/495/1/012023

[34] Smith B. Managing a remote workforce: Best practices for MRO aviation companies. International Journal of Aviation Management. 2019;**5**(2):87-98

Chapter 10

Mental Workload for Bank Advisers Due to the Use of Digital Technologies

Edith Galy and Klara Nano Hormez

Abstract

For several years now, an increasing proportion of bank advisers' work has been carried out using digital technologies. The COVID health crisis led to the development of videoconferencing meetings, and despite the end of the crisis, many appointments with customers are still offered by videoconferencing. A study of 349 bank advisers was carried out to examine the effect of the use of digital technologies on perceived mental workload as a function of some contextual and individual factors. Results show a change in the temporal and organizational workload and in the implementation of activity regulation strategies due to the use of digital technologies.

Keywords: mental workload, bank advisers, digital technologies, digital fluency, IWA model

1. Introduction

With the integration of digital tools in the workplace, the work activity has changed. Saadi Lahlou describes this change as a kind of complete reengineering of the service sector, with far-reaching and serious changes [1]. The digitization of companies was accelerated by the arrival of the COVID-19 health crisis. This acceleration in digitalization has affected all sectors, but the banking sector has undergone real upheaval more than any other has. During the March 2020 lockdown, almost 90% of employees in the banking sector were placed in teleworking, greatly altering not only the way banks operate but also customer relations. In this context, the interaction between advisers and their customers has been mediated by digital tools more largely than before. In fact, during the period of lockdown, all banking appointments were made remotely, online, using videoconferencing, email, the messaging application, and so on. This digital transformation has continued despite the end of lockdown. It is now increasingly common for customers to demand online appointments, whether by telephone call or videoconference. This creates more work for bank advisers, receiving emails all the time, expecting an immediate or very rapid response. This digitalization therefore tends to expose employees to psychosocial risks, with a higher mental workload, compared to less digitalized sectors [2].

The aim of the study presented is to understand the relationship between the use of digital tools and mental workload and how the use of digital tools affects the mental workload of a bank adviser. The literature review is composed of a first part on mental workload and a second part on digitalizing of the customer relation. Data issued of this review will allow elaborating a hypothetical model tested by a survey. Results will be treated by generalized linear models and are discussed. Finally, we will conclude and propose some recommendations in the light of results.

2. Theoretical background

2.1 Mental workload

According to [3], mental workload can be defined as cognitive demand of a task and be estimated by psychophysiological records, performance to the task, and self-reports. Leplat [4] added that this cognitive demand varied as a function of individual resources and context of task execution. Mental workload will be thus the perception of effort necessary to perform a task. Galy [5] proposes the Individual—mental Workload—Activity Model (IWA) to describe mental workload perceived by operator. This model is centered on identification of factors responsible of the mental workload allowing to categorize it. It considers three components: individual, activity, and mental workload. Individual characteristics can be affective, cognitive, social, and physiological. Thus, as a function of affective or emotional state, available resources of individual will be too more or less high to perform a task. Work activity is defined by specific characteristics that determine a first category of mental workload and intrinsic mental load, as well as by execution context. This context integrates organizational factors (work schedules, time to shift, equip composition, etc.) that influence functional state of individuals and work conditions (work rhythm, time pressure, work-family conflict, etc.) determining extraneous mental workload. Previous studies showed that two subcategories of extraneous mental workload can be distinguished: temporal mental workload and organizational mental workload [6]. Temporal workload concerns temporal aspects of work in terms of work rhythms, cadences, task interferences, or temporal constraints. Organizational load corresponds to work organization (planning, clarity of instructions, autonomy in work, etc.) and social ambience (relation with hierarchy and colleagues, job recognition, etc.). A last category of mental workload is characterized, which is the germane load. It corresponds to mental cost of adaptation strategies. Implementation of these strategies of work activity regulation allows individuals to adapt to the constraints imposed by task or context and maintain performance. Germane load depends thus on task characteristics (an easy task will mobilize little germane load because meta-cognitive processes or particular strategies will not be necessary) and individuals' characteristics (expertise to task will permit to implement easier adapted strategies; on the contrary, stereotype threat, for example, will prevent implementation of adapted strategies). Relationships between these categories of mental workload and factors of load are represented in **Figure 1**.

As a function of task characteristics and work context, intrinsic and extraneous loads will be more or less high and draw on the available resources of individuals. Remaining resources can be allocated to germane load. Temporal workload and organizational workload have opposite effects on germane load. A study conducted by Galy [6] on 616 participants showed that germane load is high when temporal aspects of external load are high and when external load due to organization and social ambiance in work is low (**Figure 2**). Organizational workload creates constraints that

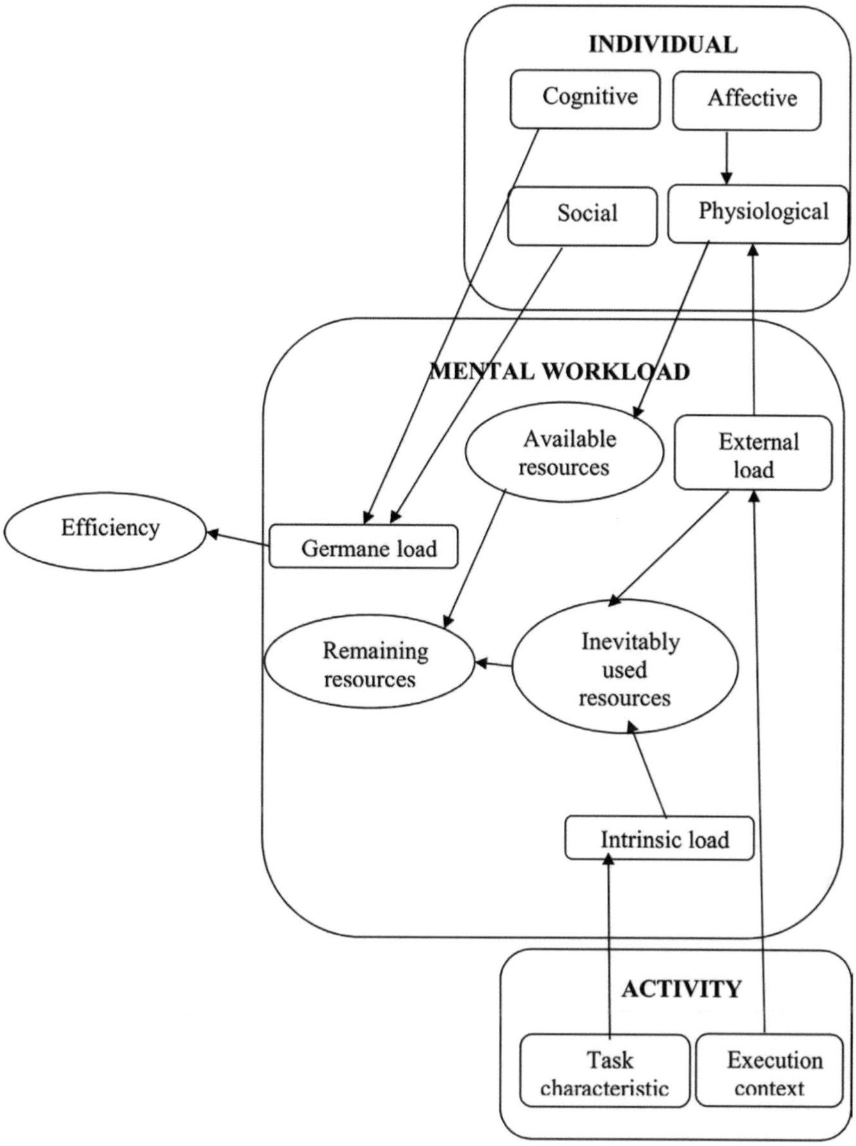

Figure 1.
Representation of IWA model.

do not allow individuals to regulate their activity, while regulatory strategies can be implemented to compensate for time constraints.

The IWA Model of mental workload has given rise to a rating scale of mental workload used in the present study [6].

2.2 Digitalizing the customer relation

Digitizing the customer relationship seems to be a matter of strategic priority because creating a lasting customer relationship is at the heart of the strategy [7]. Customers are connected to all types of digital media, computers, tablets,

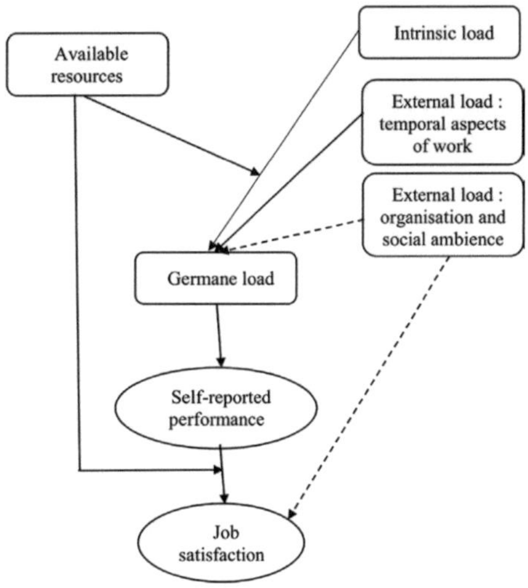

Figure 2.
Schematic representation of relationships between mental workload categories revealed by generalized additive models analyses. Full lines represent positive relationships. Dotted lines represent negative relationships.

smartphones, and so forth, and can interact 24/7. The customer therefore requires an instantaneous customer relationship. The health crisis has played a role in accelerating the digitalization of the banking sector by promoting digital contacts, whether by telephone, videoconference, or *via* their applications, to communicate with their customers. The aim is to consider customers in their own environment, that is, from their smartphone, computer, and so on. To achieve this, companies are making new resources available to customers to maintain and develop their customer relationships.

In the case of banks, we can talk about "multi-channeling," which is the integration of all communication channels in order to offer customers a harmonious experience [8]. Multi-channeling suggests the possibility for customers to contact their adviser by different channels: telephone calls, messages, emails, video-conferencing, and so forth. Multi-channeling creates a fusion of channels and therefore meets the customer's need for fluidity [9], giving them the feeling of being present in all places simultaneously [10].

The concept of meta-work is increasingly present because of digital tools. Meta-work is defined as "any work that makes work possible" [11]. It represents work added on top of the main work. This leads to an increase in activities such as organizing tasks and coordinating activities. Meta-work therefore corresponds to factors of extraneous workload and particularly organizational workload. New activities are also emerging, such as immediate exchanges and the management of permanent information flows, and employees can easily find themselves with an information overload to be processed very quickly, increasing work cadences. They have several digital tools at their disposal (computers, tablets, and mobile phones) that enable them to carry out many tasks simultaneously, but their activity is fragmented by the constant influx of new information. These elements participate in an increase of temporal mental workload.

A previous study conducted on teleconsultants highlighted the constraints, as well as the advantages, associated with the use of digital tools [12]. These tools made employees more efficient but required a learning and adaptation phase, which can be likened to an additional task. This new task consumes resources and requires voluntary effort, which can contribute to exhaustion and lead to poor working conditions [13]. Employees need to be supported and given time to assimilate [14]. Thus, in the present study, we consider digital fluency like a factor of mental workload.

These effects of digitalization are likely to be more pronounced in women than in men. Because even today, in the context of long-term planning and decision-making, women devote more mental energy to anticipating the demands of parenthood and reconciling partners' competing career needs [15, 16].

3. Hypotheses

The hypothetical model tested the interaction between individual characteristics and task characteristics to explain perceived mental workload. The details of this model are shown in **Figure 3**.

Individual characteristics were gender, digital fluency, age, and length of service. Task characteristics were task difficulty, number of videoconference appointments, and number of face-to-face appointments.

Considering the presented background, we assume that gender will determine available resources with lower resources for women than for men. Task difficulty will determine intrinsic mental workload. Intrinsic load will be higher when task difficulty will be perceived high. Number of videoconference and face-to-face appointments will determine the organizational and temporal mental workloads. Particularly, we assume that temporal workload increases with an increase of number of videoconference and face-to-face appointments and that a high number of video-conference appointments will be related to a high organizational workload. Finally, available resources, digital fluency, age, length service, and other categories of mental workload will determine germane mental workload. Thus, according to IWA model, germane load will be high when intrinsic and temporal loads will also be high and when available resources and organization load will be low. Digital fluency, age, and length of service will have a positive effect on germane workload because these factors are the reflection of an expertise that favors the implementation of regulatory strategies responsible for a high germane load.

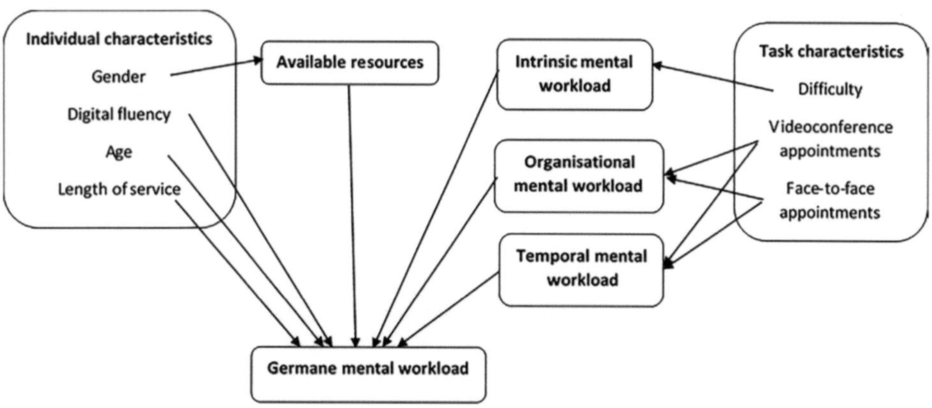

Figure 3.
Hypothetical model.

4. Methods

4.1 Participants

About 349 participants composed the final sample, all bank advisers aged between 21 and 56, with an average age of 33.7 and a median of 33. Of these, 276 were women and 73 were men. They had 10.2 years (±7.09) of length of service.

4.2 Materiel

A questionnaire was elaborated. The first part was the consent to participate in the study. The second part interrogated on the use of digital tools. It comprised questions on the frequency of face-to-face and videoconference appointments expressed as a number of appointments by day and on digital fluency (How comfortable do you think you are with the digital tools you use in your day-to-day work? By asking on an eight-degree scale from not very comfortable to very comfortable). A third part was the IWA questionnaire [5] composed of five dimensions: available resources (9 items), intrinsic mental workload (4 items), organizational mental workload (10 items), temporal mental workload (7 items), and germane mental workload (10 items). For each item, participants answered on a scale of eight degrees from strongly disagree to strongly agree. Finally, participants were asked some sociodemographic questions (gender, age, and length of service).

4.3 Procedure

The questionnaire was distributed mainly on a group dedicated to bank advisers on Facebook and was also sent to bank advisers *via* LinkedIn. The questionnaire remained available for 1 week. Participants were informed of their right to data processing anonymity and their right of withdrawal at the start of the survey. All questions were required, and participants could not move on to the next questions if they had forgotten to answer a question. Once they had answered the questions, participants could not go back. At the end, a thank-you message appeared, indicating that the participant's answers had been recorded.

5. Results

Recollected data have been treated by generalized linear models with the software Jamovi.

5.1 Descriptive analyses of mental workload dimensions

Table 1 presents mean and standard error for available resources, intrinsic load, organization load, temporal load, and germane load. With single-sample T-test, we compare the obtained means and reference values described by Galy [6] in order to determine the criticality of work situation. The reference value is 4 for available resources, organization load, and temporal load and 6 for germane load. No reference value is reported for intrinsic load.

Dimensions	Mean	Standard Error	T-test
Available resources	3.38	1.40	−8.18**
Intrinsic load	5.66	1.10	
Organization load	4.25	1.25	3.78**
Temporal load	6.88	.988	54.54**
Germane load	6.37	.873	7.85*

**indicates p<.01; ** indicates p < .001.*

Table 1.
Descriptive analyses.

For each dimension, minimal score was 1 and maximal score was 8. Results show that available resources are low and significantly lower than reference value. Organizational and temporal loads are high and significantly higher than reference value. Finally, germane load seems near to reference value (6), but it exists a significant difference between mean of germane load and reference value indicating a germane load higher than this one.

5.2 Determinants of available resources

The model explicating the most part of variance and with the best statistical powerful was composed of digital fluency, gender, and task difficulty perception (r^2 = .318; AIC = 997.772). Available resources were higher when participants were more comfortable with the use of digital tools (β = .144; $p < .01$), for men than for women (β = −.791; $p < .001$), and when task was perceived easier (β = −.328; $p < .001$).

5.3 Determinants of intrinsic mental workload

Concerning the factors explaining intrinsic workload variation, only task difficulty perception is significant (r^2 = .0627; AIC = 923.9360). Intrinsic mental workload increased when the task difficulty was perceived higher (β = .131; $p < .001$).

5.4 Determinants of organizational mental workload

The better model indicates two factors determining the organizational mental workload, digital fluency, and task difficulty perception (r^2 = .0985; AIC = 994.9030). These factors were acting in opposite directions with an increase of organizational workload when the digital fluency was low (β = −.178; $p < .001$) or when task was perceived difficult (β = .158; $p < .001$).

5.5 Determinants of temporal mental workload

Generalized linear model shows a significant effect of age, gender, task difficulty perception, and number of videoconference appointments on temporal workload (r^2 = .197; AIC = 832.123). Temporal workload is estimated higher by women than by men (β = .278; $p < .05$), when participants are older (β = .029; $p < .05$), when tasks are perceived difficult (β = .165; $p < .001$), and when the videoconference appointment number is low (β = −.049; $p < .001$).

5.6 Determinants of germane mental workload

Finally, the last analysis reveals that gender, length of service, digital fluency, task difficulty perception, available resources, and organizational workload are a significant effect of germane mental workload (r^2 = .161; AIC = 849.128). Results show that germane load is higher in women than in men (β = .249; $p < .05$), when participants are more comfortable with digital tools (β = .194; $p < .001$), when the task is perceived difficult (β = .055; $p < .05$), when available resources are high (β = .107; $p < .01$), and when organizational load is low (β = −.116; $p < .01$).

5.7 Mediation analyses

Previous generalized linear models highlight the probable mediation of available resources of the effect of task difficulty on germane load, mediation of organizational load of this same effect, and mediation of organizational load of effect of digital fluency on germane load. Analyses of mediation reveal a partial mediation of available resources on the effect of task difficulty on germane mental workload (indirect effect: z = −4.078, $p < .001$, % mediation = 46.7) and a partial mediation of organizational load on effect of task difficulty on germane load (indirect effect: z = −3.514, $p < .001$, % mediation = 44.1). Thus, the effect of task difficulty on germane load is mediated by available resources and organizational load. When the task difficulty is high, available resources are low and organizational load is high, resulting in a decrease of germane load.

5.8 Observed model

With all the obtained results, we can represent the model presented in **Figure 4**.

Globally, our results reveal direct effects of individual characteristics on germane mental workload and indirect effects of task characteristics. Three individual

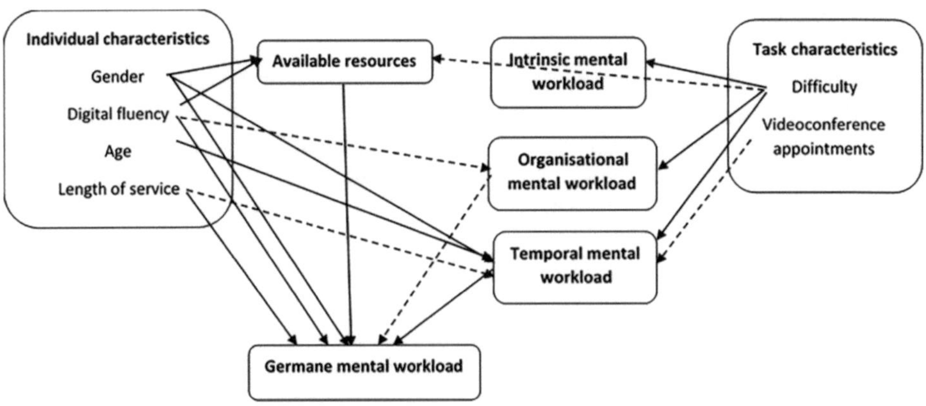

Figure 4.
Observed model. Full lines represent positive relationship and dotted lines represent negative relationship.

characteristics (gender, digital fluency, and length of service) determine germane load. Participants are able to regulate activity when they are males, comfortable with technology, and long-standing. The phenomenon is reinforced by the presence of high resources, themselves determined by gender, digital fluency, and task difficulty. Resources decrease when task difficulty increases. Task difficulty determines intrinsic mental workload as well as organizational and temporal loads. When task difficulty increases, these three categories of mental workload increase too. Concerning the appointments, only the number of videoconference appointments seems to play a part in the model with a negative relationship with temporal load indicating that a high number of videoconference appointments decreases the temporal load.

6. Discussion

The obtained model, while different from the hypothetical model, is quite close to it. It confirms that mental workload can be categorized in several dimensions because these dimensions are determined by different factors and that different categories of mental workload have asymmetric relationships. Indeed, germane load is determined by others categories of mental load (organizational and temporal loads) and available resources. These results are in agreement with previous studies [5, 6].

Data show that surveyed bank advisers experience problematic work situations in term of mental workload. Indeed, they express high organizational and temporal mental loads associated with low resources. However, this seems to be compensated by activity regulation, since the germane load is higher than the threshold value of 6. This ability to regulate activity varies according to the resources available to individuals and the organizational and temporal constraints they face. When constraints are severe, the individuals with the most difficulty are those with the fewest resources.

Two factors related to technology use seem to reduce constraints. Contrary to our expectations, the deployment of videoconferencing leads to a reduction in temporal workload, while the face-to-face appointment number has no effect on mental workload. Thus, videoconferencing appointments would reduce the need to implement regulation strategies by decreasing temporal mental load. Consequently, for our population, contrary to what Bonneau and Enel [11] report, the use of these digital tools does not appear to be at the origin of additional meta-work tasks. There are, however, inter-individual differences.

Digital fluency has a negative relationship with organizational load and a positive relationship with germane load. This result is in line with those obtained by Le Gonidec and collaborators [12], which show that when tools are mastered, they help maintain work performance. Indeed, different levels of digital fluency can be considered like different levels of expertise in technology use. Experts are able to have high efficiency in some tasks because they develop specific strategies to the task, allowing to decrease the cognitive cost of information processing. Thus, the experts are able to establish an efficacy planning and to adopt behaviors making them efficient in the task execution [17]. They elaborate schemes allowing to categorize and to aggregate elements. The more an individual is expert in a field, the more he has schemes in memory and the less the task will be cost cognitively. The experience permits experts to elaborate new schemes more quickly, and the knowledge permits them to apply the best strategies as a function of the task [18]. Thus, the implementation of strategies by experts favoring performance to the task would correspond effectively to the solicitation of germane load of IWA model. This result highlights the importance of formation to reduce mental workload of workers. In our case, the mastery of digital tools is at the root of a reduction in organizational workload and favors the implementation of more efficient regulation strategies. This interpretation is reinforced by the effect of length of service on temporal and germane loads too. High length of service is associated to a more important expertise, and the longest-serving bank advisers have the lowest temporal mental workload and the highest germane mental workload.

According to our hypotheses, gender determines available resources, as well as temporal load and germane load. They report higher temporal and germane loads despite lower resources. Work situation seems be more critical for women than for men. These differences can be explained by the fact that mental workload is added to that generated by family activities [15, 16].

7. Conclusion

Our study highlights that the use of new technologies actually represents a cognitive cost for bank advisers since poor skills in the use of new technologies increase the organizational workload and reduce available resources. However, when the tools are mastered, they can reduce the external mental load and promote the implementation of regulation strategies improving professional satisfaction and subjective performance at work [6]. Thus, these results show that the introduction of digital technologies needs to be considered in the context of overall work organization. Bank advisers' training prior to deployment seems to be essential to ensure that a work situation is not created that generates a deleterious workload with repercussions on individual work performance.

Author details

Edith Galy* and Klara Nano Hormez
Côte d'Azur University, LAPCOS, Nice, France

*Address all correspondence to: edith.galy@univ-cotedazur.fr

References

[1] Lahlou S. La cognition au travail et ses outils: débordement, révolution, distribution. Intellectica: Revue de L'Association Pour la Recherche Cognitive. 2000;**3**:7-17

[2] Castillo JM, Galy E, Thérouanne P. Technostress and its relationship with mental load in the professional context. Psychologie du Travail et des Organisations. 2023;**29**(4):197-213. DOI: 10.1016/j.pto.2023.06.001

[3] Miyake S. Multivariate workload evaluation combining physiological and subjective measures. International Journal of Psychophysiology. 2001;**40**:233-238. DOI: 10.1016/S0167-8760(00)00191-4

[4] Leplat J. Eléments pour une histoire de la notion de charge mentale. In: Jourdan M, Theureau J, editors. Charge Mentale: Notion Floue et Vrai Problème. Toulouse: Octarès; 2002

[5] Galy E. Consideration of several mental workload categories: Perspectives for elaboration of new ergonomic recommendations concerning shiftwork. Theoretical Issues in Ergonomics Science. 2017;**24**(2):176-188. DOI: 10.1080/1463922X.2017.1381777

[6] Galy E. A multidimensional scale of mental workload evaluation based on individual–workload–activity (IWA) model: Validation and relationships with job satisfaction. The Quantitative Methods for Psychology. 2020;**16**(3):240-252. DOI: 10.20982/tqmp.16.3.p240

[7] Chakor A, Belhara O. La contribution du digital au développement de la relation client: Cas de l'opérateur Orange Maroc. Revue Marocaine de Recherche en Management et Marketing. 2020;**12**(1):48-73. DOI: 10.48376/IMIST.PRSM/remarem-v12i1.19758

[8] Rigby D. The future of shopping. Harvard Business Review. 2002;**89**(12):64-75

[9] Belveaux B, Noteebaret J. Crosse canal omnicanal, la digitalisation de la relation client. Paris: Dunod; 2015

[10] Badot O, Lemoine JF. Du paradigme dichotomique de l'expérience d'achat au paradigme ubiquitaire. Recherche et Applications en Marketing. 2013;**28**(3):3-13. DOI: 10.1177/0767370113499286

[11] Bonneau C, Enel S. Caractériser le méta-travail des nomades numériques: un préalable à l'identification des compétences requises. Lien social et Politiques. 2018;**81**:138-155. DOI: 10.7202/1056308ar

[12] Le Gonidec N, Dubois C, Fenzy C, Galy E. Identification des facteurs de charge mentale de travail des conseillers en centre d'appels à l'aide d'entretiens semi-directifs. Psychologie du Travail et des Organisations. 2023;**29**(3):183-195. DOI: 10.1016/j.pto.2023.05.004

[13] Korunovska J, Spiekermann S. The effects of digitalization on human energy and fatigue: A review. ArXiv. 2019. DOI: 10.48550/arXiv.1910.01970

[14] Béguin P, Rabardel P. Concevoir pour les activités instrumentées. Revue d'intelligence artificielle. 2000;**14**(1-2):35-54

[15] Bass BC. Preparing for parenthood? Gender, aspirations, and the reproduction of labor market inequality. Gender and Society. 2015;**29**(3):362-385. DOI: 10.1177/0891243214546936

[16] Wong JS. Competing desires: How young adult couples negotiate moving for career opportunities. Gender and Society. 2017;**31**(2):171-196. DOI: 10.1177/0891243217695520

[17] Hung SY. Expert versus novice use of the executive support systems: An empirical study. Information and Management. 2003;**40**:1777-1189. DOI: 10.1016/S0378-7206(02)00003-4

[18] van Gog T, Paas FGWC, Van Merrienboer JJG. Uncovering expertise-related differences in troubleshooting performance: Combining eye movement and concurrent verbal protocol data. Applied Cognitive Psychology. 2005;**19**(2):205-221. DOI: 10.1002/acp.1112

Chapter 11

Supporting Non-Clinical Staff through the Use of Clinical Supervision

Nadjete Natchaba

Abstract

Clinical supervision is a commitment from supervisors to ensure the provision of quality services and nurture the professional growth of supervisees. Clinical supervision is made up of formative, normative, and restorative domains. While supervisors naturally focus on administrative and formative domains of clinical supervision, there needs to be a shift to focus more on clinical supervision's restorative (self-related/self-care) domain. Given the workforce crisis, the unrest in the U.S., and post-pandemic residues, organizations must formalize clinical supervision to attend to their workforce. The study to assess the effectiveness of clinical supervision among non-licensed care coordinator, findings affirmed best clinical practices in the administrative and formative domains, while clinical supervision covering the restorative domain pointed to practices that were not deemed effective. Both care coordinators' and supervisors' views aligned on experiencing clinical supervision that did not prioritized discussions of "self" in supervision. Effective clinical supervision must equally focus on discussion in the three domains of clinical supervision, and supervisors must be equipped with the right tools to adopt the best clinical supervision practices. Crisis-based clinical supervision is one of the models supervisors can apply through the Just Practice framework to lean in more on the restorative domain of clinical supervision for non-licensed staff.

Keywords: clinical supervision, workforce, restorative, crisis-based, just practice

1. Introduction

Before the COVID-19 pandemic, the United States struggled with the discord between high healthcare costs and poor health outcomes for people with behavioral needs. Social and economic conditions, workforce shortages, physical environment challenges, and healthcare system barriers are the main culprits of poor health outcomes in the United States [1]. The shortage of behavioral staff, burnout, and compassion fatigue are some of the residues of the pandemic and present a threat to achieving the triple aim, which goal is to offer better healthcare experience and health outcomes and decrease the per capita cost of Care for people with chronic behavioral health needs [2]. Data reported in June 2020 showed that over half of the adults in

America reported having unhealthy sleep hygiene, experiencing deteriorating chronic conditions, increased substance misuse, and suicide risks because of the COVID-19 pandemic [3]. Consequently, we face the reality of managing an increased and acute behavioral population mental health with a scarce and fatigued workforce. Continued attention to workforce development and readiness is critical for stabilizing the behavioral health subset of the U.S. adult population. The acknowledgment of the crucial role of the workforce in achieving the triple aim bore the fourth aim, which concentrates on improving the work-life of physicians, clinicians, and staff [4]. Clinical supervision has often been advanced as an effective intervention to support clinical staff in their role. What happens to non-licensed behavioral health staff who are not considered clinicians but work in the behavioral setting? This subset of the workforce is the front line and the largest group of behavioral health professionals, and they should be offered clinical supervision to better equip and support them in their role.

The following pages will explore delivering clinical supervision to non-licensed staff. The sections will describe the role and professional needs of the non-licensed workforce, define and discuss the three domains of clinical supervision, summarize the methodology and findings of the study, and provide recommendations for a clinical supervision model to support non-licensed staff in the behavioral health arena effectively. Specifically, we will explore the crisis-based clinical supervision model and the just practice framework to illustrate supporting non-licensed staff.

2. Clinical supervision for non-licensed workforce

2.1 Non-licensed workforce in behavioral healthcare

In behavioral healthcare, licensed staff operate as clinicians, and non-licensed staff work as care coordinators, case managers, patient navigators, etc. Their scope of work includes identifying treatment providers in the community, establishing connections to care, outreaching, arranging/brokering transportation to and from appointments, assisting with social service needs (benefits, housing, etc.), participating in hospitalization discharge planning, as well as keeping accurate documentation in the electronic health record. Non-licensed staff are essential in getting service users to clinicians to receive the necessary treatment. Non-licensed staff often engage service users who are not in the best mental health state and/or are disconnected from Care. The role requires a high level of engagement with the patient, an understanding of mental health needs, and an awareness of the staff's needs. It is necessary to broaden the definition of clinical work and not limit it to only diagnosing, assessing, and treating. We should consider including the engagement work as preliminary clinical work preparing service recipients to enter Care. Staff needs to be knowledgeable about primary mental health signs, determine the best way to build trust and rapport, decide when to discuss treatment options, make a referral, be a listening ear, or escalate to 911. Non-clinical staff are not only ill-prepared for their task, but they also do not receive clinical supervision despite experiencing some of the same stressors clinicians experience when dealing with service users. Case managers have admitted their lack of skills [5] in managing the job responsibilities. Ironically, clinicians equipped for their role receive continued support via clinical supervision, while the ill-equipped workforce receives the least structured support. It is time to shift our views of the work of non-clinical staff in behavioral health and commit to providing them with the clinical supervision licensed clinicians receive.

2.2 What is clinical supervision?

Clinical supervision (C.S.) is a continuous supportive learning process for clinicians at different career stages to help them function optimally in their duties [6]. The National Association of Social Workers also defines clinical supervision as establishing a co-learning alliance between a supervisor and a supervisee to promote the development of skills, knowledge, attitudes, and ethical standards in clinical practices [7]. Falender et al. [8] emphasized that "the effectiveness of supervision encompasses not only changes in the client outcomes but also changes in therapist's competencies (e.g., in session skills and professionalism" (p.14). Further, there is an apparent advantage to using clinical supervision to ease supervision for supervisees through experiential learning and promote evidence-based positive clinical outcomes [9]. Regardless of the clinical supervision model supervisors use, all three domains recommended in Proctor's model of clinical supervision and discussed by Kadushin and Harkness [10] should be discussed. Those domains are normative/administrative, formative/educational), and restorative/supportive.

Normative/administrative supervision involves bringing staff on board, determining their workload, evaluating performance, etc. In this role, the supervisor operates in the capacity of a manager. This domain emphasizes understanding clients' rights, standards, professional ethics, and casework management [11]. The subdomains under the normative domain are "Importance/Value of Clinical Supervision (IMV)" and "Finding time (F.T.)" [12].

Formative/educational supervision entails educating, training, sharing experiences, promoting professional growth, and helping subordinates solve problems related to their cases. The supervisor's role is equivalent to that of the teacher. Similarly, Proctor [11] and Kadushin and Harkness [9] advanced skills such as teaching, facilitating, training, sharing experiences, and personal integration as formative or educational tasks. The subdomains under the formative domain are "Improve Care/skill (IMP)" and "Reflection (REF)" [12].

Restorative/supportive supervision encompasses the supervisor playing a role similar to that of a counselor. The supervisor must help the supervisee manage job-related stress, which directly influences people's decision to leave the workplace [11]. Haarman [13] noted that adequate supervision should not be limited to reviewing notes and approving forms and reports; it should aim to foster mutuality, workers' rights, appraising, and self-monitoring [10, 11]. The subdomains under the restorative domains are "Trust/Support (T.S.)" and "Support advice/Support (SAS)" [12].

Studies have affirmed that the few advantageous aspects of supervision can be seen in the supervisory relationship, and those tend to yield the most beneficial outcomes for supervisees and clients [14, 15]. Yet, supervision literature still highlights the scarcity of training, lack of mentors, and inadequate organizational structure as roadblocks to implementing clinical supervision in social service organizations [16–18].

2.3 Methodology

This research study inspected the perceptions of care coordinators and care coordinators' supervisors of the effectiveness of clinical supervision in care coordination within the Heath Homes context in New York State. It examined the alignment of the perceptions of care coordinators and care coordinators' supervisors within each domain of clinical supervision. The study also evaluated if current clinical supervision practices mirror best practices of effective clinical supervision. A Care

Coordinator, as defined by The New York State Department of Health, is a staff member with a bachelor's degree and two years of experience supporting people with behavioral health needs. On the other hand, a supervisor is defined as a master's level clinician with experience supervising staff working directly with people with behavioral health needs. Participants in this study did not have any clinical licenses like the norm group used by Winstanley and White to set the standard scores for Allied health staff.

Participants responded to a two-part survey using an anonymous survey-based approach. The first part of the survey consisted of Manchester Clinical Supervisor Scale-26 questions using a Likert-like scale to describe respondents' experiences of clinical supervision within the three domains of clinical supervision. The MCSS-26 solely captures a supervisee's perception, in this case, the care coordinator's. However, in this study, care coordinators' supervisors answered the MCSS-26 questions as supervisors by referring to themselves as the supervision providers. It needs to be noted since the study occurred during the COVID-19 pandemic, a second part of the survey was added to include questions about clinical supervision sessions before and during the COVID-19 pandemic. The following were the research questions:

RQ1: Is the clinical supervision provided to care coordinators perceived as effective by care coordinators?

RQ2: Is the clinical supervision provided to care coordinators perceived as effective by care coordinators' supervisors?

RQ3: Is there alignment between perceptions of a care coordinator and a care coordinator supervisor of the effectiveness of clinical supervision as measured by the six subscales (value of C.S., finding time for C.S., trust, and support of C.S., support and advice of C.S., improve skills/care of C.S. and reflective of C.S.)?

RQ4: To what extent has COVID-19 impacted the clinical supervision received by care coordinators?

RQ5: To what extent has COVID-19 impacted the clinical supervision provided by care coordinators' supervisors?

RQ6: What are the perceptions of care coordinators and care coordinators supervisors on the effectiveness of providing care coordination remotely during this COVID-19 pandemic?

RQ7: Do current practices of clinician supervision in the health home mirror best practices of clinical supervision?

The study's participant target population was a range of 100–300 care coordinators and a range of 30–75 care coordinators' supervisors. This researcher elected to use a purposive sample and projected that a sample of 30 participants in each category would permit preliminary exploration of the clinical supervision phenomenon in human services. Care coordinators and care coordinators' supervisors self-selected to participate in the study. The study secured a license to gather up to 100 surveys and got 68 responses without missing information. Care coordinators completed 35 surveys, and Care coordinators' supervisors completed 33 surveys. The researcher used

Qualtrics to collect the data and preserved the anonymity of all study participants by preventing the sharing of information such as I.P. or e-mail address. IBM's Statistical Package for Social Sciences tool (SPSS) for analysis was used to input the survey data. Upon completing the survey, the researcher used descriptive statistics, the chi-square test of independence, and a series of *t*-tests to analyze the data and answer all identified research questions.

As required by the MCSS-26, the researcher gathered the following: gender, frequency of clinical supervision sessions (every week, every two weeks, monthly, 2–3 months, over three months apart), place of clinical supervision (within the workplace, away for the workplace, both), type of clinical supervision sessions (one-to-one basis, group sessions, 1:1, group, triad) and length of clinical supervision sessions (< 15 mins; 15–30 mins; 31–45 mins; 46–60 mins, >60 mins).

2.4 Findings

The findings indicated that Care coordinators and Supervisors perceived the clinical supervision received as effective based on the overall respective mean scores ($M = 84.6$; M 93.4). With the MCSS-26, the effectiveness of clinical supervision is represented by an overall mean score between 74 and 102.

Results of the study indicated that the mean scores of both Care Coordinators and Supervisors were higher than the norm group of allied health professionals ($M = 74.7$). The study's result revealed that Care coordinators' supervisors' mean scores ($M = 93.4$) are higher than care coordinators' ($M = 74.7$). A statistical difference of ($p < 0.006$) was noted in the overall mean scores of care coordinators and care coordinators' supervisors. Therefore, the null hypothesis of alignment of the perceptions of care coordinators and care coordinators' supervisors of the effectiveness of clinical supervision was not accepted. The survey also examined alignments between the Care coordinators and supervisors within the six sub-domains (Importance/Value of clinical supervision [IMV], Finding time [F.T.], Improve Care/skill [IMP], Reflection [REF], Trust/Support [T.S.]and Support advice/Support [SAS]). A statistical difference ($p < 0.03$) was noted in the supervisor advice/support subscale, hence rejecting the null hypothesis that there was an alignment of perceptions of the care coordinators and care coordinators' supervisors in the SAS subscale. The data also revealed a statistical significance (p < 0.01) in the formative domain, therefore rejecting the null hypothesis of alignment of perceptions of care coordinators and care coordinators' supervisors of clinical supervision in the formative domain. However, due to the lack of statistical significance in the normative domain and the trust/rapport subscale, the hypothesis of alignment in the perceptions of care coordinators and care coordinators' supervisors in the normative domain and T.R. subscale was accepted.

The analysis for RQ4 consisted of two paired *t*-tests to compare care coordinators' responses before and during COVID-19 on the frequency and duration of clinical supervision. Of the two paired-sample *t*-tests, the statistical significance ($p > 0.019$) was observed in the duration of clinical supervision; the data pointed to a decrease in the duration of clinical supervision during COVID-19. However, no statistical significance was noted in the frequency of clinical supervision ($p < 0.726$). The null hypothesis that COVID-19 did not impact the frequency and quality of clinical supervision was accepted due to the lack of statistical significance ($p > .726$, $p > 0.290$). Similarly, for RQ5, two paired *t*-tests were used to compare care coordinators' supervisors' responses before and during COVID-19 on the frequency, duration, and satisfaction with clinical supervision sessions. The two paired sample *t*-tests yielded a statistical significance ($p < 0.022$) in the duration of clinical supervision sessions. In contrast, no statistical significance was revealed in the frequency of clinical supervision ($p > 0.666$) and the satisfaction with clinical supervision provided ($p > 0.148$). The paired sample *t*-test with statistical significance ($p < 0.022$) permitted the null hypothesis that COVID-19 impacted the duration of clinical supervision sessions not to be accepted. Clinical supervision sessions duration decreased during COVID-19. The null hypothesis that COVID-19 did not impact the frequency of clinical supervision and satisfaction with clinical supervision was accepted due to the lack of statistical significance ($p > .666$; $p > 0.148$).

Although the study did not seek an alignment of the perceptions of care coordinators and care coordinators' supervisors on the effectiveness of the provision of remote care coordination during COVID-19, it was interesting to look at the comparative responses. Overall, there was a lower percentage of care coordinators (37%) and Care coordinators' supervisors (45%) who perceived the provision of remote care coordination as effective. Further findings revealed that 9% of care coordinators, compared to 6% of care coordinators' supervisors, perceived remote care coordination as not effective.

Finally, the researcher used mean scores to determine if current practices of clinician supervision in the health home reflect best practices of clinical supervision. The mean scores in the restorative (36.1) and formative domains (25.0), trust rapport, supervisor advice/support (17.8), improved skills/care (14.2), and reflection (10.7) subscales pointed to the prevalence of best clinical supervision practices. However, the mean score of care coordinators in the normative domain (23.5) was lower than the norm group (24.1), which warrants further analysis. Care coordinators scored lower (13.1) than the norm group (15.1)in the importance/value (IMV) of clinical supervision but scored higher (10.4) on the finding time (FT) subscales compared to the norm group (8.4). The score on IVM attested that care coordinators did not see much value in clinical supervision sessions. The score on the FT subscale signals that care coordinators struggle to find time to engage in clinical supervision sessions.

Additional results showed that while clinical supervision practices in care coordination mirror best practices in the formative and restorative domains, only 22% of care coordinators reported receiving weekly supervision compared to 54% of the care coordinators who admitted to receiving monthly clinical supervision; 82% of care coordinators noted that clinical supervision sessions were between 30 to 60 minutes in length. The data indicated that clinical supervision was provided consistently and for the recommended duration. Related to the topic discussed in clinical supervision, care coordinators ranked patient care and documentation as 1st the 2nd most frequently covered topics in supervision. The primary goal of supervision is to prepare supervisees to offer Care to impact client outcomes effectively [8], and the study's findings affirmed that client care remains the focus of clinical supervision sessions. On the contrary, current practices in clinical supervision in the restorative domain did not reflect the best practices of clinical supervision. Findings revealed that the topic of self-related was classified as the third or fourth topic discussed in supervision. Clinical supervision endorses that much more attention be given to the supervisee than to documentation.

Supportive/restorative supervision is vital in helping staff handle job-related stress and trauma in managing clients' crises [10, 11]. Skills development is another discussion topic that fits under the category of self-related in the formative domain; clinical supervision sessions are intended to teach supervisees skills to improve client care. When topics around self-related are seldomly discussed, it may highlight that clinical supervision sessions are not focused enough on addressing staff competency and skills development. Findings indicated that discussion on the topic of self-related was rated as 3rd most frequently discussed topic in supervision by both care coordinators and care coordinators' supervisors. This finding does not mirror best practices of clinical supervision, as existing literature notes that proper supervision does not only involve reviewing notes and approving forms and reports [13]. Supervisees view supervisors who show empathy, understand the importance of an honest relationship with the supervisee, and demonstrate a commitment to the supervision process as "best" supervisors [13]. Further, it is known that the degree to which the supervisee feels supported by the supervisor impacts the supervisee's perceptions of effective supervision [12]. Discussions related to self should adequately help address supervisees' needs and make them feel supported.

It is alarming to see that discussions around documentation were more frequent than discussions of self-related/self-care, such as managing job-related stress before the COVID-19 pandemic, and this pattern did not change during this COVID-19 pandemic. It behooves the community to propose a supervision model that provides a simplistic framework to help supervisors offer clinical supervision using a more balanced approach. The model discussed below was deduced from the study's findings, which mirror a few current workforce challenges.

2.5 Worker-centered clinical supervision

Post the COVID-19 pandemic, the behavioral health workforce shortage is a crisis that organizations, government, academia, etc., are committed to solving. Staff recruitment and retention are among the most discussed topics in many workgroups. Incentive programs such as healthcare worker bonuses, loan repayment, training programs, or professionalization of non-clinical staff were proposed as solutions to attracting and retaining staff in the behavioral health sector. These incentives would not solve the crisis if not coupled with support to help the workforce feel equipped to manage the day-to-day stress of their job duties. Many clinical supervision models can be used to create a supportive and co-learning environment for staff. Based on the known residues of the post-pandemic and the birth fourth aim of attending to staff work-life [4], I would like to suggest crisis-based clinical supervision, a model that requires supervisors to lean more on the restorative domain of clinical supervision.

During the post-pandemic phase, while staff servicing clients and clients are still dealing with residues of the crisis, it is valuable to engage in crisis-based supervision. The crisis-based supervision model was developed to equip staff with the right tools to manage clients' crises, a primary responsibility of behavioral health staff [19]. James and Gilliland [20] suggested that supervisors should focus on addressing burnout, vicarious trauma, and compassion fatigue that supervisees may experience due to their clinical work. The restorative domain of clinical supervision strongly encourages supervisors to minimize supervisees' job-related stress and trauma [10, 11]. Supervisors should commit to learning more from supervisees about their perception of support to be emotionally equipped to engage in critical reflection about their work [21]. One model recommended to implement crisis supervision effectively is the CARE (context, action, response, and empathy) supervision model; it attempts to understand supervisees' needs related to crisis-trauma and disaster-based counseling situations (Abassary & Goodrich, 2014) [22].

The context component in this model factors in the impact elements such as time, location, and logistics in a crisis. Context affords supervisees the opportunity to detect that everyone is part of systems that intersect and touch various people differently. Vicarious trauma experiences of supervisees significantly influence supervisees' comprehension and assessment of their client's context. Safety factors for both clients and supervisees should be reviewed within the context of applicable situations. The safety assessment must address all matters, including race, gender, ethnicity, religion, sexual orientation, socioeconomic class, etc. Supervisors need to be comfortable and equipped to manage these conversations that often are seen as challenging or uncomfortable.

"Action" which follows the first component, requires supervisors to tackle any arising needs and concerns of the supervisees and assist them with coming up with an intervention to take Care of the clients. The supervisor is expected to engage in check-ins to gauge the success of the selected interventions and avail themselves to offer immediate assistance. The response component tackles the post-crisis and follow-up; supervisors should review the crisis and interventions and determine gaps in Care if applicable. The last component is empathy, which requires the supervisor to respond with compassion and empathy to the supervisee's concerns. Supervisors show empathic responses by cultivating a safe space for supervisees to engage in self-reflection around experiencing vicarious trauma; the supervisor will also underscore the critical value of self-care [22]. Empathy is presented as an element that enables emotional growth for supervisees working with clients in crisis and is considered the most vital aspect of the supervisor in engaging in the supervisory process [23].

Providing effective clinical supervision can be very challenging for supervisors without the right tools. Just Practice is a framework developed by Finn [24] to ensure that connection with others is done methodically to honor the full agency of the person with the least power in the relationship dynamic. The framework is comprised of five components: meaning, context, power, history, and possibilities. It aligns well with the CARE (context, action, response, and empathy) supervision model and the domains of clinical supervision. **Table 1** illustrates tasks supervisors can engage in to provide supervision that helps supervisees feel seen, heard, supported, and psychologically safe.

2.6 Clinical supervision in a hybrid world

During this workforce crisis, organizations need to be creative in creating flexible work environments that promote work-life balance and a supportive culture. Crisis clinical supervision can be facilitated virtually, providing the supervisor's context and supervisee's support it. Tele-supervision is the provision of clinical supervision via technology, and recently, there has been a notable increase in the use of such methods [25]. During the COVID-19 pandemic, telesupervision became many providers' primary vehicle of clinical supervision. Telesupervision is a promising approach to attain results similar to in-person supervision in situations where face-to-face contact is impossible [26–28]. Martin et al. [29] outlined the following steps for the practitioner to be effective and efficient when engaging in clinical supervision: (a) clear expectations and goals for supervision must be established; (b) there is no size fit all medium and mode of telesupervision- adjustment must be made to address the need of the supervisee appropriately; (c) embed tele-supervision in a comprehensive framework rounded in educational principles; (d) focus on the supervisory relationship; (e) formulate a plan to manage technical problems; (f) pay attention to communication by not multitasking during the supervision session; (g) rethink continuity by the supervisor making themselves more available outside of scheduled supervision time; (h) protect online security, safety, and confidentiality; (i) build in additional time and; (j) review supervision arrangements frequently.

DOI: http://dx.doi.org/10.5772/intechopen.1004408

Just practice [24]	**Clinical supervision domains and sub-domain [12]**	**Supervisory tasks**
Meaning: What assumptions are shaping one's interpretation of the situation? How are those interpretations different from one another? What is the significance of the encounter/relationship	• *Normative* • Importance/value of C.S.	*Assess supervisee's* • Past experiences with supervision • Current views on supervision • Workload to help supervisees allocate time for supervisory sessions. • Ability to be available for routine scheduled sessions
Context: How is this context shaping me as a supervisor/staff/co-worker? How are macro systems impacting my struggles? How do organizational and social contexts impact the workplace's relation, trust, and psychological safety?	*Restorative* • Trust and rapport *Formative* • Finding time	*Assess* • How do interpersonal and social contexts shape the relation in the workplace? • If context needs to be adjusted to facilitate the supervisory alliance • If the context facilitates mutual learning
Power: How do we remain mindful of our own power and power imbalances? How do our histories shape our perspectives? How are power and inequality structured in our organizations and macro systems shaped?	*Restorative* • Supervisor advice/support	*Assess* • What forms of power need to be addressed in this process • How can you use power to promote justice/belonging in the relationship? Practice Cultural humility (*consider your bias, accountability, respect, and embrace difference*). Encourage the supervisee to develop the goal of C.S. Promote self-care, self-compassion and
History: How does where we have been shaped where we are going? How do peoples' past histories and experiences shape relationship-building?	*Formative* • Reflective practice	*Create an opportunity for the supervisee to* • Learn from and about their Practice with persons served • Evaluate change over time in their practice • Assess their critical consciousness about systemic challenges affecting the people served • Reflect on conscious use of self • Practice
Possibility: What can I learn from others? How can we learn from old decisions made?	*Formative* • Improve care/skills	• Assess the supervisee's skills, needs, and learning style • Teach clinical skills • Helps supervisee with managing persons served effectively

Table 1.
Application of the just practice framework to clinical supervision domains and sub-domain.

3. Conclusion

Despite high healthcare spending, people with chronic behavioral issues do not have great health outcomes. The triple aim of improving patients' experience with healthcare systems, health outcomes, and reducing the cost per capita birthed the fourth aim, which focuses on the staff's support and development. Supporting the workforce after the pandemic is necessary to attract and retain staff. Clinical supervision is one of the interventions often used to support clinicians in effectively managing job-related stress and competencies. Of the three domains of clinical supervision (normative, formative, and restorative), the restorative domain is the least discussed yet most important in addressing self-care-related matters. Considering that non-clinical staff like clinicians deal with the same trauma and stressors in their work, it is imperative to provide this group with clinical supervision using the crisis-based CARE (Context Action Response Empathy) supervision model through the just practice framework. This model leans toward restorative supervision, emphasizing self-care, empathy, and reflection. Knowing supervisors' challenges with focusing on the restorative domain of clinical supervision, supervisors need the right tools to support their staff effectively. Supervisors can use The Just Practice framework to navigate through supervision models to include issues such as power, race, gender, religion, context, and history, which organically fall under the restorative domain of clinical supervision.

Author details

Nadjete Natchaba[†]
Silberman School of Social Work at Hunter College Bronx, New York, USA

*Address all correspondence to: natchaba@gmail.com

† The author is a licensed clinical social worker employed as chief program officer in a not-for-profit organization in New York City, New York. The author has over 20 years of professional experience providing residential and treatment services to people with behavioral health conditions and a history of homelessness. She is a faculty member at the Silberman School of Social Work, teaching a practice lab course and serving as a field advisor.

References

[1] Ridic G, Gleason S, Ridic O. Comparisons on health care systems in the United States, Germany, and Canada. Materia Sociomedica. 2012;**24**(2):112-120. DOI: 10.5455/msm.2012.24.112-120

[2] CMS. Health Homes for Enrollees with Chronic Conditions. Department of Health & Human Services: Center for Medicare & Medicaid Services; 2010

[3] Czeisler ME, Lane RI, Petrosky E, Wiley JF, Christensen A, Njaiz R, et al. Mental health, substance use, and suicidal ideation during the COVID-19 pandemic – United States, June 24-30, 2020. MMWR;**69**(32):1049-1057. DOI: 10.15585/mmwr.mm6932a1

[4] Itchhaporia D. The quadruple aim. Journal of the American College of Cardiology. 2018 Available from: https://www.acc.org/membership/sections-and-councils/cardiovascular-management-section/section-updates/2018/04/26/12/07/the-quadruple-aim

[5] Tenille J, Solomon P, Blank M. Case managers discovering what recovery means through an HIV prevention intervention. Community Mental Health Journal. 2010;**46**(5):486-493. DOI: 10.1007/s10597-010-9326-0

[6] Bernard JM, Goodyear RK. Fundamentals of Clinical Supervision. 5th ed. London, England: Pearson; 2014

[7] National Association of Social Workers. NASW Code of Ethics. Washington, DC: Author; 2008

[8] Falender C, Ellis MV, Burnes TR. Response to reactions to major contribution: Multicultural clinical supervision and benchmarks. The Counseling Psychologist. 2013;**41**(1):140-151. DOI: 10.1177/0011000012464061

[9] Milne D, Watkins. Jr, C.E. In: Milne DW, editor. Defining and Understanding Clinical Supervision: A Functional Approach. Hoboken, NJ: Wiley; 2014

[10] Kadushin A, Harkness D. Supervision in Social Work. 5th ed. Columbia: Columbia University Press; 2014

[11] Proctor B. Supervision: A cooperative exercise of accountability. In: Marken M, editor. Enabling and Ensuring: Supervision in Practice. National Bureau and Council for Education and Training in Youth and Community Work. Leicester, UK; 1986. pp. 21-34

[12] Winstanley I, White E. MCSS-26 User Manual. Manchester, UK: White Winstanley Ltd.; 2019

[13] Haarman G. Clinical Supervision: Legal, Ethical, and Risk Management. Valley, CA: Createspace Independent Publisher; 2013

[14] Tebes JK, Matlin SL, Migdole SJ, Farkas MS, Money RW, Shulman L, et al. Providing competency training through an interactional supervision approach. Research on Social Work Practice. 2011;**21**(2):190-191. DOI: 10.1177/1049731510385827

[15] Toredi S, Gaggia A, Balducci C, Sarchielli G. Reducing psychosocial risks through supervisors' development: A contribution for a brief version of the "Stress Management Competency Indicator Tool.". Science of the Total Environment. 2015:345-351. DOI: 10.1016/j.scitotenv.2015.02.082

[16] Carmago C, Millar K. Promoting supervisory practice change in public welfare: Lessons from university/agency collaborative research in four states. Child Welfare. 2012;**91**(1):101-124

[17] Chen S, Scannapieco M. The influence of job satisfaction on child welfare workers's desire to stay: An examination of the interaction effect of self-efficacy and supportive supervision. Children and Youth Services Review. 2010:482-486

[18] Barak M, Travis DT, Pyun H, Xie B. The impact of supervision on worker outcomes: A meta-analysis. Social Service Review. 2009;**83**(1):3-32

[19] McAdams CR III, Keener HJ. Preparation, action, recovery: A conceptual framework for counselor preparation and response in client crises. Journal of Counseling & Development. 2008;**86**(4):388-398. DOI: 10.1002/j.1556-6678.2008.tb00526.x

[20] James RK, Gilliland BE. Crisis Intervention Strategies. 7th ed. Pacific Grove, CA: Brooks/Cole; 2013

[21] Wachter CA, Minton CAB, Clemens EV. Crisis-specific peer supervision of school counselors: The P-SAEF model. Journal of Professional Counseling: Practice, Theory & Research. 2008;**36**(2):13-24

[22] Abassary C, Goodrich KM. Attending to crisis-based supervision for counselors: The care model of crisis-based supervision. The Clinical Supervisor. 2014;**33**(1):63-81. DOI: 10.1080/073225223.2014.918006

[23] Brockhouse R, Msetfi RM, Cohen K, Joseph S. Vicarious exposure to trauma and growth in therapists: The moderating effects of sense of coherence, organizational support, and empathy. Journal of Traumatic Stress. 2011;**24**(6):735-742. DOI: 10.1002/jts.20704

[24] Finn JL. Just Practice: A Social Justice Approach to Social Work. New York: Oxford University Press; 2021

[25] Brandoff R, Lombardi R. Miles apart: Two art therapists' experience of distance supervision, art therapy. Journal of the American Art Therapy Association. 2012;**29**(2):93-96. DOI: 10.1080/07421656.2012.683729

[26] Milne D, Aylott H, Fitzpatrick H, Ellis MV. How does clinical supervision work? Using a "best evidence synthesis" approach to construct a basis model of supervision. The Clinical Supervisor. 2008;**27**(2):170-190. DOI: 10.1080/07325220802487915

[27] McColgan K, Rice C. An online training resource for clinical supervision. Nursing Standards. 2012;**26**(24):35-39

[28] Rousmaniere T, Abbass A, Frederickson J. New developments in technology assisted supervision and training: A practical overview. Journal of Clinical Psychology. 2014;**70**(11):1082-1093

[29] Martin P, Kumar S, Lizarondo L, Tyack Z. Factors influencing the quality of clinical supervision of occupational therapists in one Australian state. Australian Occupational Therapist Journal. 2016;**63**(5):338-346. DOI: 10.1111/1440-1630.12314

Section 3

Diversity and Immigration Trends

Chapter 12

Readiness to Manage More Diversity and Inclusion to Gain Competitive Advantage in Changing Landscape of the Workplace

Ume Rubaca

Abstract

The increasing globalization of the world is bringing forward the research agenda that could help the top management to effectively deal with the more diverse workforce. Diversity brings potential competitive advantage and, at the same time, impedes challenges to equality and inclusion; however, its benefits are not ignorable. Therefore, a committed top management that is equipped enough to deal with a more diverse workforce in alignment with human resource management is a way forward to face the upcoming challenges that range from recruitment, retention, and performance management to downsizing in tomorrow's workplace. This chapter covers the topic through the following two lenses: What does top management need to carry forward to deal with the upcoming challenges? What do human resource managers need to do in attracting, retaining, and developing a diverse workforce? We will continue through in-depth, open-ended interviews with 14-panel experts to dig down the topic and, thus, refine a roadmap to accomplish organizational goals.

Keywords: diversity, inclusion, top management, human resource management, globalization, digital economy, competitive advantage, strategic intelligence

1. Introduction

Today's knowledge-based economy is dependent on strategic management of human resources and, in this way, on human capital, skills, knowledge, intellect and potential [1]. An organization's sustainable competitive advantage and innovative progress depend on its assets, mainly human capital, which is largely comprised of the human skills of its workforce and management [2]. Human resources are the most complicated and unique resources to be assessed and researched as compared to tangible and financial resources [3]. In recent years, the focus of top management has been switched to human resources due to their significant role and overall share of the firm's assets to gain a competitive advantage. In short, human resources are a cohesive collection of education, knowledge, skills, cultural values, and experience that are related to organizational efficiency. However, the game of human resource management has become ever more challenging due to globalization, digital transformation, political changes, income inequality, and job rotation, which have evolved quite steadily [4]. Alongside job restructuring, hybrid business models, environmental focus, global climate issues, diversity, inclusion, and justice perception have shifted traditional human resource management's reactive responses to proactive strategies [5]. A successful business relies on market competition, finances, and interrelationships among its stakeholders, where stakeholders dominate in defining its destiny. Therefore, the workforce employed by a successful business has an enormous impact on its survival, which brings human-centric ethos as the mainstream challenge for HR. The over-reliance of a business on the human dimension demands the loop of all aspects to devise business strategies apart from business metrics, statistics, goals, profit, and loss [6, 7].

The increasing globalization of the world is bringing forward the research agenda to help the top management effectively deal with the more diverse workforce. Diversity brings potential competitive advantage and, at the same time, impediments challenges to inclusion [8]. Its benefits are not ignorable; therefore, committed top management that is equipped enough to deal with a more diverse workforce in alignment with human resource management is a way forward to face the upcoming challenges from the perspective of recruitment, retention, and performance management in a changing workplace [9]. The changing demographics of the existing workforce have become a global challenge due to the dramatic shift to diversity. The diverse workforce differs visibly or invisibly in many ways such as color, gender, marital status, age, culture, ethnicity, sexual orientation, and religion [10]. Diversity brings about several issues despite competitive advantage, which puts an extra responsibility on the management to manage them at the workplace [11]. It starts from recruitment and selection to job performance and retention. Workforce diversity enjoys a remarkable position due to its benefits for organizational decision-making and the progress through innovation it brings [12]. In this regard, the literature highlights the prominent role of human resource management in managing a diverse workforce and puts this responsibility on HR managers to devise such strategies and policies that cater for the needs of the diverse workforce without compromising a firm's performance. Diversity management is distinct from Equal Employment Opportunity (EEO) and Affirmative Action (AA), being a positive approach towards individual differences and harnessing their true potential for mutual gains solely based on business motives. In short, it is about acknowledging individual differences [13, 14].

Western countries like New Zealand, Australia and EU countries hold the most prominent diverse workforce due to an enormous number of migrants having diverse cultural backgrounds, which has become a significant thread of Western economies [15]. However, a diverse workforce neither brings quality in managerial decisions nor competitive advantage. This puts the responsibility on management to take necessary initiatives for inclusion by actively managing and valuing diversity. It demands people-centred policies and strategic thinking in integration with effective HRM strategies [16].

In recent years, the uncertain work context, political and economic crises, pandemics and wars have become the question mark of HR practices and, at the same time, posing challenges for business owners/managers regarding business survival and performance [17]. Nevertheless, organizations take proactive measures rather than becoming passive recipients of surprises that come along with uncertainty.

These issues become more pressing when it comes to the human resource management of the organization. The globalized world which is interconnected too is vulnerable to the unpredicted scenarios of workplace challenges and its changing landscape [18]. The discussion entails that although the workplace has been facing a constant change since then, the role of HRM is also unfolding contextually. In a similar vein, literature on HRM is exceptionally bundled with a long list of variables that play a crucial role in the strategic management of human resources. However, contextual and cultural differences sometimes bring unforeseen challenges and demand practitioners to take necessary actions to bridge the gap between theory and practice. Therefore, the main motive of the current study was to identify the factors that can assist top management and human resource managers in dealing with unanticipated difficulties associated with changing workplace. At the same time, the study intends to provide a practical solution to what is achievable and more workable while dealing with known and unknown challenges by making swift decisions. In this way, predicting what could be done with existing tools for the unpredictable future to remain competitive is the biggest challenge for top management; for example, the use of social media and technology in a post-COVID context has its benefits and disadvantages [19].

In short, a firm's response to a crisis or an opportunity depends on its strengths and weaknesses along with the strategic choices of its manager, which at times intensify the complexities in the decision-making process [20]. At the same time, such challenges demand managers to think out of the box with a focus on dealing with exceptional workplace threats rather than just keep doing day-to-day business [21]. Every firm, whether small or large, multinational, or local encounters challenges to some extent due to dramatic shifts in the international market, sociopolitical changes, crises, and wars. What is in control of the firms is their capacity to manage and prepare their workforce due to their reliance on them [22]. Similarly, in hard times, while adopting a low-road strategy [23] due to financial pressure amid economic crisis, firms cut costs by reducing short-term spending on training and development of their human resource [24]. However, their reliance on human capital dominates the human resource management aspect as well. The discussion sets the stage to perceive that organizations should be prepared to adapt to the changing workplace scenario by keeping the trust, commitment, performance, and motivation of their workforce high [25].

To conclude, the bar is raised on HRM practitioners to inculcate such practices that help gain a competitive advantage due to employing inimitable resources in a constantly changing work environment [26]. However, due to the prevailing vacuum in the HRM literature guidance is lacking regarding strategic choices and induction and retention of employees. Literature usually suggests three distinct HRM streams due to crises, namely natural, economic and political [17] with different sets of solutions to deal with every type of disaster, which seems impossible due to its practicality. Therefore, this study sought to provide a comprehensive set of tools to deal with expected and unexpected challenges posed by different crises by providing managers with a way forward with upcoming surprises. In a similar vein, diversity management in an ever-changing workplace is the most controversial issue that demands thought-provoking discussion regarding the ability of organizations to respond [27].

Therefore, we have tried to present an extended overview that can guide in choosing the right options among many to be multiculturally inclusive by utilizing the best potential of the worker, thus enhancing the ability to compete. To elaborate, this chapter attempts to answer two broad research questions, followed by details on data collection and methodology. The later section of this chapter includes results, discussion, and conclusion. We continue through in-depth, open-ended interviews with 14 HR panel experts to have a deep understanding of the topic and, thus, refine a roadmap to accomplish organizational goals.

1.1 Research questions and methodology

1. *What qualities/power skills are needed by top management to carry forward in the new era of changing workplaces to deal with workplace diversity?*

2. *What necessary measures should the HR managers take to make things work?*

2. Sample and data collection

We conducted open-ended, in-depth, face-to-face interviews of HR professionals and executives across Pakistan to collect qualitative data, thus employing a key informant approach. The key informant approach is advantageous to gather information from experts. In this way, we engendered an in-depth understanding by gathering extensive but relevant information [28]. We started with the pilot study with two HR professionals to ensure the appropriateness and content validity of the interview guide. Additionally, the study's advisory committee, comprising three professors in HRM agreed to the study data and methodology for collection fit to meet the study objectives.

We prepared a list of 25 workplace diversity HR experts based on the criterion that their names appeared repeatedly in the diversity management literature, involved in diversity work and consultation through public and private platforms such as communities of practice.

Out of 25, 14 experts agreed to take part in the interview after formal approval, date and time adjustments and complying with the formal arrangements. We sent an introductory email to every participant explaining the purpose and questionnaire of the study 2 weeks before the interview. The actual interviews were conducted from June to July 2023. Extensive notes were taken, and with the permission of the participants, we tape-recorded the interviews. The average time of the interview was one and a half hours.

The collected data was content analyzed manually and computer-assisted to systematically examine the content of communications, thus independently putting it together as quotations and arranging fields per topic addressed. We analyzed the responses through thematic analysis and categorized the emerging themes by their frequency. This provided quantitative support to the qualitative data [29].

2.1 Demographics

We collected demographic data on age, gender, educational background, work experience, present position, race, and ethnicity. Of the 14 participants, eight (57%) were women and six (43%) were men. All had graduate degrees, five (35%) were university professors, seven (50%) were professional HR managers of well-known international firms including Coca-Cola, ICI, Habib Bank Ltd., Siemens and Engro Corp, and two (15%) were independent HR consultants. The average age of participants was 48.21, and 12 (85%) were local, whereas 2 (15%) were foreigners with an average work experience of 29.18 years.

3. Results

The results are comprised of two sections as per the research questions. We invited two of the diversity managers to review the data from two interviews to establish its reliability. The consensus between researchers and reviewers regarding identified factors from the text ensured the credibility of the study findings. **Figure 1** summarizes the results of the thematic analysis containing a list of the factors essential for diversity management in a changing workplace.

3.1 Top management

3.1.1 Power skills

All the participants (100%) agreed that a company's financial success directly depends on its managerial practices dealing with employees as assets. The way management manages its people defines the culture and competencies of the business, leading to competitive advantage. According to experts, putting people first requires a shift in leadership style as human abilities are becoming increasingly in demand and important. In previous years, recruiters and executives remained ignorant of this fact, which will also be a component of the future workforce and a new way of thinking about leadership. Interviewee No. 6, "It's all about the human abilities of leading, empathizing, caring, organizing, and motivating, no matter what sector or organization you work in". The emphasis on human capabilities has a long-term dimension that adds to the overall sustainability of the firm. Experts endorsed the fact that business executives should hire people with abilities, competencies, teamwork, flexibility, adaptability, knowledge absorptive capacity and job resourcefulness.

Referring to Interviewee No. 5 about changing demographics: "A country's population determines its long-term economic, social and political future due to its size, composition and growth, demography is destiny, which suggests that societies face

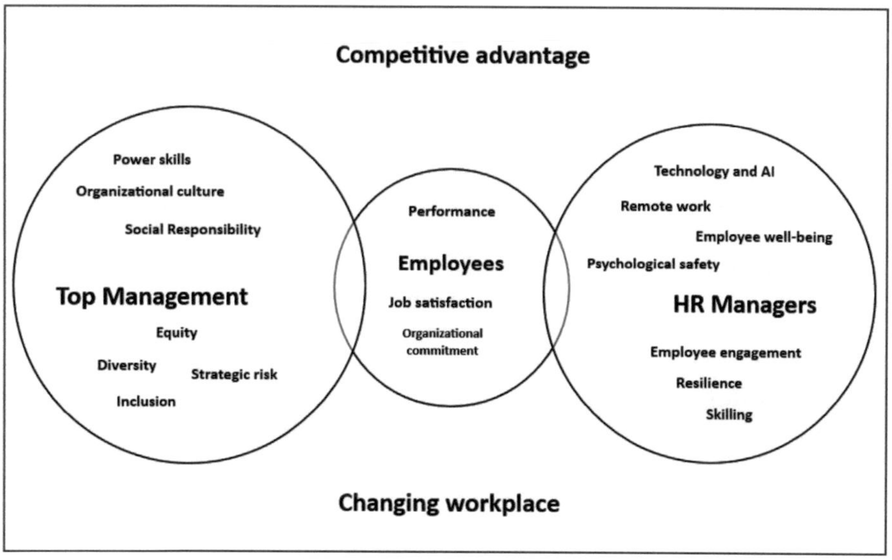

Figure 1.
Thematic analysis results.

intricate problems and opportunities shaped by demographics of their population, thus, playing a tremendous role in its societal development and economic growth". According to the opinion of nine (65%) experts, the changing demographics scenario suggests that the millennials, who are about to take on significant leadership roles in the upcoming era, shall have to deal with remote workers. The predicted challenges could be organizational commitment, productivity, and job satisfaction. The good thing about millennials is that they favor collaboration and prefer a healthy work-life balance. Managers with excellent communication and interpersonal skills could serve better by upholding trust, fostering effective mentoring, a strong organizational culture, and ensuring effective delegation and conflict resolution. Interviewee No. 3, "It is also noteworthy that active listening and empathy boost social support at the workplace leading to enhanced productivity and well-being".

The power skills identified by the HR experts for executives are as follows: optimism, learning, time management, followership, empathy, ethics, curiosity, patience, kindness, forgiveness, flexibility, integrity, and humility.

3.1.2 Organizational culture

Referring to Interviewee No. 2 (an international HR consultant): "A successful organization's culture depends on the broad set of beliefs supported by structure and strategy and in this way inculcate: mutual trust among employees and on top management's policies and procedures, upholding values with expected outcomes and rewards and expectations of top management". Eight (58%) experts supported that it is now time for organizations to concentrate on developing a culture that captures their unique personalities and distinguishes them from competitors. However, why culture, you ask? Consider culture as a bottom-up strategy that begins with the individual at its core, moves to team levels, and then reaches the entire organization. The experts advocate that culture has long been a corporate buzzword, but recent advancements in digitization have made it clear how crucial a role culture plays in the success of businesses. Beyond the fundamentals, many businesses make the error of neglecting to listen to their staff. The organic value of culture results from putting into practice and upholding the principles that a business claims to uphold and from realizing the importance of dialog in creating a culture. Ten (71%) participants favored that in a successful organization, cultural shifts typically occur in response to both internal and external changes, and most of the time, it takes tricky situations to remind both large and small businesses of just how ingrained a company's culture is. Interviewee No. 1, "We must realize that building a strong culture is a continuous process that enriches learning and development at every step rather than an attempt to hit the bullseye in one shot".

All experts agree that the effectiveness of an organization's culture depends on its capacity to give meaning to what is written down and to transform the immaterial into something. HR leaders are juggling several challenges as the world recovers from the pandemic, including the emergence of a hybrid workforce and the requirement to put employee well-being first. In hindsight, the nature of work is changing, and HR professionals need to stay on top of developments to stay competitive. The role of HR professionals is constantly changing along with the workplace. Understanding and incorporating the most recent HR trends into HR strategies helps organizations stay competitive in the labour market as we gradually transition ourselves into accepting the new challenges of the workplace. Referring to Interviewee No. 11, "A company's culture upheld its overall performance by offering a strategic competitive advantage. A strong culture steadfastly and widely nurtures increased cooperation, reduction in conflicts, effective decision making, informal control mechanism and a strong sense of identification, in short, it is an essence of what is needed by employees".

3.1.3 Social responsibility

Among 14 participants, nine (64%) were proponents of corporate social responsibility (also known as CSR) and favored the implementation of CSR strategies for business success. From a strategic angle, it can be viewed as top management's vision which helps organizations to stand out from the competition as a strategic initiative. Referring to interviewee No. 4 (HR professor), "Businesses success is bound on incorporating social responsibility in their strategies along with high-quality goods and services to gain competitive advantage in a market". Experts endorsed that strategic CSR enables organizations to do anything not as an expense but as a strategic move to improve their business for their stakeholders. Stakeholders could be the direct or indirect beneficiaries of such actions taken under top management's umbrella of strategic CSR. It is a need and demand of time that organizations should pay attention to the strategic issues related to CSR, which can have a robust association with diversity initiatives, thus playing a significant role in reducing firms' risks. Referring to interviewee No. 12 (HR consultant), "A company's responsible attitude towards society and environment makes it distinguished among competitors and open ways for collaboration. The idea of CSR is recognized by the business world, as a result, it is an important strategic initiative for sustained competitive edge and a great opportunity to attract and retain loyal customers and potential employees".

3.1.4 Diversity

All experts (100%) agreed that it should be management's ulterior motive to create and implement policies that favor disadvantaged groups (such as racial/ethnic minorities and women) to combat social inequality. Given their impact, control groups (the ones who are the direct beneficiaries of the inequality) can hinder their implementation, leading to continued inequalities, wasted resources and potential conflicts within the organization. It happens due to the perceived threat of losing control over resource distribution, change in organizational culture or values and power delegation to the new members. Therefore, it is the utmost responsibility of the top management to take care of this issue by implementing a fair merit system based on justice for all. In this regard, the control group focus should be switched to the broader and collective interests of all the stakeholders, this will help reduce the perceived threats associated with diversity initiatives. Nurturing multiculturalism with inclusion and a positive focus on underprivileged groups is also a solution that can be implemented with confidence. As one of the interviewees (No. 8) and diversity expert says, "Diversity paves the path for new contacts in new communities, expanding business networks, drawing in people who were not previously a part of the company's ecosystem. The company appeals to non-minority employees who want to work for a diverse company, as well as to women, minorities, and women in general".

3.1.5 Equity

All (100%) experts favor equity as an integral part of any business and the key to success. However, it is an equal responsibility of both HR managers and business leaders to inculcate it in organizational culture. Organizations with equity fabricated in their practices and procedures gain a competitive edge over their competitors. Active listening and paying attention to the voices of the workers help support them to be their authentic selves. In this regard, mutual efforts by HR managers, business leaders and partners can help invest and motivate equity. Ranging from supply chains to overall organizational learning and leadership programmes should be focused on equity. Five (35%) HR experts supported the notion that anonymous resumes, looking for talent away from top schools, use of technology to monitor equity in recruitment, selection, pay and performance, and recognition of HR for hiring and appraising minorities will help inculcate it.

Interviewee No. 2, "The strategic business imperatives of diversity, equity, and inclusion are fundamental to every facet of our operations, including interactions with clients, suppliers, and the communities in which we operate. Companies that prioritize DEI enjoy higher profits, increased sales, greater innovation and better employee job satisfaction, which is quite a clear business case".

3.1.6 Inclusion

All experts (100%) agreed that inclusion depends on the strategic initiatives of the firm to provide equal opportunities and access to organizational resources to marginalized groups. It is crucial to comprehend where they are getting their opposition from. Everything must be done inclusively; we must look for underrepresented or underprivileged people in an equal way to everyone else. Interviewee No. 5 "Inclusion efforts run the risk of losing priority in strategy as international leaders continue to face a tangle of problems. However, we have learned from previous crises that diversity and inclusion are essential elements of any economic strategy aimed at resilience and recovery and that a company's ability to perform well financially is correlated with its level of diversity and inclusion". However, the focus should be towards the control group's opposition to the DEI policies and the marginalized group to help them regarding perceived threats, which may affect their well-being and may prevent them from joining such an organization. Interviewee No. 1 "I feel comfortable with my team, and I feel like people listen to me, that's really about inclusion". In this regard, top management needs to focus on certain factors including personal characteristics, such as political ideology, prejudice, education, social context such as organizational environment and leadership qualities, and strategy itself such as group membership. A considerable amount of attention is required to find out factors that shape threatful attitudes towards DEI policies.

3.1.7 Strategic risk

It was a common consensus among all experts (100%) that the most important aspect of a successful business highly depends on the strategic decisions of top management regarding diversity. Management considering financial constraints, competitive markets and operational efficiencies while ignoring strategic risk (which is attributed as a misfit of business strategy with goals) may face trouble at any stage. However, this risk can be minimized with structured decision-making. In this regard, SWOT analysis, scenario planning, and balanced scorecard approaches are helpful to make structured decisions. However, big data analytics helps broaden the knowledge base by expanding the human capabilities to make optimum decisions in uncertain and complex situations. Interviewee No. 9, "In the organizational paradigm, every business takes risks. They must do it, or they won't understand the market's direction and how they must improvise to keep their ship afloat in this vast, constantly shifting ocean". Interviewee

No. 11, "A company's financial performance highly depends on its diversity initiative, it is a profitable investment with greater returns. Additionally, while interacting with like-minded individuals might help a person's social life, it can cause businesses and investors to lose a lot of money. Similarly, different viewpoints, skill sets, and life experiences of their personnel are the fuel that propels successful organizations".

3.2 HRM

3.2.1 Technology and AI

According to six experts (43%), companies have invested a lot of time in HR technology and will continue to put more effort into this red area. Today's HR should be aimed at making the systems more user-friendly, intelligent, and capable of voice or chatbot interaction, as well as increasing the number of recommendations the system makes for what you should do. They all agreed that what might create trouble for HR executives and can make them up at night are the dreadful issues related to employee mental health, economic crisis and downsizing, social unrest, and layoffs. The abrupt changes in the new normal due to switching to remote work have placed HR professionals to effectively manage and implement fair and consistent procedures from recruitment to performance management, appraisals, and layoffs. According to nine (64%) experts, HR executives need to conduct behavioral assessment tests to examine skills and cultural fits to be able to evaluate employees' job-relevant skills. This will help organizations to create an equitable and transparent process for attracting and retaining potential applicants. Not only this, but the skill-based assessment approach will provide a legal cushion to downsizing in an objective and quantifiable manner. All agreed that recent advancements in DEI initiatives are urging firms to step ahead of mere promises to actual strategic moves by cultivating each action they take in this regard to be coherent.

Interviewee No. 14, "To make employees feel safe at the workplace, provide them with needed support, and autonomy is an HR's job that leads to their workplace safety and outstanding performance. Today HR practices are benefiting from cutting-edge technologies like artificial intelligence that have resulted in a greater scope of strategic implementation. It helps process greater volumes of data, so we can say, AI has revolutionized the HR duties from talent management, recruitment, and performance appraisals".

A consensus was found among all 14 experts that HR leaders must consider the use of tech-driven HR tools such as pre-employment testing and behavioral assessment tests to create an equitable, diverse and inclusive workplace to manifest to promote DEI. This dream can come true by combining human-centric strategy with tech-powered solutions, all possible due to today's rapid digital transformation. By doing so, they will move forward with an unbiased objective procedure of talent attraction and selection. This will also help to avoid subjective job-fit criteria as data-drive insights accelerate innovation, decision-making and implementation of resilient and sustainable processes leading to operational efficiencies. These technology-driven steps help accelerate the HR professionals ride the wave of radical changes by creating procedures of equal deployment of organizational resources for internally verified talent.

3.2.2 Remote work

Interviewee No. 13, "Remote work, whether it be fully remote or a hybrid model, is here to stay as we enter a new era". Among 14 participants, four (28%) were of the view that although many businesses made technology investments to allow employees to work and collaborate remotely, there are still difficulties. As we transition into the "next normal" and beyond, HR leaders must now promote social cohesiveness and regularly update remote working policies. However, a global health crisis, social unrest, and economic downturn that abruptly shifted to remote work and resulted in a mental health crisis have changed how HR functions. The future of work must be strategically planned by HR leaders, who must shift from reaction to resilience.

Interviewee No. 5, "While the move to remote working gave professionals the freedom they needed, it also had drawbacks, including isolation, decreased teamwork, and fatigue. According to research, remote workers are working longer hours, attending more meetings, and managing more communication channels".

3.2.3 Employee well-being

All the participants emphasized the importance of employee well-being in the workplace. The evolution of employee well-being from health to what is referred to as "overall performance" is another notable change that future organizations will carry forward. Health and well-being are going to be the most important aspects of future jobs that millennials will take over. What matters most is what encourages greater productivity among individuals. Healthy employees are a huge plus for businesses due to reductions in insurance and medical costs. Job performance, which includes task and contextual performance, is directly impacted by well-being. Happiness and well-being are used synonymously. Employee well-being improves decision-making and gives workers strong interpersonal skills, more optimism, and greater resilience. They are therefore more adept at fulfilling.

Interviewee No. 10, "In the workplace, maintaining one's health is crucial for both managers and businesses as well as for specific individuals. This is due to the relationship that exists between employee satisfaction and business performance".

3.2.4 Psychological safety

All participants agreed that organizations working in a post-pandemic context are facing a complex and uncertain environment with unpredictable business opportunities. This situation is quite challenging from a strategic point of view to be able to survive and compete by relying on human capital. Similarly, it is threatful for the employees to find a candid way to contribute their knowledge with uncertain job security and job loss threats. The problem can be addressed by maintaining psychological safety. Employees perceiving positive psychological safety have a positive relation to their context which helps reduce conflicts and helps reduce burnout, stress and feelings of loneliness and detachment. Interpersonal communication strategies can play a vital role in building employee confidence and connection with the organization.

Interviewee No. 13, "However, fostering psychological safety involves more than just urging others to speak up. It also covers the employer's perspective on work-life balance. Making people feel safe allows them to focus on their task without worrying about their survival, which is the goal of great leadership".

3.2.5 Employee engagement

Interviewee No. 6, "The number-one driver of employee engagement is belonging". The work environment plays a significant role in influencing employee engagement, which in turn leads to productivity, innovative work behavior and well-being. In this regard, the human resource practices of the firm play a significant role by having a positive association with employee engagement. In the new normal, remote work has become so common it requires more engagement. Communication, diversity and inclusion and quality of work life are important determinants that can be improved through artificial intelligence (AI). Experts agree that AI can improve the work conditions and thus the perception of workers by providing a healthy work environment, fair compensation, equal use of firm resources and access to opportunities, working of human skills and capacities, assessing, and enhancing employee work engagement, thus, their well-being and productivity.

3.2.6 Resilience

Nine (64%) out of 14 experts proposed that one thing is certain as organizations fight the effects of the global pandemic: this storm has permanently altered us all. The way we do business, how we organize our workforce, and how we build cultures are all drastically changing. Organizations now need to adapt and change a variety of things to build a sustainable model that can withstand crises like this one in the future. The necessity and significance of placing people at the "heart" of digitization have become abundantly clear over the past few months. Without any test cases or reference points, organizations must respond to a variety of complex and rapidly changing needs of their most valuable business assets.

Interviewee No. 13, "The good news is that while some people appear to have higher levels of resilience than others, those who have lower levels may acquire strategies to increase their capacity to survive, thrive, and flourish in trying times. Resilience can therefore be improved".

Twelve (85%) experts highlighted that the real drivers of any change, particularly in the digital sphere, are people because they are resilient and adaptable by nature. All aspects of business operations, including value creation, are determined by them. Organizational strategies are determined by how people, or more specifically customers, engage and interact with one another. People hold the keys to any business's ability to expand and thrive, both internally and externally. Both customers and employees contribute to the creation of the parameters that map the company's trajectory and orientation. And it has been demonstrated that employees play a bigger role in this regard.

3.2.7 Skilling

Interviewee No. 9, "Key abilities obtained in an academic context are quickly becoming obsolete as our jobs change more quickly than ever. More and more companies are no longer requiring college degrees. Retraining and upskilling are more than just the newest buzzwords in learning and development and "nice to have" advantages. They are now essential for a company to succeed. Future-focused businesses predict their skill gaps and integrate them into their succession plans. They are starting to realize how beneficial internal upskilling and reskilling projects can be".

Two (14%) HR experts suggested that HR professionals need to find ways to embrace it to stay relevant in the business. Despite challenges like the difficulty in creating a sense of community and the limited access to resources, this trend is here to stay. Opportunities for skill development and reskilling have undergone a remarkable evolution, becoming a significant HR trend in recent years. The need to adjust to a constantly changing work environment has resulted in a significant shift in the emphasis on continuous learning and development when compared to previous years. Interviewee No. 8, "HR professionals have been at the forefront of driving creative skilling and reskilling programmes during the changing times". To make the process more dynamic and engaging, they are utilizing online platforms, virtual classrooms, and AI-driven learning tools. This trend will keep developing, assisting businesses that adopt it early to stay ahead of the curve. Organizations now understand the significance of building more inclusive workplaces while addressing inequalities, which has caused a noticeable shift in the trend of embracing Diversity, Equity, and Inclusion (DEI) initiatives.

4. Discussion and conclusion

In recent years, jobs and the workforce have shifted dramatically from conventional workplace and classical management strategies to technology-driven, information-based decisions [30]. Globalization, flexible work arrangements, telecommuting and hybrid business models have surprisingly taken the forefront while generating huge challenges for HR professionals to plan for the drastic changes coming [31–33]. Since everyone will have uniquely reacted to the pandemic, the meaning of diversity and inclusion and what it means to an organization have also changed. The findings of the qualitative study are compatible with previous similar studies that direct that businesses that have strong diversity and inclusion policies can navigate through the storm [34]. So, what exactly constitutes a diverse and inclusive organization in the modern era? Consider diversity in the workplace as honoring and valuing the differences among people, such as those based on age, gender, ethnicity, religion, education, and/or origin [35, 36]. On the other hand, inclusion refers to a company's efforts to treat all its employees fairly and with respect. The findings suggest that HR managers must begin creating settings that make people feel comfortable no matter where they are, it is in accordance with the recent trends in HRM research [37].

A diverse team can promote innovation, provide a variety of viewpoints and ideas, enhance worker productivity, and bring out a range of skills across the organization. As a result, an organization must promote diversity and inclusion. Habits, attitudes, and behaviors have changed somewhat because of digitization, but society is now acknowledging newer challenges, which are introducing a new set of communities. Being inclusive and diverse is increasingly important in the modern world [38].

Similarly, the findings of the study indicate that it is time for employees and organizations to be resilient, inventive, and responsive to the new world in these times when change is accelerating [39–41]. All the practices have been made possible by the pandemic and the enormous changes it has brought about. Therefore, if you have not given them much thought in the past, do so right away. Therefore, working on employee resilience by enhancing it to harness its benefits in times of crisis is an important implication and relatable to HRM, which demands to initiate it as an essential component of HR practice [42].

Employee engagement, retention, and general satisfaction have all increased because of the evolution of DEI because employees feeling inclusion display more trust in organizational diversity practices, resulting in enhanced well-being and work engagement [43, 44]. Additionally, it has improved brand recognition and helped organizations attract a diverse talent pool. By encouraging diverse hiring practices, offering unconscious bias training, and fostering an inclusive culture through ongoing education and awareness programmes, HR professionals are the ones who launch comprehensive DEI strategies. A thorough DEI strategy will assist businesses in developing workplaces that embrace diversity and spur technological advancements in the coming years [45].

Similarly, the findings highlight the role of artificial intelligence. As AI has transformed how businesses approach their HR management, it is a prominent HR trend [46–48]. By enabling tasks like automated resume screening, the introduction of chatbots for candidate interactions, and AI-driven performance evaluations, AI is increasingly transforming different areas of HR operations. It has aided HR departments in the present by streamlining operations, reducing manual errors, and improving data-driven decision-making abilities. Additionally, AI-powered tools assist HR in data analysis for long-term workforce planning. So, in the upcoming year, AI will aid businesses in gaining new efficiencies and maintaining an edge in the constantly changing HR landscape. The potential of virtual reality (VR), augmented reality (AR), and mixed reality (MR) to improve various HR operations is also being recognized by HR professionals. It can assist with conducting online job fairs, offering interactive training stimulators, and providing remote onboarding experiences, for example [49, 50].

To conclude, despite being in its initial stages, this debate holds a lot of ambitious potential. HR professionals must keep up with the most recent developments in the industry and assess how they might affect HR practices as they navigate challenges like data privacy and security. Impactful rewards and recognition programmes will become much more prominent in the coming years in the HR landscape. Organizations are starting to understand how important this is for increasing motivation and engagement. As a result, the traditional one-size-fits-all strategy has been given away.

By creating and managing a strong talent ecosystem, businesses can access a wider talent pool that includes gig workers, freelancers, and remote workers. While HR specialists use technology to speed up the hiring and management of talent, they play a critical role in fostering a culture of collaboration. Organizations must embrace partnerships with educational institutions, use data to inform decisions and foster a culture of ongoing learning and development if they hope to move in the right direction. Therefore, in the constantly shifting business environment of 2023 and beyond, organizations can create a work environment that attracts and retains top talent by utilizing the true potential of interconnected talent networks.

Author details

Ume Rubaca
COMSATS University Islamabad, Pakistan

*Address all correspondence to: lucky4being@yahoo.com

References

[1] Ricceri F. Intellectual Capital and Knowledge Management: Strategic Management of Knowledge Resources. New York: Routledge; 2008

[2] Evanschitzky H et al. Knowledge management in knowledge-intensive service networks: A strategic management approach. Management Decision. 2007;**45**(2):265-283

[3] Chowdhury S et al. Unlocking the value of artificial intelligence in human resource management through AI capability framework. Human Resource Management Review. 2023;**33**(1):100899

[4] Walmsley P. Playing the workforce generation game: Meeting the HR challenges of changing workforce expectations. Strategic HR Review. 2007;**6**(5):32-35

[5] Dutta D. Social Media and Technology Trends in HRM: Cases in Recruitment and Talent Management, in Social Media and Journalism-Trends, Connections, Implications. London, UK: IntechOpen; 2018

[6] Hewins-Maroney B, Williams E. The role of public administrators in responding to changing workforce demographics: Global challenges to preparing a diverse workforce. Public Administration Quarterly. 2013;**37**(3):456-490

[7] Farndale E et al. A Global Perspective on Diversity and Inclusion in Work Organisations. Taylor & Francis; 2015. pp. 677-687. [Online]

[8] Ivancevich JM, Gilbert JA. Diversity management: Time for a new approach. Public Personnel Management. 2000;**29**(1):75-92

[9] Newman A et al. Human resource management in times of crisis: What have we learnt from the recent pandemic? The International Journal of Human Resource Management. 2023;**34**(15):1-19

[10] Meena K, Vanka S. Developing an empirical typology of diversity-oriented human resource management practices. Journal of Management Development. 2017;**36**(7):915-929

[11] Jackson SE. Diversity in the Workplace: Human Resources Initiatives. New York: Guilford Press; 1993

[12] Herriot P, Pemberton C. Competitive Advantage through Diversity: Organizational Learning from Difference. APA PsycInfo. NE, Washington, DC: Sage Publications, Inc; 1995

[13] Green KA et al. Diversity in the workplace: Benefits, challenges, and the required managerial tools: HR022/HR022, 7/2002. Edis. 2002;**2002**(2)

[14] Flory JA et al. Increasing workplace diversity: Evidence from a recruiting experiment at a fortune 500 company. Journal of Human Resources. 2021;**56**(1):73-92

[15] Laurent A. The cultural diversity of western conceptions of management. International Studies of Management & Organization. 1983;**13**(1-2):75-96

[16] Urbancová H, Hudáková M, Fajčíková A. Diversity management as a tool of sustainability of competitive advantage. Sustainability. 2020;**12**(12):5020

[17] Ererdi C et al. International HRM in the context of uncertainty and

crisis: A systematic review of literature (2000-2018). The International Journal of Human Resource Management. 2022;**33**(12):2503-2540

[18] Wood G et al. International HRM in an Uncertain World. Taylor & Francis; 2022 [Ebooks]

[19] Holland P, Dowling P, Brewster C. HRM and the smart and dark side of technology. Asia Pacific Journal of Human Resources. 2022;**60**(1):62-78

[20] Vorst JGVD, Beulens AJ. Identifying sources of uncertainty to generate supply chain redesign strategies. International Journal of Physical Distribution & Logistics Management. 2002;**32**(6):409-430

[21] Coutts A. Good news and bad news are still news: Experimental evidence on belief updating. Experimental Economics. 2019;**22**(2):369-395

[22] Pfeffer J, Salancik G. External control of organizations—Resource dependence perspective. In: Organizational Behavior 2. California, United States: Stanford University Press; 2015. pp. 373-388

[23] Cook H, MacKenzie R, Forde C. HRM and performance: The vulnerability of soft HRM practices during recession and retrenchment. Human Resource Management Journal. 2016;**26**(4):557-571

[24] Hauff S, Alewell D, Hansen NK. HRM systems between control and commitment: Occurrence, characteristics and effects on HRM outcomes and firm performance. Human Resource Management Journal. 2014;**24**(4):424-441

[25] Wall TD, Wood SJ. The romance of human resource management and business performance, and the case for big science. Human Relations. 2005;**58**(4):429-462

[26] Wright PM, McMahan GC, McWilliams A. Human resources and sustained competitive advantage: A resource-based perspective. International Journal of Human Resource Management. 1994;**5**(2):301-326

[27] Stockdale MS, Crosby FJ. The Psychology and Management of Workplace Diversity. APA PsycInfo. Blackwell Publishing; 2004

[28] Kumar N, Stern LW, Anderson JC. Conducting interorganizational research using key informants. Academy of Management Journal. 1993;**36**(6):1633-1651

[29] Bogdan R, Biklen SK. Qualitative Research for Education. MA: Allyn & Bacon Boston; 1997

[30] Cheng MM, Hackett RD. A critical review of algorithms in HRM: Definition, theory, and practice. Human Resource Management Review. 2021;**31**(1):100698

[31] Harel GH, Tzafrir SS. HRM practices in the public and private sectors: Differences and similarities. Public Administration Quarterly. 2001;**25**(3):316-355

[32] Whicker LM, Andrews KM. HRM in the knowledge economy: Realising the potential. Asia Pacific Journal of Human Resources. 2004;**42**(2):156-165

[33] Wolfe R, Wright PM, Smart DL. Radical HRM innovation and competitive advantage: The Moneyball story. Human Resource Management: Published in Cooperation with the School of Business Administration, The University of Michigan and in Alliance with the Society of Human Resources Management. 2006;**45**(1):111-145

[34] Kossek EE, Markel KS, McHugh PP. Increasing diversity as

an HRM change strategy. Journal of Organizational Change Management. 2003;**16**(3):328-352

[35] Mathews A. Diversity: A principie of human resource management. Public Personnel Management. 1998;**27**(2):175-185

[36] Benschop Y. Pride, prejudice and performance: Relations between HRM, diversity and performance. International Journal of Human Resource Management. 2001;**12**(7):1166-1181

[37] Triana MdC et al. Sixty years of discrimination and diversity research in human resource management: A review with suggestions for future research directions. Human Resource Management. 2021;**60**(1):145-204

[38] Alcázar FM, Fernández PMR, Gardey GS. Workforce diversity in strategic human resource management models: A critical review of the literature and implications for future research. Cross Cultural Management: An International Journal. 2013;**20**(1):39-49

[39] Goodman M. Creativity and Strategic Innovation Management: Directions for Future Value in Changing Times. Taylor & Francis; 2013 [Online]

[40] Carvalho A, Areal N. Great places to work®: Resilience in times of crisis. Human Resource Management. 2016;**55**(3):479-498

[41] Dahles H, Susilowati TP. Business resilience in times of growth and crisis. Annals of Tourism Research. 2015;**51**:34-50

[42] Bardoel EA et al. Employee resilience: An emerging challenge for HRM. Asia Pacific Journal of Human Resources. 2014;**52**(3):279-297

[43] Downey SN et al. The role of diversity practices and inclusion in promoting trust and employee engagement. Journal of Applied Social Psychology. 2015;**45**(1):35-44

[44] Chandani A et al. Employee engagement: A review paper on factors affecting employee engagement. Indian Journal of Science and Technology. 2016;**9**(15):1-7

[45] Itam U, Bagali M. Diversity and inclusion management: a focus on employee engagement. In: Gender and Diversity: Concepts, Methodologies, Tools, and Applications. USA: IGI Global; 2019. pp. 1771-1788

[46] Leavy S. Gender bias in artificial intelligence: The need for diversity and gender theory in machine learning. In: Proceedings of the 1st International Workshop on Gender Equality in Software Engineering. New York, NY United States: Association for Computing Machinery; 2018

[47] Cohen T. How to leverage artificial intelligence to meet your diversity goals. Strategic HR Review. 2019;**18**(2):62-65

[48] Roche C, Wall P, Lewis D. Ethics and diversity in artificial intelligence policies, strategies and initiatives. AI and Ethics. 2022:1-21

[49] Budhwar P et al. Artificial intelligence–challenges and opportunities for international HRM: A review and research agenda. The International Journal of Human Resource Management. 2022;**33**(6):1065-1097

[50] Malik A, Srikanth N, Budhwar P. Digitisation, artificial intelligence (AI) and HRM. Human Resource Management: Strategic and International Perspectives. 2020;**88**:103

Chapter 13

Assessing the Challenges of Medical Practitioners' Retention and Its Implications in a Developing Economy

Hezekiah O. Falola and Oluwatunmise O. Ojebola

Abstract

The high turnover rate of medical personnel in Nigeria is becoming alarming as many of them are leaving the country for developed nations for better job opportunities. This has contributed to the shortage of doctors and nurses in the Nigeria health sector. The study's objective is to crystallise the challenges of health worker retention in Nigeria through a critical literature review. The study used data from previously published peer-reviewed articles published in recognised and credible scientific journals. Relevant information was obtained from these sources, conceptualised, and discussed alongside existing literature. Key findings from the research are attributed to a lack of competitive pay, state-of-the-heart medical equipment deficiency, security, and lack of political will by the government. To this end, there is a need for restructuring of the health sector in Nigeria to address issues relating to poor remuneration, infrastructure, training opportunities, and the well-being of the health workers.

Keywords: employee turnover and retention, health workers well-being, employee voice, employee recognition, OCB

1. Introduction

Nigeria is often hailed as the Giant of Africa due to its population and a strong economy. Moreover, the World Bank has acknowledged it as an emerging market [1]. Nigeria, an African country in the Gulf of Guinea currently has a population of 224,217,577 million people based on a recent report from the United Nations Department on Economics and Social Affairs [2]. The healthcare system, in Nigeria faces challenges such as the quality of public sector health services leading to health outcomes. There is a lack of targeted strategies to reach populations resulting in disparities between the rich and the poor. Insufficient availability of drugs limited human resources and managerial capabilities contribute to the quality of government healthcare services. Also, there is a need for an environment that encourages collaboration between private and public sector providers. Inadequate public funding and inefficient resource allocation further exacerbate these issues. Furthermore, there

IntechOpen

is ambiguity regarding the roles and responsibilities within the three tiers of government concerning healthcare provision and financing.

Looking back historically modern medical services in Nigeria have their origins in expeditions during the early to mid-century [3].

A severe scarcity of healthcare providers resulted from the colonial deployment of doctors and other medical specialists in the army during World War I, which brought home the necessity for indigenously trained healthcare providers. Only 10–15% of the population of Nigeria had access to contemporary healthcare facilities in 1960, according to Ref. [4] estimates. Foreign donors like WHO, UNICEF, and BTA contributed significantly to the creation and upkeep of medical facilities in Nigeria, but little was accomplished due to the Nigerian federal government's deceit and apathy [3, 5]. More so, Nigeria had several years of military rule since it gained independence in 1960 from the British and was characterised by poor economic management and a decline in public institutions which made Nigeria's health system bereft of long-term sustainable development plan characterised by impulses and deviations from what is expected from Nigerian leadership [6, 7]. Realistically, the present state of Nigeria's health system is far from the minimum standard according to WHO [8], that all members must provide its citizens with the right to enjoy the highest attainable standard of health and provide basic, affordable, and universal healthcare to her citizens according to WHO retention in developing economies through a critical review of Nigeria's Health Sector. This chapter therefore focused on the concept of health workers retention, migration of medical personnel, possible reasons for migration, strategies for mitigating medical workers migration, incentives, and work environment/infrastructure.

2. Methodology

An inductive approach and a qualitative research approach were both used for the data analysis. The findings of this investigation are based on previously released data. The major goals of the literature review are to extend the scope of potential future research and to offer a critical assessment of the state of the art now. The study follows the guidelines provided by Kitchenham [9] for carrying out a literature review. To find related articles, search terms are utilised. The primary objective of this search is to compile as much relevant research data as is practical to assist with the identified study subjects. It must be noted that only articles published in indexed scientific journals, peer-reviewed, and written in English as well as tertiary sources such as newspaper reports relevant to the subject of health workers retention, and turnover intention were considered for inclusion and exclusion criteria. It is important to highlight that the choice of the papers was based on the evaluation of the articles, information collecting, categorisation of the peer-reviewed works, and identification of empirical research.

3. Literature review

3.1 The concept of employee turnover and retention

The drive for employee turnover is associated with the unsatisfactory and ineffectiveness of policies and existing retention strategies. Retention and turnover can be described as pull-push strategies. Pull factors can be referred to as retention strategies while push factors can trigger or motivate the intention to leave according to Ref. [10].

Workers are an essential part and key to organisational existence. More so, as organisations are experiencing migration of their workforce globally especially their key employees to other organisations, the more organisations are keen on placing priority on the retention of their workforce as opined by Ref. [10].

Employee turnover (ET), as defined by Ref. [11], is the act of leaving a company for one or more reasons, including discontent and unequal access to the company's resources. ET refers to the migration of personnel away from the company. Employee retention, on the other hand, is a process whereby staff members are persuaded to remain with their organisations for an extended amount of time, according to Ref. [12]. According to Ref. [12], organisations struggling to retain their staff must deal with problems such as additional training for new hires, higher recruitment costs, employees with insufficient skills, and interruption of organisational processes.

3.2 Migration of medical practitioners

The International Council of Nurses (ICN) and the WHO published a cautionary statement regarding the global lack of medical personnel following the COVID-19 pandemic in 2020. Due to its impact on the healthcare sector of both the economy and the overall economy of the nation, which has left the healthcare system in the nation in a precarious position, the migration of medical professionals from Nigeria to advanced nations is of major concern to all stakeholders. Health worker's migration from Nigeria is a disturbing trend in a country already experiencing critically low medical practitioner numbers and extremely poor health thereby creating a vacuum for those who chose to remain and negatively impacting their job satisfaction and well-being [13].

However, it was not so before independence as extant studies assert that during the era of Dr. Nnamdi Azikiwe in 1924 only three (3) Nigerian students were schooling in the USA and all of them returned home after the completion of their education [14]. After independence, Nigerians abroad were still exhibiting patriotic fervour by returning home after completing their studies even until the 1980s. Nigerian medical doctors that schooled abroad are eager to return home because of adequate employment and a vibrant economy [14].

3.3 Reason for migration

In Nigeria, the major reason for migration is usually an economic factor as the economy was mismanaged by successive governments especially when the military governments were in power between the 1990s and 2000s. Push factors are the low standard of living, political instability, insecurity, excessive workload and stress, low income, inadequate facilities, irregular payment of allowances and salaries, inadequate funding, preferential treatment among health workers, and irregularities during recruitment to mention but a few as asserted by Refs. [15–18]. According to Ref. [19], the outflow of doctors from sub-Saharan Africa, and specifically Nigeria, started to rise alarmingly over time. The majority of immigrants and foreign-trained medical professionals in Trinidad and Tobago and South Africa between 2011 and 2015 came from Nigeria, which indicates that not all African nations are experiencing migration patterns in their health sectors or are unable to effectively handle their health workforces [8].

The WHO reports that 600 healthcare professionals emigrated from Nigeria on average each year between 2010 and 2016, with roughly 50% of those emigrants travelling to Europe, which was followed by North America and then Africa. Nigerian doctors made up 45.02% of all medical graduates from other countries (IMGs) working in the US who completed medical colleges in sub-Saharan African nations. According to reports, over 9000 medical professionals left Nigeria between 2016 and 2018 in quest of better opportunities in the USA, Canada, and the UK [20].

The Nigeria Medical Association (NMA) expressed regret in 2021 that fewer than half of the more than 80,000 doctors registered with the Medical and Dental Council of Nigeria (MDCN) were actively practising in the nation, translating to a doctor-to-population ratio of 1 between 4000 and 5000, as opposed to the WHO recommendation of 1 doctor to 600 people [21]. According to Ref. [21], the Medical and Dental Consultants Association of Nigeria (MDCAN) expressed regret over the departure of more than 100 medical professionals from 17 Nigerian tertiary health institutions during the previous 2 years. A member poll done a few months later by the association found that over 500 medical and dental professionals had left Nigeria for developed countries in the 2 years prior, with nine out of ten doctors with less than 5 years of work experience departing the country. This unfavourable trend in doctor exodus highlights a serious condition of a long-standing, unresolved issue in the Nigerian health system. The necessity of national action, however, cannot be overemphasised to reverse the terrible trend and avert the anticipated medical professional shortage in Nigeria. Little wonder, a former governor in southwest Nigeria predicted that native doctors would manage Nigeria's health if Nigeria fails to curb medical workers' brain drain [22]. He further describes the trend as an emergency and the government must disincentivize the rate at which medical personnel are migrating out of this country.

According to Ref. [23], claims that Nigeria is the most populated country in Africa, has the biggest economy in Sub-Saharan Africa and also has the continent's highest gross domestic product (GDP). This suggests that Nigeria ought to be facing a brain drain from other nations. Nigeria, the biggest oil exporter in Africa, has a history of poor financial management, including misusing donations from other countries. The mismanagement by the government has affected the development of Nigeria's strategic sectors including the health sector. Categorically, by Ref. [24], extreme poverty was classified as $2.15 per person per day and the current exchange rate is #768.267 to $1. This suggests an average of #1600.00 per day is available for a low-income earner in Nigeria bearing in mind the minimum wage of #30,000.00 without tax deducted at the end of the month. It is worth noting that this #1600.00 per day includes feeding, transportation, housing, and other expenses.

3.4 Mitigating strategies for medical workers migration—Nigeria in perspective

In the wake of the 2020 COVID-19 pandemic, the WHO and ICN warned about a global scarcity of medical workers. Nigeria has seen an increase in the number of medical practitioners leaving the country in recent years, but there are no obvious efforts to stop or mitigate the harm this trend is doing to the country's already precarious healthcare sector. Better job opportunities and living circumstances, competitive pay, and the chance for career progression in the destination country are major motivators for Nigerian health professionals to relocate to industrialised nations [25]. Nigeria has not only a severe lack of medical personnel but also a sizable share of the global disease burden [26]. Relocation is becoming an increasingly difficult issue since more and more chronic diseases like diabetes and hypertension are contributing to the spread of infectious diseases like malaria, TB, and HIV/AIDS [27]. Additionally, whereas other countries are responding to the recent COVID-19 outbreak by taking proactive steps to make up for this shortage of health personnel, Nigeria is not acting appropriately because people in control seem unconcerned [28]. The few health professionals' job happiness, general well-being, and most importantly, their desire to stay in the nation, were all negatively impacted by this gap.

Remittances, one of the most important sources of money influx into Africa over the years, today support the continent's economic development and standard of living. Nigeria is the nation in Sub-Saharan Africa that receives the greatest remittances [29, 30]. As a result, Nigeria is now a significant source of labour exports to developed nations, particularly from the healthcare sector [29]. This labour is both unskilled and, more crucially, skilled, and professional [29]. The loss of manpower that the healthcare industry experiences and the loss of income that the government invests in training these experts are the results of this ongoing movement of qualified health professionals [25]. Another result of this is that people are now more likely to recommend their fellow countrymen for medical care abroad in areas where these highly qualified doctors have migrated, resulting in a loss of income for the healthcare system [25].

It was recently revealed that Nigeria ranks fourth in the world in terms of the number of medical physicians [31] during the 17th Annual Scientific Symposium and All Fellows Conference hosted by the National Postgraduate Medical College of Nigeria in August 2023. This implies that Nigeria has training medical doctors for the advantage of other countries. However, the factors responsible for pull and push migration are presented in **Table 1**.

Issues push	Reasons for migration	Suggested mitigating strategies-pull
Disregard for medical employee voice	The medical workforce must be heard by their management whenever issues are raised. They do not care about their yearnings.	They should be given a sense of belonging by listening to them and having a harmonious relationship through communication.
Little or no concern for medical employee well-being	This posits subjective and psychological well-being as criteria for employee mental health. However, stress and burnout as a result of excessive workload on employees can trigger the intention to migrate.	The well-being of employees must be promoted and preserved as it improves performance and satisfaction.
Inadequate medical employee recognition	When employees are not intrinsically and extrinsically satisfied, they can intend to migrate.	Since recognition is a vector for motivation, it can foster job satisfaction.
Absence of organisational citizenship behaviour	Workload that results in stress and job burnout	Encourage organisational citizenship behaviours like altruism, sportsmanship, etc.
Limited/no incentive for overseas medical practitioners willing to work and relocate	Policies & laws are not in place to attract employees in this context back home or not to migrate as employees will weigh the pull options against the push options	Tax holidays can be given to employees in this regard if they relocate back home or given to those that remain to stay.
Inadequate work environment, infrastructure, and Security	Inadequate facilities, Insecurity, and porous environment.	Provision of medical infrastructure, conducive environment, and adequate security

Table 1.
Pull and push factors.

3.5 Employee voice

If the Nigerian government had been listening to the yearnings of medical workers as depicted in **Table 1**, most of the protests and strikes witnessed in the industry would have been averted [32, 33]. According to Ref. [34], a voice mechanism benefits both the employer and the employee because it has a conflictual and consensual image. Similarly, participation through voice may have a favourable impact on worker quality and efficiency. It could also distract concerns that would otherwise erupt, like in Nigeria. For this study, a collective voice would be preferred as the Nigeria health workers are unionised. According to Ref. [35], voice consists of two components. Employee participation in organisational processes for making decisions and the expression of concerns or grievances at the workplace to management are examples of this. More so because a company still heavily relies on human influence. Since the performance of a company depends on the contributions of the individuals who work there, many organisational executives consider that its personnel are its most valuable asset [36].

Two significant factors influencing employee morale in an organisation are leadership values and style [37]. For workers to be devoted and effective, organisations must encourage them to express their thoughts. To stay a devoted employee, one must feel comfortable expressing their thoughts, worries, beliefs, and statements. However, earlier research has demonstrated that there is consistently a link between the leadership style and the voice of the workforce [37].

3.6 Employee well-being

Our aim in this study is to bring constructs together capable of bringing a paradigm shift to solving or mitigating the identified problem by strongly suggesting connectedness of the effect of happiness (well-being) on productivity while devoting attention to the specific mechanisms through which happiness may foster positive work outcomes. According to Ref. [38] personal characteristics, level of perception, and cognitive variables that may trigger stress are all elements that influence employee well-being in the workplace as depicted in **Table 1**. Employee well-being is defined as the degree of satisfaction that people have with their jobs and work lives [38]. Managers in this context must create interventions intended at raising employee productivity geared toward the key drivers of employee well-being. This can be achieved through building social relationships at work, making jobs more interesting, and improving the work-life balance of health workers [39, 40].

3.7 Employee recognition

Non-recognition of the value of medical workers is having a devastating impact on Nigeria's health sector. The level at which Nigerian medical doctors and nurses are migrating calls for an emergency to be addressed [1]. Statistics show that around 11,550 Nigerian-trained doctors are practising in the UK alone, ranking Nigeria as the country with the third highest percentage of foreign medical doctors in the country [41]. Undoubtedly, the need for the Nigerian government to urgently address the issue of migration of health workers cannot be overemphasised. In the last 2 years, over 2800 workers relocated abroad excluding medical consultants and other specialist doctors. It is also sad to note that of the remaining health workers remaining in Nigeria about 74% of them intend to migrate [28]. The implication of this is that

Nigerians will have limited access to the best healthcare if nothing is done to discourage the exodus movement of her medical personnel.

One of the panaceas to this problem is the provision of an improved welfare package for healthcare workers. As noted by Ref. [42] posited that one of the reasons why medical personnel usually migrate to developed nations is attributed to poor remuneration and well-being. This is also supported by Ref. [43], who noted that when employees are not satisfied with the pay that they receive in exchange for work performed, the turnover intention will be high. In Nigeria for instance, many health workers particularly medical doctors and nurses are migrating in numbers to other countries because of a lack of competitive pay, lack of infrastructure, and insecurity, as represented in **Table 1** [44]. Meanwhile, Ref. [45] posited that if medical personnel are not given the required recognition in terms of their valuable contributions to the well-being of the citizenry and are treated unceremoniously, they tend to lose interest in such an environment, thus, job satisfaction diminishes which will give spur turnover intention.

Additionally, it is evident and almost invariably positive that financial incentives are successful, particularly when linked to behavioural and performance outputs [46]. The value of giving employees non-cash benefits, including acknowledgement and attention, which are typically very effective and efficient, is, however, sometimes overlooked. People enjoy praise and appreciation. Formally recognising someone in a group or coworkers is extremely valuable, even if you only give them an award or commendation certificate [47].

4. Organisational citizenship behaviour

Current research has confirmed that an organisation's people resources are the most important factor in determining its success. In light of this, employees' attitudes and conduct toward their work and the organisation have a significant impact on their performance [48]. For an organisation to move from an undeveloped economy to a developing economy, there must be improvements in income growth, health, life span, and the standard of living of the populace [49].

According to Ref. [50], contends that severe personnel ineptitude, malfeasance, and shortage are the root causes of Nigeria's development issues rather than a lack of natural, financial, or technological capacities. Prior studies in this context have emphasised the absence of motivation, pay increase, and opportunity for growth, research, and development as impediments to the growth of Nigeria's health sector [51, 52]. However, scant studies underscored the judicious use of human resources which is assumed to be the most important resource that controls other resources in the sector.

Specifically, the management of Nigeria's health sector is expected to align the strategic objective of the sector stakeholders with the reality on the ground by optimising the use of available manpower through OCB. OCB is defined as individual discretionary activity that, taken as a whole, supports the efficient operation of the organisation but is not explicitly or immediately recognised by the official incentive system [53]. According to Refs. [53, 54], conscientiousness, sportsmanship, civility, altruism, and civic virtue are the five categories that makeup OCB. Altruism involves aiding coworkers or staff members who are experiencing challenges at work, whereas conscientious behaviour involves going above and beyond what is required. More so, courtesy refers to having a polite manner that prevents the creation of problems at the workplace. Nevertheless, sportsmanship refers to having magnanimous behaviours that avoid too many complaints at work. Civic virtue is defined as having behaviours that demonstrate one's participation in organisational activities [53, 54].

According to research by Ref. [55] on the relationship between job stress and nurses' intention to leave their positions, it was found that nurses gave their jobs a high level of stress and that factors contributing to this stress included inadequate pay, workplace inequality, an excessive amount of work, a staffing shortage, a lack of promotion opportunities, job insecurity, and a lack of management support as illustrated in **Table 1**. However, if they could find another work, more than 35% of nurses said they would consider quitting the hospital [56].

The results of the OCB have inspired public organisations to use civic engagement to improve organisational performance [48, 57]. Public organisations must balance maintaining a quality of service that is attainable with meeting the citizens' growing demands for performance and expectations [58, 59]. Because OCB encourages individuals to go above and beyond officially defined duties, extra-role behaviour may be a crucial element in building organisational responses to such difficulties [60, 61].

5. Incentives for returning and home healthcare workers

One of the panaceas to this problem is the provision of an improved welfare package for healthcare workers. For instance, via strategy, preparation, and the execution of new solutions including both financial and non-monetary rewards for keeping and inspiring health professionals, the chronic shortage of medical professionals in Asian countries was solved. While benefits and compensation, along with the environment of work, oversight, and management, as well as learning and development opportunities, are critical factors in determining whether employees choose to stay in the health sector, previous investigations in that context have found that these factors are also important [62, 63]. This suggests that government commitment to health workers' well-being will compel them to stay in the country as described in **Table 1**.

6. Work environment, infrastructure, and security

Effective healthcare service delivery requires a favourable atmosphere referred to as a Positive Practice Environment (PPE). PPEs are needed to foster excellent and decent work that will ensure the safety and health of personnel including patients and their visitors, support quality care to patients, and improve the motivation and productivity of individuals and organisations [64]. Furthermore, PPEs are essential variables such as job and human security, access to adequate equipment, decent staff welfare packages, fair and manageable workloads, and job demand, as posited by Ref. [65]. In a related development, Ref. [66] posited that good infrastructure and equipment drive health workers' motivation and job satisfaction. The medical personnel's experience concerning the state of infrastructure and state-of-the-heart equipment to work with is nothing to write home about. According to Refs. [67, 68], they posited that employees are more likely to be engaged if they are provided with necessary support and initiatives. This implies that medical doctors and nurses in Nigeria can be encouraged to stay in the country if they have access to what is obtainable in developed countries in terms of competitive pay, equipment, security, and well-being initiatives as shown in **Table 1**.

7. Final thoughts and conclusion

Nigerian researchers' findings corroborate with other researchers in Africa findings based on this context. During this study, we observed that some few African countries were able to curb this migration problem of medical workers and even lured Nigerian medical workers to their home countries. This fact was validated recently when a stakeholder in Nigeria confirmed that countries like Sierra Leone and Gambia are now offering $3000 to $4000 to lure Nigerian doctors which is about three to four times higher than what they earn in Nigeria [69].

What is observed is that there are many causes why Nigerian medical workers are leaving Nigeria which are predominantly triggered by Nigeria's weak economy and socio-political inadequacies coupled with bad leadership. It cannot be overemphasised that the migration of health workers in Nigeria needs a holistic approach as the problem is multi-faceted. Nigeria leaders must investigate the past when our health workers having trained abroad, come back home to practice. We need a social leadership style driven by emotional and emphatic leadership components that focus on connection, collaboration, and communication. This type of leadership style is needed in this sector to enable a strong relationship and positive work with stakeholders as there is a lack of political will on the part of our leaders to curb this ugly trend.

Recent information gathered identified the root causes of this focus in Nigeria's health sector which include excessive workload, insecurity, inadequate facilities, and inadequate compensation. Despite the growing and alarming awareness of the devastating consequences of medical workers relocating to good economies, there is scant empirical and qualitative research on how leaders with a social leadership component can bring about a paradigm shift needed in the sector. Moreover, the influence of a high-power distance culture is restraining medical workers from challenging the status quo, as the Nigerian government and employers from the private sector are unworried about the worker's plight.

Author details

Hezekiah O. Falola and Oluwatunmise O. Ojebola*
Department of Business Management, Covenant University, Ota, Ogun State, Nigeria

*Address all correspondence to: oluwatunmise.ojebola@stu.cu.edu.ng

References

[1] Agba AM, Ogaboh HT, Udom IT. Why brain drain in the Nigerian health sector? Asian Journal of Applied Sciences. 2020;**8**(2):95-104

[2] United Nations Department on Economics and Social Affairs. Capacity Development Assistance for Developing Countries. 2023. Available from: https://www.un.org/development/desa/dpad/ [Accessed: August 22, 2023]

[3] Scott-Emuakpor A. The evolution of health care systems in Nigeria: Which way forward in the twenty-first century. Nigerian Medical Journal. 2010;**51**:53-65. Available from: https://www.nigeriamedj.com/text.asp?2010/51/2/53/70997

[4] Chuke PO. Nigeria. In: Saltman RB, editor. The International Handbook of Health Care Systems. New York: Greenwood Press; 1988

[5] Alonge SK. Primary health care in Nigeria: An appraisal of the effect of foreign donations. African Journal of Health, Safety and Environment. 2020;**1**(2):86-100

[6] Okonjo-Iweala N, Osafo-Kwaako P. Nigeria's Economic Reforms: Progress and Challenges. Washington, DC: The Brookings Institutions; 2007

[7] Ogaji D, Brisibe SF. The Nigerian health care system, evolution, contradictions and proposal for future debates. Port Harcourt, Medical Journal. 2015;**9**:S79-S88

[8] World Health Organization. A Dynamic Understanding of Health Worker Migration. 2021. Available from: https://www.who.int/publiccations/m/item/a-dynamic-understanding-of-health-worker-migration [Accessed: August 9, 2023]

[9] Kitchenham B. Procedures for Performing Systematic Reviews. Keele: Keele University; 2004. p. 33

[10] Okafor L, Ifekwem NE, Adeyi AO. Employee retention strategies and organizational performance in selected private universities in Ogun State Nigeria. Pacific Journal of Science and Technology. 2019;**20**(2):123-131

[11] Idowu OF. Retention strategy and Employee's turnover among academic staff of Lagos State Owned Tertiary Institutions. LASU Journal of Employment Relations & Human Resources Management. 2018;**1**(1):2018

[12] Xuecheng W, Qaisar I, Bai S. Factors affecting employee's retention: Integration of situational leadership with social exchange theory. Frontier in Psychology. 2022;**13**:872105

[13] Yakubu K, Blacklock C, Adebayo KO, Peiris D, Joshi R, Mondal S. (2023). Social networks and skilled health worker migration in Nigeria: An ego network analysis. International Journal of Health Planning Management. 2023;**38**(2):457-472. DOI: 10.1002/hpm.3595

[14] Ike S. The health workforce crisis: The brain drain scourge. Nigerian Journal of Medicine. 2007;**16**(3):204-211

[15] Adebayo O, Labiran A, Franklin Emerenini C, Omoruyi L. Health workforce for 2016-2030: Will Nigeria have enough? International Journal of Innovation Health Research. 2016;**4**(1):9-16

[16] Premium Times. LUTH deteriorating, in crisis – Report. 2018. Available from: https://www.premiumtimesng.com/health/health-news/283171-luth-deteriorating-in-crisis-report.html [Accessed: August 2023, and July 30, 2023]

[17] Abubakar DS. Unemployment among medical doctors. In: Balogun JA, editor. The Nigerian Healthcare System: Pathway to Universal and High-Quality Health Care. Nigeria: Springer Link; 2021

[18] Al Jazeera C. Nigerian Doctors Strike Over Pay and Inadequate Facilities. 2021. Available from: https://www.aljazeera.com/news/2021/8/2/nigerian-doctors-begin-strike-over-pay-inadequate-facilities [Accessed: July 30, 2023]

[19] Tankwanchi ABS, Ozden C, Vermund SH. Physician emigration from sub-Saharan Africa to the United States: Analysis of the 2011 AMA Physician Masterfile. PLoS Medicine. 2013;**10**(9):e1001513

[20] Fatunmole M. In two years, Nigeria lost nearly 9,000 doctors to the UK and others. Int. Cent. Investig. Report. 2021. Available from: https://www.icirnigeria.org/in-two-years-Nigeria-lost-nearly-20000-doctorrs-to-uk-others/ [Accessed: July 29, 2023]

[21] Onah CK, Azuogu BN, Ochie CN, Akpa CO, Okeke KC, Okpunwa AO, et al. Physician emigration from Nigeria and the associated factors: The implications to safeguarding the Nigeria health system. Human Resources for Health. 2022;**20**:85. DOI: 10.1186/s12960-022-00788-z

[22] Daily Post. Stakeholders Demand Immediate Action against Brain Drain. 2023. Available from: https://dailypost.ng/2023/07/21/brain-drain-stakeholders-demand-immediate-action/ [Accessed: August 14, 2013]

[23] Africa Business Insider. Africa Giants; The Ten Largest Economies on the Continent. 2023. Available from: https//africa.businessinsider.com/local/markets/Africa-giants-the-10-largest-economies-0n-the-continent/1w6srcq [Accessed: August 11, 2023]

[24] World Bank. Factsheet: An Adjustment of Global Poverty Lines. 2022. Available from: https://www.worldbank.org/en/news/factsheet/2022/05/02/fact-sheet-an-adjustment-to-global-poverty-lines

[25] Adebayo A, Akinyemi O. What are you doing in this country?: Emigration intentions of Nigerian doctors and their policy implications for human resource for health management. Journal of International Migration and Integration. 2022;**23**:1377-1396

[26] WHO. Achieving the Health-Related MDGs. It Takes a Workforce! 2017. Available from: https://www.who.int/hrh/workforce_mdgs/en/ [Accessed: July 22, 2023]

[27] WHO. 2017 World Health Statistics 2017: Monitoring Health for the SDGs, Sustainable Development Goals. Geneva: World Health Organization. Available from: http://apps.who.int/iris/bitstream/10665/255336/1/9789241565486-eng.pdf?ua=1 [Assessed: July 22, 2023]

[28] Daily Post. Native doctors will manage our health if Nigeria fails to curb medical workers brain drain. 2023. Available from: http:/dailypost.mg/2023/06/10/native-doctors-will-manage-our-health-if-Nigeria-fails-to-curb0medical-workers-brain-drain-Kimiko/

[29] Isiugo-Abanihe UC, IOM. Migration in Nigeria: A Country Profile 2014. 2016. Available from: https://publications.iom.

int/system/files/pdf/mp_nigeria.pdf [Accessed: August 4, 2023]

[30] KNOMAD. Migration and Remittances: Recent Developments and Outlook Migration and Development Brief 30. 2018. Available from: https://www.knomad.org/sites/default/files/2018-12/Migration%20and%20Development%20Brief%2030.Pdf [Accessed: August 12, 2023]

[31] Vanguard. Nigeria ranks 4th in world's population of medical doctors. 2023. Available from: https://www.vanguardngr.com/2023/08/nigeria-ranks-4th-in-worlds-population-of-medical-doctors [Accessed: August 11, 2023]

[32] Daily Trust. Strike Continues, the Health Ministry Hasn't Spoken to Us. 2023. Available from: https-//dailytrust.com/srike-continue-health-ministry-hasn't-spoken-to-us-resident-doctors [Accessed: August 7, 2023]

[33] Roche W. The end of new industrial relations? European Journal of Industrial Relations. 2000;**6**(3):261-282

[34] Dundon T, Wilkinson A, Marbhington M, Ackers P. The meaning and purpose of employee voice. International Journal of Human Resource Management. 2004;**15**(6):1149-1170

[35] McCabe D, Lewin D. Employee voice: A human resource management perspective. California Management Review. 1992;**34**:112-123. DOI: 10.2307/41167427

[36] Joseph S, Shetty N. An empirical study on the impact of employee voice and silence on destructive leadership and organizational culture. Asian Journal of Business Ethics. 2022;**11**(Suppl. 1):S85-S109. DOI: 10.1007/s13520-022-00155-0

[37] Oyerinde OF. Leadership style, work environment, organizational silence and institutional effectiveness of polytechnic libraries, South-West Nigeria. The International Information and Library Review. 2020;**52**(2):79-94

[38] Cignitus C, Arevalo J, Crusells J. Balanced scorecard: The key to employee wellbeing is the impact of a balanced scorecard on employee wellbeing. The case of state of Michigan-USA. The International Journal of Business Management. 2021;**9**(12):175-197

[39] Ward KC, de Jan-Emmanuel C. Global Happiness and Wellbeing Report. 2019 [Assessed: August 12, 2023]

[40] Fishbein M, Ajzen I. Belief, Attitude, Intention and Behaviour: An Introduction to Theory and Research. Reading, MA: Addison-Wesley; 1975. Available from: https://www.researchgate.net/publication/233897090 [Accessed: August 14, 2024]

[41] Premium Times. The UK Restricts Recruitment of Health Workers from Nigeria, and Other Countries. 2023. Available from: https://www.premiumtimesng.com/news/top-news/592642-uk-restricts/recruitment-of0workers-fromnigeria-other-countries.html [Accessed: August 14, 2023]

[42] Li N, Zhang L, Xiao G, Chen J, Lu Q. The relationship between workplace violence, job satisfaction and turnover intention in emergency nurses. International Emergency Nursing. 2019;**45**:50-55

[43] Falatah R, Almuqati J, Almuqati H, Altunbakti K. Linking nurses' job security to job satisfaction and turnover intention during reform and privatization: A cross-sectional survey. Journal of Nursing Management. 2021;**29**(6):1578-1586

[44] Nguyen QA, Tran AD. Job satisfaction and turnover intention

of preventive medicine workers in northern Vietnam: Is there any relationship? Health Services Insights. 2021;**14**:1178632921995172

[45] Alam A, Asim M. Relationship between job satisfaction and turnover intention. International Journal of Human Resource Studies. 2019;**9**(2):163-194

[46] De-Oliveira LB, Cavazotte F, Alan Dunzer R. The interactive effects of organizational and leadership career management support on job satisfaction and turnover intention. The International Journal of Human Resource Management. 2019;**30**(10):1583-1603

[47] Luthans F. Organizational Behaviour. 8th ed. New York: McGraw-Hill, Mosby; 2000

[48] Geus C, Ingrams A, Tummers L, Pandey S. Organizational citizenship behavior in the public sector: A systematic literature review and future research agenda. Public Administration Review. 2020;**80**:259-270. DOI: 10.1111/puar.13141

[49] Organ D. Organisational citizenship behaviour: Recent trends and developments. Annual Review of Organisational Psychology and Organisational Behaviour. 2018;**5**(1):296-306

[50] Olowookere EI. The relevance of industrial and organisational psychology to national development in Nigeria. Continental Journal of Social Sciences. 2012;**5**(2):32-38

[51] Daniel O, Ijeoma O, Benjamin U, Obinna O. Determinants of job satisfaction and retention of public sector health workers in southeast Nigeria. International Journal of Medicinal Health Development. 2016;**21**:2

[52] Ojebola O, Osibanjo O, Adeniji A, Salau O, Falola H, Atolagbe T. Organisational citizenship behaviour and its influence on employee turnover intentions in Nigeria health sector: A systematic review. In: Proceedings of INTCESS 2020—7th International Conference on Education and Social Sciences, 20-22 January 2020; Dubai (UAE): OCERINT's online e-library; 2020

[53] Organ W. Organisational Citizenship Behaviour: The Good Soldier Syndrome. Lexington, KY: Lexington Books; 1988

[54] Konovsky MA, Organ DW. Dispositional and contextual determinants of organizational citizenship behavior. Journal of Organizational Behavior. 1996;**17**(3):253-266

[55] Mosadeghrad AM. Occupational stress and turnover intention: Implications for nursing management. International Journal of Health Policy and Management. 2013;**1**(2):169-176. DOI: 10.15171/ijhpm

[56] Cao J, Jia Z, Zhu C, Li Z, Liu H, Li F, et al. Nurses' turnover intention and associated factors in general hospitals in China: A cross-sectional study. Journal of Nursing Management. 2021;**29**(6):1613-1622. DOI: 10.1111/jonm.13295

[57] Vigoda-Gadot E, Golembiewski RT. Citizenship behavior and the Spirit of new Managerialism: A theoretical framework and challenge for governance. American Review of Public Administration. 2001;**31**(3):273-295

[58] Pandey SK. Cutback management and the paradox of publicness. Public Administration Review. 2010;**70**(4):564-571

[59] Hassan S. The importance of ethical leadership and personal control in promoting improvement-Centered voice

among government employees. Journal of Public Administration Research and Theory. 2015;**25**(3):697-719

[60] Bolino MC, Klotz AC, Turnley WH, Harvey J. Exploring the dark side of organizational citizenship behavior. Journal of Organizational Behavior. 2013;**34**(4):542-559

[61] Koopman J, Lanaj K, Scott BA. Integrating the bright and dark sides of OCB: A daily investigation of the benefits and costs of helping others. Academy of Management Journal. 2016;**59**(2):414-435

[62] Henderson L, Tulloch J. Incentives for retaining and motivating health workers in Pacific and Asian countries. Human Resources for Health. 2008;**2008**(6):18

[63] Francetic I, Tediosi F, Salari P, de Savigny D. Going operational with health systems governance: Supervision and incentives to health workers for increased quality of care in Tanzania. Health Policy Plan. 2019;**34**(Suppl. 2):ii77-ii92. DOI: 10.1093/heapol/czz104

[64] International Council of Nurses (ICN). Positive practice environments: Quality workplaces = quality patient care. In: Information and Action Tool Kit developed by Andrea Baumann for ICN. Geneva: International Council of Nurses; 2007. Available from: http://www.icn.ch/indkit2007.pd [Accessed: August 11, 2023]

[65] Manion J. Create a Positive Healthcare Workplace!: Practical Strategies to Retain today's Workforce and Find tomorrow's. Chicago Health Forum, Inc; 2005. [Accessed: August 11, 2023]

[66] Lee YO, Kang JH. Related factors of turnover intention among Korean hospital nurses: A systematic review and meta-analysis. Korean Journal of Adult Nursing. 2018;**30**(1):1-17

[67] Ahmed S, Dalhatu A, Garba A, Irinoye O, Suberu A, Timothy G, et al. Trends and challenges of public health care financing system in Nigeria: The way forward. IOSR Journal of Economics and Finance. 2014;**4**(3):28-34

[68] Falola HO, Ogueyungbo OO, Ojebola OO. Workplace management initiatives and talent engagement in Nigerian pharmaceutical industry. F1000Research. 2020;**9**(699):1-12

[69] Punch NG. We Shed Tears of Joy after Receiving Our First Pay in Suadi Arabia, UK, Others. 2023. Available from: https://punchng.com/we-shed-tears-of-joy-after-receiving-first-pay-in-Saudi-Arabia-uk-others-Nigerian-doctors/